Applying Statistical Concepts Workbook

Dennis E. Hinkle
Towson University

Leping Liu
University of Nevada–Reno

John R. Cox
Southwest Virginia Community College

APPLIED STATISTICS FOR THE BEHAVIORAL SCIENCES

Fifth Edition

Dennis E. Hinkle
Towson University

William Wiersma
University of Toledo

Stephen G. Jurs
University of Toledo

HOUGHTON MIFFLIN COMPANY   BOSTON   NEW YORK

Senior Sponsoring Editor: Kerry T. Baruth
Development Editor: Sara Wise
Project Editor: Robin Hogan
Senior Manufacturing Coordinator: Jane Spelman
Senior Marketing Manager: Katherine Greig

Printed in the U.S.A.

ISBN: 0-618-12406-3

23456789-VG-06 05

CONTENTS

PREFACE

This student workbook is to be used in conjunction with the textbook *Applied Statistics for the Behavioral Sciences,* Fifth Edition, by Dennis E. Hinkle, William Wiersma, and Stephen G. Jurs. Its purpose is to help students refine their knowledge and understanding of the basic statistical procedures used in research. In addition, students will have the opportunity to perfect their computational skills.

ORGANIZATION OF THE WORKBOOK

The subject content of the twenty-two workbook chapters parallels that of the textbook chapters. Every chapter is divided into two sections. Each begins with a programmed review of the concepts presented in the corresponding textbook chapter. In the reviews, called Comprehension Checks, numbered blanks replace words or phrases that reflect major concepts. By supplying the missing words, students play an active role in reviewing these concepts. Answers are provided at the end of each programmed review section.

The programmed review section is followed by a section that contains multiple exercises. These exercises supplement those in the textbook and are designed to help students work typical problems. They are structured logically to maximize the student's understanding of statistical procedures and, most important, of the underlying concepts. For the first exercises in each chapter, some initial calculations are provided for the students as they work through the various steps to the solutions. Later exercises in each chapter have fewer of these initial calculations. Thus the student is required to learn from the early examples and work systematically to solve the later exercises without the initial calculations. As in the textbook, step-by-step solutions and answers are provided for each exercise.

CHAPTER 1
Introduction

COMPREHENSION CHECK

The following summary reviews the material presented in this chapter. To check your understanding of key concepts, supply the missing words indicated by the numbered blanks.

In order to understand statistics, a basic knowledge of elementary mathematical concepts and ___(1)___ is necessary. Of primary importance are the four arithmetic operations, and the three postulates and the three rules of ___(2)___ that govern the use of these operations in statistics. The four basic arithmetic operations are ___(3)___ , ___(4)___ , ___(5)___ , and ___(6)___ . The result of addition is called the sum; the result of subtraction is called the ___(7)___ . Similarly, the result of multiplication is called the ___(8)___ ; the result of division is called the ___(9)___ . When applying these operations to real numbers, we must take into consideration the algebraic ___(10)___ that precedes the number. The ___(11)___ value of a number is the value of the number without regard to the ___(12)___ sign.

The rules of summation are also important in the study of statistics. The first rule, ___(13)___ , implies that the sum of the products of a set of numbers multiplied by a constant is equal to multiplying the ___(14)___ by the sum of the numbers. The second rule, ___(15)___ , implies that the sum of a series of constant scores is equal to ___(16)___ times the constant. Finally, the third rule, ___(17)___ , states that the sum of two (or more) numbers for each individual summed over N individuals is equal to summing each of the two (or more) numbers over the N individuals and summing the ___(18)___ .

Now that the mathematical ___(19)___ and operations have been presented, it is possible to discuss the ___(20)___ of statistics. The word statistics means the procedures used to enhance our understanding of ___(21)___ . Data are some characteristics of individuals or things that can be assigned a ___(22)___ . A characteristic that can take on different values for different members of the group under study is called a ___(23)___ . If a characteristic has the same value for all members of the group under study, it is called a ___(24)___ . Variables can be categorized as either ___(25)___ variables or ___(26)___ variables. A quantitative variable is one that can take ___(27)___ value on the measurement ___(28)___ under consideration. A qualitative variable can take only ___(29)___ values.

Variables are often identified as a(n) ___(30)___ variable or a(n) ___(31)___ variable. Variables over which the researcher has control are ___(32)___ variables. The different ___(33)___ of the independent variable reflect the different ___(34)___ under study; for example, different teaching methods. The ___(35)___ variable depends on, or is the consequence of, the independent variable. For example, achievement in mathematics (dependent variable) ___(36)___ on the teaching method (independent variable).

Measurement, or the assignment of ___(37)___ to characteristics according to a defined rule, is an important concept in statistics. The hierarchy of measurement scales reflects the ___(38)___ of the measurement of the dependent variable. The first level or least precise is the ___(39)___ scale. The properties of this scale are that data categories are mutually ___(40)___ and have no logical ___(41)___ . The next level in the measurement hierarchy is the ___(42)___ scale. An additional property of this scale is the ___(43)___ of the data categories. For the ordinal scale, data categories are mutually exclusive, logically ordered, and ___(44)___ according to the amount of some characteristic they possess. The next higher level of measurement is the ___(45)___ scale. This scale has all the properties of the ___(46)___ scales with one additional property. This property is that ___(47)___ between the various levels of the categories on any part of the scale reflect ___(48)___ differences in the characteristic measured. The last level or most precise scale in the measurement hierarchy is the ___(49)___ scale. This scale has all the properties of the other scales and in addition has the property that zero is ___(50)___ or is a ___(51)___ that represents the absence of the ___(52)___ measured. With this added property, statements can be made about the ___(53)___ amounts of a characteristic possessed by different individuals or things.

In statistics we often talk about groups of people or things. By definition, a ___(54)___ includes all members of some explicit group. A subset or a ___(55)___ of a population is called a ___(56)___ . A characteristic of a population is defined as a ___(57)___ . And a characteristic of a sample is called a ___(58)___ .

The study of statistics is often described by two broad categories: ___(59)___ statistics and ___(60)___ statistics. Methods that classify and summarize numerical data are ___(61)___ statistics. The use of inferential statistics allows us to make generalizations about a ___(62)___ by studying a ___(63)___ or subset of that population. In inferential statistics, measures are computed on sample data, and inferences are made from the ___(64)___ to the ___(65)___ .

Comprehension Check: Answers

1. operations
2. summation
3. addition
4. subtraction
5. multiplication
6. division
7. difference
8. product
9. quotient
10. sign
11. absolute
12. algebraic
13. $\Sigma CX_i = C\Sigma X_i$
14. constant
15. $\Sigma C = NC$
16. N
17. $\Sigma(X_i + Y_i) = \Sigma X_i + \Sigma Y_i$
18. sums
19. concepts
20. meaning
21. data
22. value

23. variable
24. constant
25. quantitative
26. qualitative
27. any
28. scale
29. designated
30. independent
31. dependent
32. independent
33. levels
34. treatments
35. dependent
36. depends
37. numbers
38. precision
39. nominal
40. exclusive
41. order
42. ordinal
43. ordering
44. scaled

45. interval
46. preceding
47. differences
48. equal
49. ratio
50. known
51. true point
52. characteristic
53. proportional
54. population
55. part
56. sample
57. parameter
58. statistic
59. descriptive
60. inferential
61. descriptive
62. population
63. sample
64. sample
65. population

CHAPTER 1 EXERCISES

1. Let $W = 5$, $X = 12$, $Y = -4$, and $Z = -9$. Solve the following:

a. $W + X =$ **i.** $(W)(X) =$
b. $Y + Z =$ **j.** $(Y)(Z) =$
c. $W + Y =$ **k.** $(X)(Y) =$
d. $Z + X =$ **l.** $(W)(Z) =$
e. $X - W =$ **m.** $X/W =$
f. $Y - X =$ **n.** $Z/W =$
g. $Y - W =$ **o.** $X/Y =$
h. $Z - W =$ **p.** $W/Z =$

2. Let $W = 12$, $X = 4$, $Y = 6$, and $Z = -8$. Illustrate the following.

a. $X + Y = Y + X$ **e.** $X + (W + Z) = (X + W) + Z$

$\quad =$ $\quad =$

$\quad =$ $\quad =$

b. $(X)(Y) = (Y)(X)$ **f.** $X(W \cdot Z) = (X \cdot W)Z$

$\quad =$ $\quad =$

$\quad =$ $\quad =$

c. $W + Z = Z + W$ **g.** $Y(W + Z) = YW + YZ$

$\quad =$ $\quad =$

$\quad =$ $\quad =$

d. $(W)(Z) = (Z)(W)$

$\quad =$

$\quad =$

3. Let

$X_1 = 4$ $Y_1 = 2$ $C = 2$
$X_2 = 5$ $Y_2 = 3$
$X_3 = 2$ $Y_3 = 1$
$X_4 = 6$ $Y_4 = 5$

Illustrate the three rules of summation.

a. Show that $\Sigma CX_i = C\Sigma X_i$ Rule 1.
b. Show that $\Sigma CY_i = C\Sigma Y_i$ Rule 1.
c. Show that $\Sigma C = NC$ (for $N = 5$)   Rule 2.
d. Show that $\Sigma(X_i + Y_i) = \Sigma X_i + \Sigma Y_i$ Rule 3.

4. Supply the missing words using the key words listed below.

constant	interval	ratio
continuous	nominal	sample
data	ordinal	sample mean
dependent	parameter	statistic
discrete	population	variable
independent	population mean	

An English teacher uses two different methods of instruction in two English classes. The effect of the different teaching methods is determined by English achievement scores. The characteristics *English teacher* and *achievement scores* are __(a)__ . The characteristic *English teacher* is a __(b)__ and the characteristic *achievement scores* is a __(c)__ . In this study, the instructional method is the __(d)__ variable and the achievement scores are the __(e)__ variable.

Miles per hour and miles per gallon are both examples of a ___(f)___ variable. The number of cylinders in an automobile engine is a ___(g)___ variable.

The number of males and females in a class is an example of a ___(h)___ scale of measurement. At a county fair, various kinds of homegrown produce are given awards, for example, first prize, second prize, and so on. This type of measurement scale is generally considered an ___(i)___ scale. The set of scores for a class on a standardized test is an example of an ___(j)___ scale. The amount of air pressure in your car tires is measured on a ___(k)___ scale.

All third grade students in a school district are considered a ___(l)___ . A characteristic of this group is called a ___(m)___ and would be identified using a Greek letter. The Greek letter μ is the symbol for the ___(n)___ . If we select 30 students from the school district, this subgroup would be a ___(o)___ . A characteristic of this subgroup is called a ___(p)___ and would be identified using a Latin letter. The Latin letter $\bar{X}$ is the symbol for a ___(q)___ .

5. A university counseling center obtains the following information on each student who comes for help: the student's gender, age, academic department, SAT scores, and cumulative grade point average.

The information obtained about students is called ___(a)___ . The gender, age, academic department, SAT scores, and cumulative grade point average are ___(b)___ .

What is the measurement scale of the following variables?
Gender ___(c)___
Age ___(d)___
Academic department ___(e)___
SAT scores ___(f)___
Cumulative grade point average ___(g)___

The variables are called either continuous or discrete. Gender and academic department are ___(h)___ variables. Age, SAT scores and cumulative grade point average are ___(i)___ variables.

Suppose that every tenth student that comes into the center is selected for a study. This group would be a ___(j)___ of the students that come to the center and the characteristics of this group would be called ___(k)___ .

6. The director of research for a school district wants to know if there is a difference in achievement between eleventh grade and twelfth grade students taking a science course for which three different textbooks are used in three classes. The director gathers different kinds of information on two groups of 30 eleventh graders and 30 twelfth graders. This information includes each student's gender, age, class standing, SAT or pre-SAT scores, grade level, the textbook used in the class, and the final examination score.

   a. What data are gathered by the director of research?
   b. What characteristic is the constant in this study?
   c. What are the variables in the data gathered?
   d. Which variables are discrete and which are continuous?

7. The director has gathered data on a number of variables. Some of the variables are needed to conduct the study outlined in this exercise, and other variables could be used to conduct other studies.

   a. For the study of science achievement differences for eleventh and twelfth grade students using three different textbooks, what are the independent variables?
   b. What is the dependent variable?
   c. Of all the data gathered, which variables are measured on the following scales?
      a) nominal
      b) ordinal
      c) interval
      d) ratio

8. We may say that the groups of eleventh and twelfth graders are ___(a)___ drawn from the ___(b)___ of all eleventh and twelfth grade students in the district. The characteristics of the selected students are called ___(c)___ .

Chapter 1 Exercises: Answers

1. a. $W + X = 17$ **i.** $(W)(X) = 60$
  b. $Y + Z = -13$ **j.** $(Y)(Z) = 36$
  c. $W + Y = 1$ **k.** $(X)(Y) = -48$
  d. $Z + X = 3$ **l.** $(W)(Z) = -45$
  e. $X - W = 7$ **m.** $X/W = 2.40$
  f. $Y - Z = 5$ **n.** $Z/W = -1.80$
  g. $Y - X = -16$ **o.** $X/Y = -3.00$
  h. $Z - W = -14$ **p.** $W/Z = -0.56$

2. a. $X + Y = Y + X$ **e.** $X + (W + Z) = (X + W) + Z$
    $4 + 6 = 6 + 4$ $4 + (12 + (-8)) = (4 + 12) + (-8)$
      $10 = 10$ $8 = 8$

  b. $(X)(Y) = (Y)(X)$ **f.** $X(W \cdot Z) = (X \cdot W)Z$
    $(4)(6) = (6)(4)$ $4(12 \cdot (-8)) = (4 \cdot 12)(-8)$
      $24 = 24$ $-384 = -384$

  c. $W + Z = Z + W$ **g.** $Y(W + Z) = YW + YZ$
  $12 + (-8) = (-8) + 12$ $6(12 + (-8)) = (6)(12) + (6)(-8)$
       $4 = 4$ $24 = 24$

  d. $(W)(Z) = (Z)(W)$
  $(12)(-8) = (-8)(12)$
     $-96 = -96$

3. a. $\Sigma CX_i = (2)(4) + (2)(5) + (2)(2) + (2)(6)$
         $= 8 + 10 + 4 + 12$
         $= 34$
    $C\Sigma X_i = 2(4 + 5 + 2 + 6)$
         $= 2(17)$
         $= 34$

  b. $\Sigma CY_i = (2)(2) + (2)(3) + (2)(1) + (2)(5)$
         $= 4 + 6 + 2 + 10$
         $= 22$
    $C\Sigma Y_i = 2(2 + 3 + 1 + 5)$
         $= 2(11)$
         $= 22$

  c. $\Sigma C = 2 + 2 + 2 + 2 + 2$
       $= 10$
    $NC = (5)(2)$
       $= 10$

  d. $\Sigma(X_i + Y_i) = (4 + 2) + (5 + 3) + (2 + 1) + (6 + 5)$
          $= 6 + 8 + 3 + 11$
          $= 28$
    $\Sigma X_i + \Sigma Y_i = 17 + 11$
         $= 28$

4. a. data
   b. constant
   c. variable
   d. independent
   e. dependent
   f. continuous
   g. discrete
   h. nominal
   i. ordinal

   j. interval
   k. ratio
   l. population
   m. parameter
   n. population mean
   o. sample
   p. statistic
   q. sample mean

5. a. data
   b. variables
   c. nominal
   d. ratio
   e. nominal
   f. interval

   g. ratio
   h. discrete
   i. continuous
   j. sample
   k. statistics

6. a. gender, age, class standing, SAT or pre-SAT scores, grade level, textbook used, and final examination score
   b. science course
   c. gender, age, class standing, SAT or pre-SAT scores, grade level, textbook used, and final examination score
   d. discrete: gender, class standing, grade level, textbook; continuous: age, SAT or pre-SAT scores, final examination score

7. a. grade level and textbook
   b. final examination score
   c. nominal: gender, textbook; ordinal: class standing; interval: SAT scores, grade level, final examination score; ratio: age

   Note: The classification of the variables into the categories provided in the answers may justifiably be questioned. How a variable is classified depends to some extent on how the data are gathered and how the data are to be used. The researcher must be able to defend the choice of the measurement scale for the data being used. For comprehensive discussion of the pros and cons of relating appropriate statistical procedures to the scales of measurement interested readers are referred to the following articles: Anderson (1961), Kaiser (1960), Lord (1953), and Stevens (1951, 1968).

8. a. samples
   b. population
   c. statistics

CHAPTER 2
Organizing and Graphing Data

COMPREHENSION CHECK

The following summary reviews the material presented in this chapter. To check your understanding of key concepts, supply the missing words indicated by the numbered blanks.

Data consist of a collection of ___(1)___ . These numbers represent the ___(2)___ of selected variables for a group of individuals. These numbers must be ___(3)___ and summarized by the researcher before beginning the data analysis. The first step involves developing a ___(4)___ file that can contain data measured on the various scales of ___(5)___ . For data measured on the ___(6)___ scale, it may be necessary to ___(7)___ the data. For example, if the data file contains the variable sex, one coding scheme may assign a ___(8)___ to males and a ___(9)___ to females. Since any coding system is somewhat ___(10)___ , males may be coded ___(11)___ and females ___(12)___ , or vice versa.

The stem-and-leaf visual display of a frequency distribution was developed by ___(13)___ . The first step is choice of the ___(14)___ of the display; the numerical values in the frequency distribution become the ___(15)___ of the display. One drawback of the stem-and-leaf display is that it works best with ___(16)___ data sets; one advantage of the technique is that it ___(17)___ all original data values as part of the visual presentation.

A tabular arrangement of numbers that shows the number of times a given score or group of scores occur is a ___(18)___ . The first step in organizing data into a frequency distribution is to order scores from ___(19)___ to ___(20)___ . This step allows us to determine the ___(21)___ of individual scores and to easily identify the highest and lowest scores. Knowledge of the highest score and lowest score allows us to determine the ___(22)___ of scores. The second step is the development of a frequency distribution.

Data are often organized into classes that combine several scores into an ___(23)___ of scores. The intervals are called ___(24)___ . A frequency ___(25)___ can be constructed using class intervals. To develop frequency distributions using class intervals that have a ___(26)___ greater than one, two assumptions are necessary: first, that for any class interval, the scores are ___(27)___ distributed between the exact limits of the interval, and second, that the ___(28)___ of the class interval adequately represents the scores within the interval. While the procedure of using class intervals makes the data more ___(29)___ and easier to ___(30)___ , some specific information is ___(31)___ .

A graphic representation may help to understand the nature of data. A bar graph in which frequencies are represented by the length of the bars is called a ___(32)___ . Another graphic display is the ___(33)___ , in which scores in any class interval are represented by the midpoint of the interval. For both types of displays, ___(34)___ are plotted along the horizontal axis and ___(35)___ along the vertical axis. In either a histogram or a frequency polygon, if many frequencies are on the right-hand side of the distribution and fewer on the left-hand side, the distribution is said to be skewed to the ___(36)___ or ___(37)___ skewed. In contrast, if there are many frequencies on the left-hand side of the distribution with fewer frequencies trailing off to the right, the distribution is said to be skewed to the ___(38)___ or ___(39)___ skewed.

A distribution is said to be ___(40)___ if the two sides will correspond exactly when the graph is folded along a central line. Distributions may be symmetrical but vary in their degree of peakedness, a distinction called ___(41)___ . A distribution with a small degree of peakedness is referred to as ___(42)___ ; a distribution with a high degree of peakedness is referred to as ___(43)___ ; and a distribution with a moderate degree of peakedness is referred to as ___(44)___ .

Comprehension Check: Answers

1. numbers	**16.** small	**31.** lost
2. measurement	**17.** uses (or preserves)	**32.** histogram
3. organized	**18.** frequency distribution	**33.** frequency polygon
4. data	**19.** highest	**34.** scores
5. measurement	**20.** lowest	**35.** frequencies
6. nominal	**21.** frequencies	**36.** left
7. code	**22.** range	**37.** negatively
8. 0	**23.** interval	**38.** right
9. 1	**24.** class intervals	**39.** positively
10. arbitrary	**25.** distribution	**40.** symmetric
11. 1	**26.** width	**41.** kurtosis
12. 2	**27.** uniformly	**42.** platykurtic
13. John Tukey	**28.** midpoint	**43.** leptokurtic
14. stem	**29.** manageable	**44.** mesokurtic
15. leaves	**30.** interpret	

CHAPTER 2 EXERCISES

1. An instructor gave a 100-point examination to a class of 25 students. The following scores resulted:

97	75	63	51	77
82	80	93	84	90
59	68	75	76	68
64	87	70	80	82
73	66	67	71	74

a. What is the range of scores?

Range = (−   ) + 1

=

b. Complete the following frequency distributions of examination scores.

Score	f	Score	f	Score	f
97	1	77	1	68	2
93	1				
80		70		51	

Hint: The column labeled f is the frequency, or number of scores, for each value. The total of all the f columns will equal the total number of scores, or 25.

c. Suppose the instructor decides to combine several actual scores and form class intervals. Using the data from the frequency distribution of scores, complete the table for a frequency distribution using class intervals with a width of 5.

Class Interval	f
96–100	1
91–95	

51–55	1

Hint: Each class interval has a width of 5 units; that is, 91 to 95 is an interval of 5. Again, the total of the *f* column should equal the number of scores.

d. Expand the frequency distribution using class intervals to include the exact limits and midpoints of the intervals.

Class Interval	Exact Limits	Midpoint	f
96–100	95.5–100.5	98	1
91–95			

51–55	50.5–55.5	

e. Using the information developed above, draw a histogram for these data. Label the horizontal and vertical axes and place values for the points on each axis.

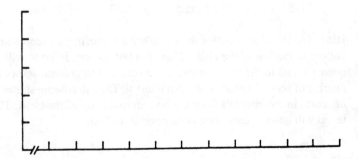

Hint: The values along the horizontal axis in a histogram are the exact limits for the class intervals, and they increase in size from left to right.

f. Draw a frequency polygon from the data in part d. Label the horizontal and vertical axes and place values for the points on each axis.

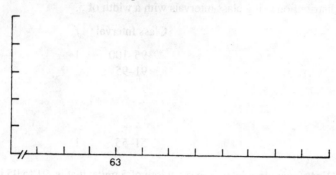

63

Hint: The values along the horizontal axis in a frequency polygon are the midpoints of the class intervals.

g. Compare your drawings of the histogram and the frequency polygon. Are they approximately the same in shape and location on the graphs?

Hint: The answer to this question should be yes, or some error in plotting has been made. They are both graphic representations of the same frequency distribution.

h. Complete the following table using the data you developed in part d, and provide the missing information for *cf*, *%* and *c%*.

Class Interval	Exact Limits	Midpoint	f	cf	$\%$	$c\%$
96–100	95.5–100.5	98	1	25	4	100
91–95	– 95.5					
51–55	50.5–55.5	53	1	1	4	4

Hint: The *cf* column shows the cumulative frequency of scores in the intervals from the bottom to the top of the chart. Thus, the last, or top, interval will have a cumulative frequency equal to the total number of scores. The % column shows the percent of the total number of scores contained in each interval. The *c%* column shows the cumulative percent of scores in the intervals from the bottom to the top of the chart. Thus, the last, or top, interval will have a cumulative percent equal to 100.

i. Draw the ogive (cumulative frequency distribution) for the data developed in part h. Label the horizontal and vertical axes and place values for the points on each axis.

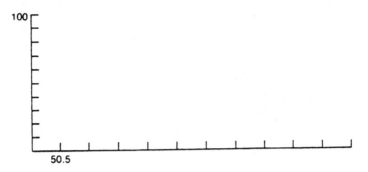

Hint: The values along the horizontal axis are the exact limits of the class intervals and increase in size from left to right. Below the exact limit of the lowest class interval (50.5–55.5) no scores exist; thus, the percent of scores below 50.5 is zero. All scores are included by the largest value of the exact limit of the highest class interval (95.5–100.5); thus the percent of scores below 100.5 is 100.

2. A traffic engineer is interested in the speed that motorists drive along a certain segment of road. A sample of vehicles was clocked to the nearest mph throughout the day, with the following results:

29	35	36	20	23
37	34	31	24	30
40	28	35	46	32
38	30	34	37	28
32	33	42	32	36
50	34	39	53	30
36	35	33	15	26
34	36	35	41	44

a. Develop the frequency distribution for the above data.

b. Suppose the engineer decides to develop a frequency distribution of class intervals with a width of 3. Complete the following table including cumulative frequencies and cumulative percentage.

Class Interval	Exact Limits	Midpoint	*f*	*cf*	%	*c*%

52

c. Draw the frequency distribution and, in general terms, describe the shape of the curve.

3. Consider the following frequency distributions of final test scores for two groups of college students in an introductory calculus course.

Class Interval	Group I Frequency	Group II Frequency
90–94	4	4
85–89	12	2
80–84	17	1
75–79	22	8
70–74	28	12
65–69	24	16
60–64	18	18
55–59	15	28
50–54	12	33
45–49	9	30
40–44	1	15
35–39	4	10
30–34	3	4

a. On the same axis, construct a frequency polygon for each of the two groups.
b. Describe and compare the two distributions.

Chapter 2 Exercises: Answers

1. a. Range = (97 − 51) + 1
              = 47

b.

Score	f	Score	f	Score	f
97	1	77	1	68	2
93	1	76	1	67	1
90	1	75	2	66	1
87	1	74	1	64	1
84	1	73	1	63	1
82	2	71	1	59	1
80	2	70	1	51	1

c, d, and **h.**

Class Interval	Exact Limits	Midpoint	f	cf	%	c%
96–100	95.5–100.5	98	1	25	4	100
91–95	90.5–95.5	93	1	24	4	96
86–90	85.5–90.5	88	2	23	8	92
81–85	80.5–85.5	83	3	21	12	84
76–80	75.5–80.5	78	4	18	16	72
71–75	70.5–75.5	73	5	14	20	56
66–70	65.5–70.5	68	5	9	20	36
61–65	60.5–65.5	63	2	4	8	16
56–60	55.5–60.5	58	1	2	4	8
51–55	50.5–55.5	53	1	1	4	4

e.

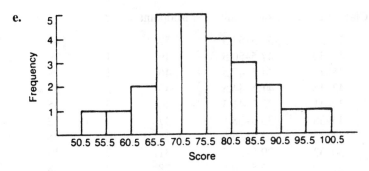

f.

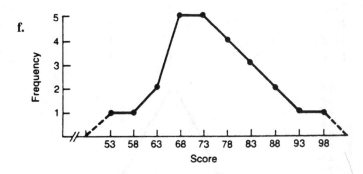

i.

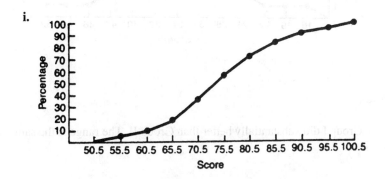

2. a.

Miles per hour	f	Miles per hour	f
53	1	34	4
50	1	33	2
46	1	32	3
44	1	31	1
42	1	30	3
41	1	29	1
40	1	28	2
39	1	26	1
38	1	24	1
37	2	23	1
36	4	20	1
35	4	15	1

b.

Class Interval	Exact Limits	Midpoint	f	cf	%	$c\%$
51–53	50.5–53.5	52	1	40	2.5	100.0
48–50	47.5–50.5	49	1	39	2.5	97.5
45–47	44.5–47.5	46	1	38	2.5	95.0
42–44	41.5–44.5	43	2	37	5.0	92.5
39–41	38.5–41.5	40	3	35	7.5	87.5
36–38	35.5–38.5	37	7	32	17.5	80.0
33–35	32.5–35.5	34	10	25	25.0	62.5
30–32	29.5–32.5	31	7	15	17.5	37.5
27–29	26.5–29.5	28	3	8	7.5	20.0
24–26	23.5–26.5	25	2	5	5.0	12.5
21–23	20.5–23.5	22	1	3	2.5	7.5
18–20	17.5–20.5	19	1	2	2.5	5.0
15–17	14.5–17.5	16	1	1	2.5	2.5

c.

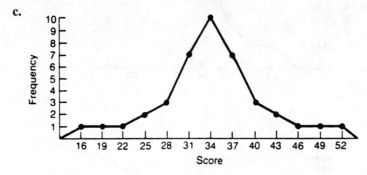

3. a.

b. Group I did substantially better than Group II. The range is the same for both groups.

CHAPTER 3

Describing Distributions: Individual Scores, Central Tendency, and Variation

COMPREHENSION CHECK

The following summary reviews the material presented in this chapter. To check your understanding of key concepts, supply the missing words indicated by the numbered blanks.

To describe a distribution of data adequately, __(1)__ kinds of information are required: knowledge of __(2)__ , __(3)__ on the measurement scale, and the __(4)__ of its scores. However, it is also important to describe __(5)__ scores because raw scores are often meaningless without knowing the __(6)__ position of an individual score. Basic tools for describing individual scores are the concepts of __(7)__ and __(8)__ . A percentile is defined as the __(9)__ in the distribution __(10)__ which a given __(11)__ of the scores are found. We may also calculate the percentile rank of a score in a distribution; that is, a value on the scale of __(12)__ . Percentiles can be used to indicate an individual's __(13)__ or position within a group. However, because many variables in the behavioral sciences tend to be __(14)__ distributed, differences between percentile points are __(15)__ uniform throughout the measurement scale. That is, percentiles are an example of a(n) __(16)__ scale of measurement, and __(17)__ be arithmetically manipulated. Thus, raw scores and percentile ranks are for the most part __(18)__ for making comparisons across distributions.

The content of this chapter included discussions of the measures of __(19)__ for a given set of scores, which tell where the scores are __(20)__ along the measurement scale. The simplest index of central tendency is the __(21)__ . It is defined as the __(22)__ score in a distribution and is determined by inspecting the data. The mode of a frequency distribution of class intervals is the __(23)__ of the class interval with the largest frequency. When a distribution has two modes, it is referred to as __(24)__ ; with more than two modes, it is called __(25)__ .

A second measure of central tendency is the median. It is defined as the __(26)__ ; that is, the point on the scale of measurement __(27)__ which 50 percent of the scores fall. A third measure of central tendency, and the most common, is the __(28)__ . It is the arithmetic average of the scores in the distribution; that is, the __(29)__ of all the scores divided by the __(30)__ of scores. There are two important properties of the mean, both pertaining to deviation scores, which are defined as the difference between a __(31)__ and the __(32)__ . First, the sum of the __(33)__ is __(34)__ . Second, the sum of the __(35)__ deviations is __(36)__ than the sum of squared deviations about any other value.

There are several considerations in choosing a measure of central tendency. Which measure is appropriate first depends on the __(37)__ of measurement of the variable. The __(38)__ is appropriate for nominal data. For ordinal data, the __(39)__ and the __(40)__ are appropriate. When the data form an interval or ratio scale, the __(41)__ , __(42)__ , and __(43)__ may be used. A second consideration in the choice of central tendency measure is the intended __(44)__ of the analysis. If the purpose is descriptive, the measure that best __(45)__ the data should be used. If the purpose is __(46)__ , then the __(47)__ has the advantage, because it can be manipulated mathematically in ways not appropriate to the __(48)__ and the __(49)__ . Finally, neither the __(50)__ nor the __(51)__ is strongly affected by extreme scores in a distribution ("outliers"). However, outliers do affect the __(52)__ .

Measures of __(53)__ are intervals on the scale of measurement that indicate the __(54)__ of the data. The simplest measure of variability is the __(55)__ . Its most serious limitation is that it tends to vary with the __(56)__ of the group. Larger groups tend to have a __(57)__ range of values than smaller groups.

A useful technique for plotting data that graphically illustrates the variability of the scores is the __(58)__ . This technique requires that we compute __(59)__ numbers from the frequency __(60)__ . Those numbers are the two __(61)__ values and the three __(62)__ . When those numbers have been calculated, a box is drawn using the median and the other __(63)__ . The median is represented by a __(64)__ line within the box. The whiskers get their name because they extend out to the __(65)__ . A very useful aspect of the box plot is its capacity to show visually the existence of __(66)__ in the frequency distribution. In addition, examination of any __(67)__ between the lengths of the two segments of the box gives a rough indication of the __(68)__ in the frequency distribution.

In order to describe the __(69)__ of scores in a distribution, a __(70)__ to all scores in the distribution must be incorporated by including the deviation of each score from the __(71)__ . Thus, the __(72)__ score is calculated as the difference between each actual score in the distribution and the mean of the scores. Consider the sum of these deviation scores; this sum __(73)__ be used to determine a measure of variation because it is __(74)__ . However, it is possible to obtain a measure of variation if the __(75)__ value of the deviation score is considered.

The __(76)__ is defined as the average of the deviation scores (in absolute value terms). It is possible to use the mean deviation to compare the variation of several distributions; the distributions with the __(77)__ deviations have the greater __(78)__ . The major problem with using the mean deviation is the difficulty of manipulating absolute values __(79)__ for advanced statistical analyses. One way to overcome this limitation is to __(80)__ the deviation scores and determine the __(81)__ of the scores. The population variance is defined as the __(82)__ of the __(83)__ deviations, that is, SS/N. To calculate the variance of a sample, we used $(n-1)$ instead of (N) in the denominator of the formula to provide __(84)__ an estimate of the __(85)__ variance. The variance is thus a measure of dispersion in __(86)__ units of the measurement scale. For example, if the measurement scale were the height of people in inches, the dispersion, or variance, would be expressed in __(87)__ inches. The square root of the variance, called the standard deviation, is the measure of dispersion expressed in the __(88)__ unit of measurement, linear inches.

Recall that raw scores and percentiles are inappropriate for comparing scores between distributions. One way that such comparisons can be made meaningfully is through the use of __(89)__ scores. The standard score, or __(90)__ , indicates the number of __(91)__ deviation units that a corresponding raw score is above, at, or below the __(92)__ . A simple rule is that a negative z score tells us that the raw score is __(93)__ the mean; a z score of __(94)__ indicates that the raw score is exactly equal to the mean; a __(95)__ z score tells us that the raw score is above the mean. If each raw score in a distribution is converted to a z score, the new distribution of scores has the identical __(96)__ , but the mean is equal to __(97)__ and the standard deviation equals __(98)__ .

A practical application of z scores involves weighting different scores. Suppose a researcher needs to combine scores from several tests into a total score and needs to weight the tests differently (for example, a final exam is weighted twice the hourly exams). The appropriate procedure would be to compute a __(99)__ average for each score. In this procedure, each of the raw scores is first converted to a __(100)__ and weighted appropriately as the researcher requires.

Lastly, there are some undesirable properties of z scores that researchers should know. Reporting z scores to two decimal places implies a precision that the __(101)__ scores clearly do not possess. Overlooking a minus sign for a z score can drastically change the __(102)__ of the score.

To overcome these undesirable characteristics, z scores can be transformed into a distribution of scores with a __(103)__ of 50 and a standard deviation of __(104)__ . The new scores are called __(105)__ scores and are all positive. Thus, a general guideline for generating new standard score distributions is to convert raw scores to __(106)__ , which are then transformed into a second distribution with the desired mean and __(107)__ . The formula for the second conversion involves first multiplying each z score by the *new* __(108)__ and then adding the *new* __(109)__ .

Comprehension Check: Answers

1. three (3)
2. shape
3. location
4. variability
5. individual
6. relative
7. percentiles
8. percentile ranks
9. score
10. below
11. percent
12. percentiles
13. rank
14. normally
15. not
16. ordinal
17. cannot (may not)
18. inappropriate
19. central tendency
20. located
21. mode
22. most frequent
23. midpoint
24. bimodal
25. multimodal
26. 50th percentile
27. below
28. mean (arithmetic)
29. sum
30. number (n)
31. score
32. mean
33. deviations
34. zero (0)
35. squared
36. smaller
37. level
38. mode

39. mode
40. median
41. mean
42. median
43. mode
44. use
45. describes (summarizes)
46. inferential
47. mean
48. median
49. mode
50. median
51. mode
52. mean
53. variability (dispersion)
54. scatter
55. range
56. size
57. larger
58. box plot
59. 5 (or five)
60. distribution
61. extreme (minimum, maximum)
62. quartiles (Q_{25}, Q_{50}, Q_{75})
63. quartiles (Q_{25}, Q_{75})
64. horizontal
65. extremes
66. outliers
67. differences
68. skewness
69. variation
70. sensitivity
71. mean
72. deviation
73. cannot
74. zero
75. absolute

76. mean deviation
77. larger
78. variation
79. algebraically
80. square
81. variance
82. average (mean)
83. squared
84. unbiased
85. population
86. squared
87. squared
88. original
89. standard
90. z score
91. standard
92. mean
93. below
94. zero
95. positive
96. shape
97. zero (0)
98. one (1.0)
99. weighted
100. z score
101. raw
102. meaning (interpretation)
103. mean
104. ten (10)
105. transformed
106. z scores
107. standard deviation
108. mean
109. standard deviation

CHAPTER 3 EXERCISES

1. Consider Exercise 1 in Chapter 2 of the workbook. In that exercise, an instructor gave a 100-point examination to 25 students. In Chapter 2, the frequency distribution for these 25 scores was developed. The original data and the frequency distribution are presented below.

97	75	63	51	77
82	80	93	84	90
59	68	75	76	68
64	87	70	80	82
73	66	67	71	74

Class Interval	Exact Limits	Midpoint	f	cf	%	c%
96–100	95.5–100.5	98	1	25	4	100
91–95	90.5–95.5	93	1	24	4	96
86–90	85.5–90.5	88	2	23	8	92
81–85	80.5–85.5	83	3	21	12	84
76–80	75.5–80.5	78	4	18	16	72
71–75	70.5–75.5	73	5	14	20	56
66–70	65.5–70.5	68	5	9	20	36
61–65	60.5–65.5	63	2	4	8	16
56–60	55.5–60.5	58	1	2	4	8
51–55	50.5–55.5	53	1	1	4	4

a. Suppose the instructor wants to determine the point below which 60 percent of the scores are found.

(1) The 60th percentile is in which interval? _____

(2) Using the general formula (3.1), calculate the 60th percentile.

$$P_{60} = ll + \left(\frac{np - cf}{f_i} \right)(w)$$

$$= \quad + \left(\frac{(25)(\quad) -}{\rule{2cm}{0.4pt}} \right)(\ )$$

$$= \quad + \left(\frac{15 -}{\rule{1.5cm}{0.4pt}} \right)(\ )$$

$$= \quad + \left(\frac{1}{4} \right)(\ )$$

$$= \quad +$$

$$=$$

(3) Calculate the 40th percentile.

b. One of the students in the class received a score of 82 and wants to know the relative position of this score in the distribution. In statistical terms, the student wants to know the percentile rank of the score 82.

(1) Using the general formula (3.2), calculate the percentile rank of the score 82.

$$PR_{82} = \left[\frac{cf + \dfrac{X - ll}{w}(f_i)}{n} \right] (100)$$

$$= \left[\frac{+ \left(\dfrac{82 - \rule{1cm}{0.4pt}}{5} \right)(3)}{\rule{2cm}{0.4pt}} \right] (\quad)$$

$$= \left[\frac{+ \left(\dfrac{1.5}{5} \right)(3)}{25} \right] (\quad)$$

$$= \left[\frac{+ (\quad)(3)}{\rule{2cm}{0.4pt}} \right] (\quad)$$

$$= \left(\frac{+ 0.9}{\rule{1.5cm}{0.4pt}} \right) (\quad)$$

$$= \left(\frac{18.9}{25} \right) (\quad)$$

$$= (\quad)(\quad)$$

$$=$$

(2) Calculate the percentile rank of the score 64.

2. A class of 20 students has the following final examination scores.

90	75	91	76	72
72	87	64	75	80
68	83	79	72	88
95	70	73	81	74

a. Develop the frequency distribution with the following headings:

Score f cf

b. What is the mode of this distribution of scores?

c. What is the median of this distribution of scores?

$$\text{Mdn} = ll + \left[\frac{n(0.50) - cf}{f_i} \right] (w)$$

$$= 74.5 + \left[\frac{20(0.50) - 8}{2} \right] (1)$$

$$= \quad +$$

$$=$$

d. What is the mean of this distribution of scores?

$$\bar{X} = \frac{\Sigma X}{n}$$

$$= —$$

$$=$$

3. a. What is the mode of the following distribution of scores?

Class Interval	Exact Limits	Midpoint	f	cf
70–74	69.5–74.5	72	8	110
65–69			12	
60–64			10	
55–59			16	
50–54			24	
45–49			18	
40–44			15	
35–39	34.5–39.5	37	7	7

b. What is the median of this distribution of scores?

$$\text{Mdn} = \quad + \left[\frac{110(\quad)-}{\rule{3cm}{0.4pt}}\right](\quad)$$

$$= \quad +$$

$$=$$

c. Assuming the midpoint of a class interval can be used to represent all scores in the interval, compute the mean for the above frequency distribution.

$$\bar{X} = [(72)(8) + (67)(12) + \cdots + (37)(7)]/110$$

$$=$$

$$=$$

4. a. In a swimming event, eight swimmers had the following times in seconds. Consider this group of swimmers to be a population. What is the variance in their scores using the deviation formula?

Time	$(X - \mu)$	$(X - \mu)^2$
28	−5	25
29		
29		
32		
32		
36		
38		
40	7	49

$$\Sigma =$$

$$\mu =$$

$$\sigma^2 = \frac{\Sigma(X - \mu)^2}{N}$$

$$= \rule{3cm}{0.4pt}$$

$$=$$

Hint: The sum of $X - \mu$ is zero.

b. Considering this group of swimmers to be a sample, what is the variance in their scores?

$$s^2 = \frac{\Sigma(X - \bar{X})^2}{n - 1}$$

$$= \underline{\hspace{3cm}}$$

$$= \underline{\hspace{1cm}}$$

c. What is the unit of measurement for the variance in parts a and b?

5. a. The times from Exercise 4 are reproduced below. Assume this group of swimmers to be a population. What is the variance in their scores using the raw score formula?

Time	X^2
28	784
29	841
29	
32	
32	
36	
38	
40	
$\Sigma =$	

$$\sigma^2 = \frac{\Sigma X^2 - \frac{(\Sigma X)^2}{N}}{N}$$

$$= \frac{- \frac{(\quad)^2}{8}}{\underline{\hspace{2cm}}}$$

$$= \frac{-}{\underline{\hspace{2cm}}}$$

$$= \underline{\hspace{1cm}}$$

Hint: Be careful of the difference between ΣX^2 and $(\Sigma X)^2$.

b. Assume the group of swimmers to be a sample. What is the variance in their scores using the raw score formula?

$$s^2 = \frac{\Sigma X^2 - \frac{(\Sigma X)^2}{n}}{n - 1}$$

$$= \frac{- \frac{(264)^2}{\underline{\hspace{1cm}}}}{8 - 1}$$

$$= \frac{-}{\underline{\hspace{2cm}}}$$

6. a. What is the standard deviation of scores for the population of swimmers in Exercise 4a?

$$\sigma = \sqrt{\sigma^2} \text{ or } \sigma = \sqrt{\frac{\Sigma(X-\mu)^2}{N}}$$

$$= \sqrt{}$$

$$=$$

b. What is the standard deviation of scores for the sample group of swimmers in Exercise 4b?

$$s = \sqrt{s^2} \text{ or } s = \sqrt{\frac{\Sigma(X-\bar{X})^2}{n-1}}$$

$$= \sqrt{}$$

$$=$$

7. a. Members of a gymnastics class, when attempting to complete a routine within a specified time limit, required 5, 6, 11, 9, 5, 7, 3, 4, 10, 8, 12, and 7 trials. What are the mean, median, and mode for this distribution?

b. Using the deviation formula, find the variance and standard deviation. Assume the class to be a population.

X	$X-\mu$	$(X-\mu)^2$
5		
6		
11		
9		
5		
7		
3		
4		
10		
8		
12		
7	_____	_____
	0	

$$\sigma^2 = \underline{}$$

$$=$$

$$\sigma =$$

c. Using the raw score formula, find the variance and standard deviation. Assume the gymnastics class to be a sample.

$$n = $$
$$\Sigma X = $$
$$\Sigma X^2 = $$

$$s^2 = \frac{- (\quad)^2}{\rule{3cm}{0.4pt}}$$

$$= \frac{-}{\rule{2cm}{0.4pt}}$$

$$=$$

$$s =$$

8. The mean of a set of six scores is 23. The first five scores are 18, 35, 26, 24, and 15. What is the sixth score?

9. Which of the three measures of central tendency lends itself most readily to mathematical manipulation?

10. For the following set of scores show that the sum of squares of deviations about the mean ($\mu = 5$) is smaller than the sum of squares of deviations about the value $\bar{X} = 6$.

X_i	$(X_i - \mu)$	$(X_i - \mu)^2$	$(X_i - 6)$	$(X_i - 6)^2$
4				
7				
3				
8				
4				
6				
3				
5	____	____	____	____

11. Computation of a variance or standard deviation requires that the data be measured on at least what scale?

12. What three types of information are needed to describe a distribution adequately?

13. What is meant by the term unbiased estimate?

14. Locate the mean, median, and mode on each of the following distributions.

a.

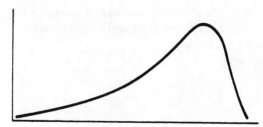

b.

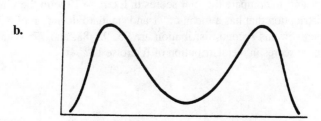

c.

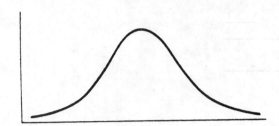

15. A distribution of final examination scores in an introductory psychology course has a mean of 73 and standard deviation of 11. What are the standard scores that correspond to the following raw scores: 80, 69, 61, and 96?

$$z = \frac{X - \bar{X}}{s}$$

$$z_{80} = \frac{80 - }{11} = 0.64$$

$$z_{69} = \frac{- 73}{} = -$$

$$z_{69} = \frac{-}{} =$$

$$z_{96} = \frac{-}{} =$$

16. Suppose the instructor in this introductory psychology course wanted to transform these raw scores in Exercise 15 to a distribution of scores that has a mean of 50 and standard deviation of 10.

$$\text{Transformed score} = (10)(z) + 50$$

Raw score	z score	Transformed score
80	0.64	56.4
69		
61		
96		

17. The mean final examination scores for all eleventh grade English students in a school district is 81 and the variance is 36 (standard deviation is 6). What are the standard scores for the raw scores of 90, 80, 70, and 60?

a. $z_{90} = \frac{-}{} =$

b. $z_{80} =$

c. $z_{70} =$

d. $z_{60} =$

18. A teacher wants to compare the four scores in Exercise 17 with the same students' scores in another distribution that has a mean of 71 and standard deviation of 8.5. The raw scores for these students in this second distribution are 95, 92, 88, and 77. What are the comparable value of these scores in the distribution of Exercise 17?

19. The following scores were achieved by the ten members of a mathematics class on a comprehensive final examination. Compute the corresponding z scores.

Theory (X)	Computation (Y)	$X - \bar{X}$	$Y - \bar{Y}$	z_x	z_y
81	88	7	10	0.54	0.97
60	75	−14	−3		
90	85				
75	78				
95	98				
55	69				
70	68				
82	82				
64	72				
68	65			−0.46	−1.26

$$\mu_X = \frac{\Sigma X}{N} = \frac{}{} =$$

$$\mu_Y = \frac{\Sigma Y}{N} = \frac{}{} =$$

$$\sigma_X = \sqrt{\frac{\Sigma(X - \mu_x)^2}{N}} = \sqrt{\frac{}{}} =$$

$$\sigma_Y = \sqrt{\frac{\Sigma(Y - \mu_y)^2}{N}} = \sqrt{\frac{}{}} =$$

20. In Exercise 19 the instructor wants to weight the mathematics computation portion of the final examination twice as heavily as the theory portion in order to arrive at a combined score. What are the combined z scores for the first four students?

z_X	z_Y	Combined score $\dfrac{\Sigma W_z}{\Sigma W} = \dfrac{1(z_X) + 2(z_Y)}{1 + 2}$
0.54	0.97	$\dfrac{1(0.54) + 2(\quad)}{3} =$
−1.08	−0.29	$\dfrac{1(\quad) + 2(−0.29)}{} = −0.55$
1.23	0.68	$\dfrac{}{} =$
0.08	0.00	$\dfrac{}{} =$

Chapter 3 Exercises: Answers

1. a. (1) 75.5–80.5

$$(2)\ P_{60} = 75.5 + \left[\frac{(25)(.60)-14}{4}\right](5)$$

$$= 75.5 + \left[\frac{15-14}{4}\right](5)$$

$$= 75.5 + \left(\frac{1}{4}\right)(5)$$

$$= 75.5 + 1.25$$

$$= 76.75$$

(3) $P_{40} = 71.5$

b. (1)

$$PR_{82} = \left[\frac{18 + \dfrac{82-80.5}{5}(3)}{25}\right](100)$$

$$= \left[\frac{18 + (0.3)(3)}{25}\right](100)$$

$$= \left(\frac{18.9}{25}\right)(100)$$

$$= (0.756)(100)$$

$$= 75.6$$

(2) $PR_{64} = 13.6$

2. a.

Score	f	cf
95	1	20
91	1	19
90	1	18
88	1	17
87	1	16
83	1	15
81	1	14
80	1	13
79	1	12
76	1	11
75	2	10
74	1	8
73	1	7
72	3	6
70	1	3
68	1	2
64	1	1

b. Mode = 72

c.
$$\text{Mdn} = 74.5 + \left[\frac{20(0.50) - 8}{2}\right](1)$$
$$= 74.5 + 1$$
$$= 75.5$$

d. $\bar{X} = \dfrac{1565}{20}$

$$= 78.25$$

3. a.

Class Interval	Exact Limits	Midpoint	f	cf
70–74	69.5–74.5	72	8	110
65–69	64.5–69.5	67	12	102
60–64	59.5–64.5	62	10	90
55–59	54.5–59.5	57	16	80
50–54	49.5–54.5	52	24	64
45–49	44.5–49.5	47	18	40
40–44	39.5–44.5	42	15	22
35–39	34.5–39.5	37	7	7

Mode = 52

b. $\text{Mdn} = 49.5 + \left[\dfrac{110(0.50) - 40}{24}\right](5)$

$$= 49.5 + \frac{15}{24}(5)$$

$$= 52.625$$

c. $\bar{X} = [(72)(8) + (67)(12) + (62)(10) + (57)(16) +$
   $+ (52)(24) + (47)(18) + (42)(15) + (37)(7)]/110$
   $= 5895/110$
   $= 53.59$

4. a.

Time	$(X - \mu)$	$(X - \mu)^2$
28	−5	25
29	−4	16
29	−4	16
32	−1	1
32	−1	1
36	3	9
38	5	25
40	7	49
$\Sigma = 264$	0	142

$$\mu = 33.0$$
$$\sigma^2 = \frac{142}{8}$$
$$= 17.75$$

b. $s^2 = \dfrac{142}{7}$

$$= 20.29$$

    c. square seconds

5. a.

Time	X^2
28	784
29	841
29	841
32	1024
32	1024
36	1296
38	1444
40	1600
$\Sigma = 264$	8854

$$\sigma^2 = \frac{8854 - \frac{(264)^2}{8}}{8}$$

$$= \frac{8854 - 8712}{8}$$

$$= 17.75$$

b. $$s^2 = \frac{8854 - \frac{(264)^2}{8}}{8-1}$$

$$= \frac{8854 - 8712}{7}$$

$$= 20.29$$

Note: Notice that you get the same answers whether you use the deviation formula or the raw score formula. However, the deviation formula requires that you determine μ or $\bar{X}$ and $(X - \mu)^2$ or $(X - \bar{X})^2$. This can be troublesome if μ or $\bar{X}$ is a fraction. Therefore, the raw score formula is more efficient and easier to compute, even though large numbers must be handled sometimes.

6. a. $\sigma = \sqrt{17.75}$

    $= 4.21$

b. $s = \sqrt{20.29}$

    $= 4.50$

7. a. Mode = 5 and 7 (bimodal)

$$\text{Median} = 6.5 + \left[\frac{12(0.5) - 5}{2}\right](1)$$

$$= 6.5 + (0.5)(1)$$

$$= 7$$

$$\text{Mean} = \frac{87}{12} = 7.25$$

b.

X	$X - \mu$	$(X - \mu)^2$
5	−2.25	5.06
6	−1.25	1.56
11	3.75	14.06
9	1.75	3.06
5	−2.25	5.06
7	−0.25	0.06
3	−4.25	18.06
4	−3.25	10.56
10	2.75	7.56
8	0.75	0.56
12	4.75	22.56
7	−0.25	0.06
	0.00	88.22

$$\sigma^2 = \frac{88.22}{12}$$

$$= 7.35$$

$$\sigma = 2.71$$

c. $n = 12$

$\Sigma X = 87$

$\Sigma X^2 = 719$

$$s^2 = \frac{719 - \frac{(87)^2}{12}}{11} = \frac{719 - 630.75}{11} = 8.02$$

$s = 2.83$

8. $\sum_{i=1}^{6} X = (23)(6) = 138$

$\sum_{i=1}^{5} X = 18 + 35 + 26 + 24 + 15 = 118$; therefore, $X_6 = 20$

9. the mean

10.

X_i	$(X_i - \mu)$	$(X_i - \mu)^2$	$(X_i - 6)$	$(X_i - 6)^2$
4	−1	1	−2	4
7	2	4	1	1
3	−2	4	−3	9
8	3	9	2	4
4	−1	1	−2	4
6	1	1	0	0
3	−2	4	−3	9
5	0	0	−1	1
		$\Sigma = 24$		$\Sigma = 32$

11. interval scale.

12. information regarding the shape, the location on the measurement scale, and the variation of scores

13. An estimate is unbiased if the mean of all possible values of the estimate for a given sample size equals the parameter being estimated.

14. a.

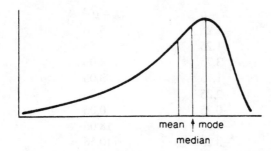

b.

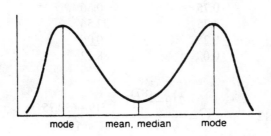

c.

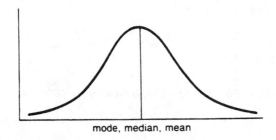

15. $z_{80} = \dfrac{80 - 73}{11} = 0.64$

$z_{69} = \dfrac{69 - 73}{11} = -0.36$

$z_{61} = \dfrac{61 - 73}{11} = -1.09$

$z_{96} = \dfrac{96 - 73}{11} = 2.09$

16.

Raw score	z score	Transformed score
80	0.64	$56.4 = 10(0.64) + 50$
69	−0.36	$46.4 = 10(-0.36) + 50$
61	−1.09	$39.1 = 10(-1.09) + 50$
96	2.09	$70.9 = 10(2.09) + 50$

17. a. $z_{90} = \dfrac{90 - 81}{6} = 1.5$

b. $z_{80} = \dfrac{80 - 81}{6} = 0.17$

c. $z_{70} = \dfrac{70 - 81}{6} = 1.83$

d. $z_{60} = \dfrac{60 - 81}{6} = -3.5$

18.

Raw score	z score	New score
95	2.82	97.92
92	2.47	95.82
88	2.00	93.00
77	0.71	85.26

19.

Theory (X)	Computation (Y)	$X - \bar{X}$	$Y - \bar{Y}$	z_x	z_y
81	88	7	10	0.54	0.97
60	75	−14	−3	−1.08	−0.29
90	85	16	7	1.23	0.68
75	78	1	0	0.08	0.00
95	98	21	20	1.62	1.94
55	69	−19	−9	−1.46	−0.87
70	68	−4	−10	−0.31	−0.97
82	82	8	4	0.62	0.39
64	72	−10	−6	−0.77	−0.58
68	65	−6	−13	−0.46	−1.26

$$\mu_X = \frac{740}{10} = 74.0$$

$$\mu_Y = \frac{780}{10} = 78.0$$

$$\sigma_X = \sqrt{\frac{1520}{10}} = 12.32$$

$$\sigma_Y = \sqrt{\frac{960}{10}} = 9.80$$

20.

z_X	z_Y	Combined score
0.54	0.97	$\dfrac{1(0.54) + 2(0.97)}{3} = 0.83$
−1.08	−0.29	$\dfrac{1(-1.08) + 2(-0.29)}{3} = -0.55$
1.23	0.68	$\dfrac{1(1.23) + 2(0.68)}{3} = 0.86$
0.08	0.00	$\dfrac{1(0.08 + 2(0.00)}{3} = 0.03$

CHAPTER 4
The Normal Distribution

COMPREHENSION CHECK

The following summary reviews the material presented in this chapter. To check your understanding of key concepts, supply the missing words indicated by the numbered blanks.

Many variables are said to be __(1)__ distributed. The normal distribution is not a single distribution but a __(2)__ of distributions, each of which is determined by its __(3)__ and __(4)__ . These distributions have similar properties: they are __(5)__ , __(6)__ , and "bell shaped," with each having a maximum height at the __(7)__ . The normal distribution is also continuous and __(8)__ to the *x* axis, when graphed.

In order to work effectively with a variety of normal distributions that have different means and standard deviations, a standardized normal distribution has been developed. The standard normal distribution or __(9)__ distribution is the distribution of normally distributed standard scores with a __(10)__ equal to zero and standard deviation equal to __(11)__ . Using the properties of the unit normal curve, we can determine the __(12)__ of scores that are between two given values in the distribution. Percentiles and percentile ranks can be calculated using the __(13)__ curve.

The ordinal nature of percentiles and percentile ranks limits their use in __(14)__ analyses. While the use of __(15)__ scores overcomes this limitation when distributions are __(16)__ or near normal in shape, __(17)__ standard scores can be generated that incorporate the advantages of both __(18)__ and __(19)__ . Computing normalized standard scores involves __(20)__ steps. The first is to convert the __(21)__ score to a __(22)__ rank. The second is to convert this percentile rank to a __(23)__ score. This normalized standard score can then be transformed using the general transformation formula. The __(24)__ score is an example of a normalized standard score.

Comprehension Check: Answers

1. normally	9. unit normal	17. normalized
2. family	10. mean	18. percentile ranks
3. mean	11. one	19. *z* scores
4. standard deviation	12. proportion	20. two
5. unimodal	13. standard normal	21. raw
6. symmetrical	14. statistical	22. percentile
7. mean	15. standard	23. *z*
8. asymptotic	16. normal	24. NCE

CHAPTER 4 EXERCISES

1. What is the height (ordinate) of the standard normal curve for the following standard scores?

Standard score	Ordinate
+1.00	0.2420
+1.35	
−0.54	
−1.83	

2. What is the area under the standard normal curve for the following z scores?

z score	Area
0.00 to +0.75	0.2734
0.00 to −0.37	
−0.67 to +1.25	
+0.35 to +1.67	

Hint: It may be helpful to draw the normal curve and identify the areas. For z score values that span 0, remember to add both the plus and minus areas for the total area.

3. Assume that the mean of a distribution of 8,500 scores is 102 and the standard deviation is 18. What score would a student have to receive so that 90 percent of the scores are lower?

$$
\begin{aligned}
X' &= (s')(z) + \bar{X}' \\
&= (18)(\quad) + \\
&= \quad + \\
&=
\end{aligned}
$$

Hint: The z in the formula needs to be determined from the area under the standard normal curve that contains 90 percent of the area.

4. What would be the percentile rank of a score of 90 in the distribution of Exercise 3?

$$z = \underline{\hspace{2cm}} = $$

Percentile rank of the score 90 is _____ .

Hint: The area between $z = -0.67$ and $z = 0$ is 0.2486.

5. Applicants for an occupational training program were administered a test designed to provide a measure of eye-hand coordination. The group mean was 65, with a standard deviation of 8. The scores were normally distributed.

a. What z scores correspond to raw scores of 49, 55, 65, and 72?

b. What raw scores were obtained by applicants with z scores of 2.0, −1.0, −0.25, and 1.50?

c. What percentage of scores is above 75?

d. What percentage of scores is between 43 and 73?

e. What is the 67th percentile?

f. What is the percentile rank of a score of 51?

6. A student's *z* scores on three separate tests are 1.78, 2.68, and 1.93.

    a. What is the student's combined *z* score if all tests are counted equally?

    b. What is the student's combined *z* score if the latter two tests are each considered twice as important as the first?

7. A student's final scores in mathematics and English are 83 and 86, respectively. Assume that the class averages are 84 and 88, with standard deviations of 5.3 and 7.2. Which is the better of the student's two scores?

8. Find the area under the standard normal curve for each of the following intervals.

    a. between $z = 1.00$ and $z = 2.00$

    b. above $z = 2.10$

    c. below $z = 1.75$

    d. between $z = -1.25$ and $z = 1.25$

    e. above $z = -2.46$

    f. below $z = -0.82$

9. The 500 members of the freshman class at College C have completed an English placement examination. Assume the scores to be normally distributed, with a mean of 72 and standard deviation of 10, and determine each of the following.

    a. The number of students who achieved a score of 88 or above.

    b. The number of students who scored less than 60.

    c. The 75th percentile.

    d. The 30th percentile.

    e. The percentile rank of a score of 75.

    f. The percentile rank of a score of 65.

Chapter 4 Exercises: Answers

1.

Standard score	Ordinate
+1.00	0.2420
+1.35	0.1604
−0.54	0.3448
−1.83	0.0748

2.

z score	Area
0.00 to +0.75	0.2734
0.00 to −0.37	0.1443
−0.67 to +1.25	0.6430 (0.2486 + 0.3944)
+0.35 to +1.67	0.3157 (0.4525 − 0.1368)

3. $X' = (18)(1.282) + 102$
$$= 23.076 + 102$$
$$= 125.076 \text{ or } 125$$

4. $z = \dfrac{90 - 102}{18} = -0.67$

The area beyond $z = -0.67$ is $0.5000 - 0.2486$, or 0.2514.
Percentile rank of the score 90 is 25.14, or 25.

5. a. $z_{49} = \dfrac{49 - 65}{8} = -2.00$ $\qquad$ $z_{55} = \dfrac{55 - 65}{8} = -1.25$

$z_{65} = \dfrac{65 - 65}{8} = 0.00$ $\qquad$ $z_{72} = \dfrac{72 - 65}{8} = 0.875$

b. $2.0 = \dfrac{X_1 - 65}{8}$ $\quad X_1 = 81$

$-1.0 = \dfrac{X_2 - 65}{8}$ $\quad X_2 = 57$

$-0.25 = \dfrac{X_3 - 65}{8}$ $\quad X_3 = 63$

$1.50 = \dfrac{X_4 - 65}{8}$ $\quad X_4 = 77$

c. $z_{75} = \dfrac{75 - 65}{8} = 1.25$

$\quad$ 10.56%

d. $z_{43} = \dfrac{43 - 65}{8} = -2.75$

$z_{73} = \dfrac{73 - 65}{8} = 1.00$

$49.70\% + 34.13\% = 83.83\%$

e. 67 percent of the scores were below $z = 0.44$

$0.44 = \dfrac{X - 65}{8}$

$X = 68.52$

$P_{67} = 69$

f. $z_{51} = \dfrac{51 - 65}{8} = -1.75$

$PR_{51} = 4.01$

6. a. Combined score $= \dfrac{1.78 + 2.68 + 1.93}{3} = 2.13$

b. Combined score $= \dfrac{1.78 + 2(2.68) + 2(1.93)}{5} = 2.20$

7. $z_{83} = \dfrac{83 - 84}{5.3} = -0.19$

$z_{86} = \dfrac{86 - 88}{7.2} = -0.28$

The mathematics score is the better of the two scores.

8. a. 0.1359   **d.** 0.7888
   b. 0.0179   **e.** 0.9931
   c. 0.9599   **f.** 0.2061

9. a. $z_{88} = 1.60$ $0.0548(500) = 27$

  b. $z_{60} = -1.20$ $0.1151(500) = 58$

  c. 75 percent of scores were below $z = 0.675$

$$0.675 = \frac{X - 72}{10}$$

$$X = 78.75$$

$$P_{75} = 79$$

  d. $P_{30} = 67$

  e. $PR_{75} = 62$

  f. $PR_{65} = 24$

CHAPTER 5
Correlation: A Measure of Relationship

COMPREHENSION CHECK

The following summary reviews the material presented in this chapter. To check your understanding of key concepts, supply the missing words indicated by the numbered blanks.

The study of __(1)__ between two variables is common in the behavioral sciences. The Pearson product-moment correlation coefficient (PPMC; r) is a common index of the relationship between two variables. The range of r is from __(2)__ to __(3)__, inclusively. The sign of the correlation coefficient indicates the __(4)__ of the relationship or the direction of the __(5)__ of data points for the two variables plotted on Cartesian coordinates. A positive sign indicates a tendency of low scores on one variable to be associated with __(6)__ scores on the second variable and for high scores on the first variable to be associated with __(7)__ scores on the second variable. On the other hand, a negative correlation coefficient tells us that low scores on the first variable are associated with __(8)__ scores on the other, while __(9)__ scores on the first variable are associated with __(10)__ on the second variable.

The absolute value of the correlation (without considering the sign) indicates the __(11)__ of the relationship between the two variables. As a rough rule of thumb, $.00 < r < .30$ (and because of symmetry, .00 to −.30) indicates little to no relationship; $.30 < r < .50$ (or, −.30 to −.50) indicates __(12)__ positive (or negative) relationship; $.50 < r < .70$ (or, −.50 to −.70) indicates __(13)__ positive (or negative) relationship; $.70 < r < .90$ (or, −.70 to −.90) indicates high __(14)__ (or negative) relationship; and $.90 < r < 1.00$ (or, −.90 to −1.00) indicates __(15)__ positive (or negative) relationship. However, we strongly caution the student that interpreting correlations is not as simple as this rule seems to indicate.

There are several equivalent conceptual and computational __(16)__ for the Pearson r. Conceptually, the Pearson r is the mean or average cross-product of the __(17)__ scores on the two variables. A second formula, easier to calculate, involves the use of __(18)__ scores. A third formula involves the use of __(19)__ scores. Lastly, the __(20)__ provides a useful conceptualization of the correlation coefficient. The covariance is defined as the average cross-product of the __(21)__ scores.

Several assumptions underlie the valid use of the Pearson r. The variables must be __(22)__ observations for the same set of objects (persons, schools, etc.). Second, because the mean and variance are used to calculate r, the variables must be measured on __(23)__ or __(24)__ scales. Other assumptions influence the size of the obtained r. One is the assumption that the variables being correlated have a __(25)__ relationship. This means that the data points on a scatterplot tend to fall along a __(26)__ . This is not to say that all the points must fall exactly along a straight line, but that the points display a __(27)__ scatter around a straight line.

There are variables in the behavioral sciences that have a nonlinear or __(28)__ relationship. However, if the Pearson r were computed for curvilinear data, the resulting coefficient would __(29)__ the actual relationship between the two variables. Thus, the Pearson r is __(30)__ for such data.

The __(31)__ of the group on one or both of the variables being correlated affects the __(32)__ of the Pearson *r*. If the group is homogeneous (meaning that the scores are similar and thus less scattered), the variance of the scores is __(33)__ . As the variance tends toward zero, a variable __(34)__ a constant. If either variable (or both) becomes a constant, the formula for *r* becomes meaningless. Therefore, when the group is __(35)__ the resulting correlation will be __(36)__ than one resulting from a heterogeneous group.

If the data are measured at the __(37)__ level, for example the rankings provided by teachers of pupils in a class, the __(38)__ correlation coefficient is an appropriate index of relationship. The numerator of the formula uses the __(39)__ between the ranks on the two variables. If there are __(40)__ in the ranks, the average of the ranks is substituted. Lastly, the __(41)__ and __(42)__ coefficients are often very similar in value, with any differences being due to the __(43)__ .

Although the correlation coefficient is an index of the __(44)__ between two variables, it does *not* follow that the scores on one variable are __(45)__ by the scores on the other variable. A third variable or combination of other variables may determine the observed relationship. Causation can be established only by careful __(46)__ of the variables in the specific context of the investigation.

An appropriate interpretation of *r* may be made in terms of shared variance of the two variables. The square of the correlation, r^2, is called the coefficient of __(47)__ and is defined conceptually as the proportion of variance in one variable that is associated with the variance in the other variable. As an example, suppose that the correlation between age and physical strength for a group of individuals is .50. Squaring *r*, we find that the coefficient of determination is .25. We can conclude that for this sample 25 percent of the variance in __(48)__ is associated with the ages of persons. The remaining 75 percent of the __(49)__ not associated with age may be attributed to other factors (unmeasured here, but potentially measurable), such as the individual's health, motivation, and physical strength training.

Comprehension Check: Answers

1. relationships	**18.** deviation	**35.** homogeneous
2. +1.00 (or −1.00)	**19.** raw	**36.** smaller
3. −1.00 (or +1.00)	**20.** covariance	**37.** ordinal
4. direction	**21.** deviation	**38.** Spearman rho
5. slope	**22.** paired	**39.** difference
6. low	**23.** interval	**40.** ties
7. high	**24.** ratio	**41.** Pearson (or Spearman)
8. high	**25.** linear	**42.** Spearman (or Pearson)
9. high	**26.** line	**43.** ties
10. low	**27.** random	**44.** relationship
11. strength (magnitude)	**28.** curvilinear	**45.** caused
12. low	**29.** underestimate	**46.** consideration
13. moderate	**30.** inappropriate	**47.** determination
14. positive	**31.** homogeneity	**48.** physical strength
15. very high	**32.** size	**49.** variance (in physical strength)
16. formulas	**33.** small	
17. *z*	**34.** reduces to (becomes)	

CHAPTER 5 EXERCISES

1. An educational psychologist wants to investigate the theoretical position that creativity has universal qualities. A study is proposed to look at the relationship between creativity in drawing and creativity in writing. The data for 10 elementary school students are below; both measures of creativity are measured on a 10-point scale.

Student	Writing (X)	Drawing (Y)	X^2	Y^2	XY
1	8	6	64	36	48
2	7	8	49	64	56
3	5	7			
4	3	5			
5	9	7			
6	8	6			
7	2	2			
8	6	7			
9	4	9			
10	7	4			
Σ	59	61	397	409	375

a. Draw the scatterplot for these data.

b. Complete the above table and compute *r*.

$$r = \frac{n\Sigma XY - \Sigma X\Sigma Y}{\sqrt{[n\Sigma X^2 - (\Sigma X)^2][n\Sigma Y^2 - (\Sigma Y)^2]}}$$

$$= \frac{10(\quad) - (\quad)(61)}{\sqrt{[10(\quad) - (59)^2][10(\quad) - (\quad)^2]}}$$

$$= \underline{\qquad\qquad}$$

$$=$$

2. Suppose an experimental psychologist is investigating the relationship between the level of stimulus (X) and subsequent performance (Y) in a controlled environment. The following data are for 12 volunteer subjects.

Student	Stimulus (X)	Performance (Y)	X^2	Y^2	XY
A	18	15	324	225	270
B	12	13	144	169	156
C	15	16			
D	14	12			
E	9	10			
F	11	9			
G	7	8			
H	11	14			
I	13	15			
J	16	17			
K	10	11			
L	17	15			
Σ	153	155	2075	2095	2065

a. Draw the scatterplot for these data.

b. Complete the above table and compute r.

$$r = \frac{n\Sigma XY - \Sigma X \Sigma Y}{\sqrt{[n\Sigma X^2 - (\Sigma X)^2][n\Sigma Y^2 - (\Sigma Y)^2]}}$$

$$= \frac{12(\quad) - (153)(\quad)}{\sqrt{[12(\quad) - (\quad)^2][12(\quad) - (155)^2]}}$$

$$= \underline{\qquad\qquad}$$

$$=$$

3. The following data are the English aptitude scores (X) and English grades (Y) for ten students. Compute the Pearson r.

Student	English aptitude	English grades
1	580	65
2	520	85
3	470	70
4	465	80
5	500	65
6	510	80
7	535	70
8	625	78
9	400	65
10	425	92

$$n = 10 \qquad\qquad \Sigma XY = 376{,}600$$
$$\Sigma X = 5{,}030 \qquad\qquad \Sigma Y = 750$$
$$\Sigma X^2 = 2{,}571{,}500 \qquad\qquad \Sigma Y^2 = 57{,}048$$

$$r = \frac{(\quad) - (\quad)(\quad)}{\sqrt{[\ (\quad) - (\quad)^2][\ (\quad) - (\quad)^2]}}$$

$$= \underline{\qquad\qquad}$$

$$=$$

4. Safety in chemistry classroom activities, specifically in the laboratory, has been a concern in many high schools. An investigation is undertaken to determine the relationship between money spent to improve safety in chemistry labs and the number of injuries sustained by students. This study covered the number of reported injuries per 1,000 students and the annual safety budget measured in thousands of constant dollars (using 1975 = 100) for the years 1971–1985. Compute the Pearson r.

Year	Safety budget (× 1000)	Injury rate
1971	10	1.30
1972	23	1.00
1973	47	.75
1974	12	.90
1975	60	.40
1976	3	1.50
1977	4	1.40
1978	6	1.20

Year	Safety budget (× 1000)	Injury rate
1979	7	.90
1980	10	1.00
1981	67	.60
1982	11	1.30
1983	2	1.65
1984	9	1.10
1985	8	.90

$$n = 15 \qquad \Sigma XY = 214.55$$
$$\Sigma X = 279 \qquad \Sigma Y = 15.9$$
$$\Sigma X^2 = 11{,}551 \qquad \Sigma Y^2 = 18.475$$

$$r = \underline{\hspace{6cm}}$$

$$= $$

5. A sociologist is investigating the relationship between years of education and income. The data for fifteen employees are as follows. Compute the Pearson r.

Employee	Education (X)	Income (× 1,000) (Y)
1	6	11.6
2	8	14.2
3	9	12.7
4	10	13.5
5	11	15.9
6	12	14.5
7	12	16.3
8	13	17.1
9	14	14.0
10	14	16.8
11	15	13.0
12	16	18.0
13	16	15.9
14	17	17.7
15	20	20.4

$$n = 15 \qquad \Sigma XY = 3{,}076.8$$
$$\Sigma X = 193 \qquad \Sigma Y = 231.6$$
$$\Sigma X^2 = 2{,}677 \qquad \Sigma Y^2 = 3{,}654.4$$

6. The fifteen graduates of a dental hygiene program are ranked according to their scores on the clinical and written portions of their state board of examination. Compute the Spearman rho correlation coefficient.

Graduate	Clinical rank	Written rank	d	d^2
A	4	5	−1	1
B	12	11	1	1
C	8	8		
D	6	3		
E	5	10		
F	1	4		

Graduate	Clinical rank	Written rank	d	d^2
G	15	13		
H	14	14		
I	11	15		
J	3	1		
K	2	2		
L	7	6		
M	9	7		
N	10	9		
O	13	12		
			$\Sigma d =$	$\Sigma d^2 =$

$$\rho = 1 - \frac{6\Sigma d^2}{n(n^2 - 1)}$$

$$= 1 - \frac{6(\quad)}{15[(\quad)^2 - \quad]}$$

$$= 1 - \frac{\quad}{15(\quad)}$$

$$= 1 -$$

$$=$$

7. In a pet show, the judging of a particular breed of dog is determined by color and body shape. Use the results of the judging to compute rho.

Dog	Color	Body Shape
1	4	3
2	8	7
3	1	4
4	5	8
5	2	1
6	6	5
7	3	2
8	7	6

Chapter 5 Exercises: Answers

1. b.

Student	Writing (X)	Drawing (Y)	X^2	Y^2	XY
1	8	6	64	36	48
2	7	8	49	64	56
3	5	7	25	49	35
4	3	5	9	25	15
5	9	7	81	49	63
6	8	6	64	36	48
7	2	2	4	4	4
8	6	7	36	49	42
9	4	9	16	81	36
10	7	4	49	16	28
Σ	59	61	397	409	375

$$r = \frac{n\Sigma XY - \Sigma X\Sigma Y}{\sqrt{[n\Sigma X^2 - (\Sigma X)^2][n\Sigma Y^2 - (\Sigma Y)^2]}}$$

$$= \frac{10(375) - (59)(61)}{\sqrt{[10(397) - (59)^2][10(409) - (61)^2]}}$$

$$= \frac{151}{\sqrt{(489)(369)}}$$

$$= .355$$

2. b.

Student	Stimulus (X)	Performance (Y)	X^2	Y^2	XY
A	18	15	324	225	270
B	12	13	144	169	156
C	15	16	225	256	240
D	14	12	196	144	168
E	9	10	81	100	90
F	11	9	121	81	99
G	7	8	49	64	56
H	11	14	121	196	154
I	13	15	169	225	195
J	16	17	256	289	272
K	10	11	100	121	110
L	17	15	289	225	255
Σ	153	155	2075	2095	2065

$$r = \frac{12(2,065) - (153)(155)}{\sqrt{[12(2,075) - (153)^2][12(2,095) - (155)^2]}}$$

$$= \frac{1,065}{\sqrt{(1,491)(1,115)}}$$

$$= .826$$

3. $n = 10$ $\Sigma XY = 376,600$

$\Sigma X = 5,030$ $\Sigma Y = 750$

$\Sigma X^2 = 2,571,500$ $\Sigma Y^2 = 57,048$

$$r = \frac{10(376,600) - (5,030)(750)}{\sqrt{[10(2,571,500) - (5,030)^2][10(57,048) - (750)^2]}}$$

$$= \frac{-6,500}{\sqrt{(414,100)(7,980)}}$$

$$= -.11$$

4. $n = 15$ $\Sigma XY = 214.55$

$\Sigma X = 279$ $\Sigma Y = 15.9$

$\Sigma X^2 = 11,551$ $\Sigma Y^2 = 18.475$

$$r = \frac{15(214.55) - (279)(15.9)}{\sqrt{[15(11,551) - (279)^2][15(18.475) - (15.9)^2]}}$$

$$= -\frac{-1217.85}{\sqrt{(95,424)(24.315)}}$$

$$= -.80$$

5. $n = 15$ $\qquad \Sigma XY = 3,076.8$

$\Sigma X = 193$ $\qquad \Sigma Y = 231.6$

$\Sigma X^2 = 2,677$ $\qquad \Sigma Y^2 = 3,654.4$

$$r = \frac{15(3,076.8) - (193)(231.6)}{\sqrt{[15(2,677) - (193)^2][15(3,654.4) - (231.6)^2]}}$$

$$= \frac{1,453.2}{\sqrt{(2,906)(1,177.44)}}$$

$$= .786$$

6. $\Sigma d = 0$ $\qquad \Sigma d^2 = 76$

$$\rho = 1 - \frac{6(76)}{15[(15)^2 - 1]}$$

$$= 1 - \frac{456}{15(224)}$$

$$= 1 - .136$$

$$= 0.86$$

7. $\rho = 1 - \frac{6(24)}{8(64 - 1)}$

$$= 0.71$$

CHAPTER 6
Linear Regression: Prediction

COMPREHENSION CHECK

The following summary reviews the material presented in this chapter. To check your understanding of key concepts, supply the missing words indicated by the numbered blanks.

The concept of linear regression refers to __(1)__ or estimating __(2)__ on one variable based on __(3)__ of the scores on a second variable. In linear regression, the slope-intercept equation of a straight line is $\hat{Y} = bX + a$, where $\hat{Y}$ is the __(4)__ score, b, is the __(5)__ of the line, and a is the Y __(6)__ . The slope is defined as the change in __(7)__ associated with a __(8)__ change in __(9)__ . The two steps involved in the process of prediction are determining the __(10)__ equation and using the equation to __(11)__ scores.

In predicting Y from X, the slope of the regression line is denoted __(12)__ and is referred to as the regression __(13)__ . The intercept is symbolized __(14)__ and is called the regression __(15)__ . Thus, the regression equation used to predict Y from X is given by __(16)__ . This line of "best fit" satisfies the __(17)__ criterion, which means that the sum of squared distances from data points to the regression line is a __(18)__ . When predicting standard scores (z scores) on Y from standard scores on X, the standard score on X is multiplied by the __(19)__ between X and Y. The formula for predicting standard scores from standard scores is __(20)__ .

An error in prediction is defined as the difference between an individual's actual score on the Y variable and the __(21)__ score ($\hat{Y}$). Symbolically, $e = $ __(22)__ . In linear regression, we are concerned with the distribution of __(23)__ scores as well as the variance and __(24)__ of these scores. The mean of this distribution of errors of prediction is __(25)__ ; the estimated standard deviation of the error scores is called the __(26)__ error of __(27)__ .

Assumptions associated with the development and use of the regression line are that the X and Y variables are __(28)__ related and that the errors of prediction are assumed to be __(29)__ distributed with a __(30)__ equal to zero and a standard deviation equal to __(31)__ . Finally, the assumption of __(32)__ is that the variances of the errors of prediction at every value of X are equal. This is the same as saying the variances of the __(33)__ distributions are equal.

Simply because we can predict Y from knowledge of X does not imply that X __(34)__ Y. However, the order or occurrence of the variables can indicate whether such a relationship is possible. The method for inferring cause-and-effect relationships is through understanding the __(35)__ under investigation.

Comprehension Check: Answers

1. predicting	**4.** predicted	**7.** Y
2. scores	**5.** slope	**8.** unit
3. knowledge	**6.** intercept	**9.** X

10. regression	19. correlation coefficient	28. linearly
11. predict	20. $z_{\hat{Y}} = (r)(z_X)$	29. normally
12. b	21. predicted	30. mean
13. coefficient	22. $(Y - \hat{Y})$	31. $s_{Y \cdot X}$
14. a	23. error	32. homoscedasticity
15. constant	24. standard deviation	33. conditional
16. $\hat{Y} = bX + a$	25. zero	34. causes
17. least squares	26. standard	35. variables
18. minimum	27. prediction	

CHAPTER 6 EXERCISES

1. A professional licensing examination contains both written and clinical components. Complete the following table and develop the regression equation for predicting clinical scores from written scores.

Examinee	Written (X)	Clinical (Y)	X^2	Y^2	XY
1	85	89	7,225	7,921	7,565
2	76	71	5,776	5,041	5,396
3	92	90			
4	60	53			
5	81	88			
6	84	85			
7	95	98			
8	56	62			
9	76	79			
10	68	62			
11	93	92			
12	71	75			
13	88	90			
14	69	78			
15	80	91			
Σ	1,174	1,203	93,838	98,927	96,154

a. Plot the data in a scatterplot.

b. Determine the regression equation for predicting the clinical scores (Y) from written scores (X).

$$b = \frac{n\Sigma XY - (\Sigma X)(\Sigma Y)}{n\Sigma X^2 - (\Sigma X)^2}$$

$$= \frac{15(\qquad) - (1,174)(\qquad)}{15(\qquad) - (1,174)^2}$$

$$= \underline{\qquad}$$

$$=$$

$$a = \frac{Y - b\Sigma X}{n}$$

$$= \frac{1,203 - (\qquad)(\qquad)}{15}$$

$$=$$

Therefore,

$$\hat{Y} = bX + a = (\qquad)X + (\qquad)$$

c. Draw the regression line on the scatterplot.

d. For an examinee who had a written score of 77, predict the clinical score.

$$\hat{Y} = bX + a = (\qquad)(77) + (\qquad)$$
$$= $$

e. Compute the standard error of prediction using formula 6.11 and formula 6.12.

$$s_{Y \cdot X} = s_Y\left(\sqrt{1 - r^2}\right)\left(\sqrt{(n-1)/(n-2)}\right) \qquad (6.11)$$

$$s_{Y \cdot X} = s_Y\sqrt{1 - r^2} \qquad (6.12)$$

where $s_Y = \sqrt{SS/(n-1)}$ (see Chapter 3)

$$= \sqrt{2446.40/14}$$
$$= 13.22$$

and $r = \dfrac{n\Sigma XY - \Sigma X \Sigma Y}{\sqrt{[n\Sigma X^2 - (\Sigma X)^2][n\Sigma Y^2 - (\Sigma Y)^2]}}$

$$= \frac{15(\qquad) - (\qquad)(1,203)}{\sqrt{[15(\qquad) - (1,174)^2][15(98,927) - (\qquad)^2]}}$$

$$= $$

Therefore,

$$s_{Y \cdot X} = 13.22\sqrt{1 - (\qquad)^2}\ \sqrt{\qquad / \qquad} \qquad (6.11)$$
$$= (5.33)(1.04)$$
$$= $$

and

$$s_{Y \cdot X} = 13.22\sqrt{1 - (\qquad)^2} \qquad (6.12)$$
$$= $$

2. A social historian is interested in the relationship between education (measured in years of formal schooling) (X) and income (Y). The data were collected from nine individuals.

Subject	Education (X)	Income $(\times 1,000)$ (Y)	X^2	Y^2	XY
1	4	6	16	36	24
2	6	12	36	144	72
3	8	14			
4	11	10			
5	12	17			
6	14	16			
7	16	13			
8	17	16			
9	20	19			
Σ	108	123	1522	1807	1606

a. Plot the data in a scatterplot.

b. Determine the regression equation for predicting income (Y) from education (X).

$$b = \frac{n\Sigma XY - (\Sigma X)(\Sigma Y)}{n\Sigma X^2 - (\Sigma X)^2}$$

$$= \frac{9(\quad\quad) - (\quad\quad)(\quad\quad)}{9(\quad\quad) - (\quad\quad)^2}$$

$$= \underline{\quad\quad\quad\quad}$$

$$=$$

$$a = \frac{Y - b\Sigma X}{n}$$

$$= \frac{-(\quad\quad)(\quad\quad)}{\quad\quad}$$

$$=$$

Therefore,

$$\hat{Y} = bX + a = (\quad\quad)X + (\quad\quad)$$

c. Draw the regression line on the scatterplot.

d. For a subject with 13 years of education, predict the income.

$$\hat{Y} = bX + a = (\quad\quad)(\quad\quad) + (\quad\quad)$$
$$=$$

e. Compute the standard error of prediction using formula 6.11 and formula 6.12.

$$s_{Y\cdot X} = s_Y\left(\sqrt{1 - r^2}\right)\left(\sqrt{(n-1)/(n-2)}\right) \quad\quad (6.11)$$

$$s_{Y\cdot X} = s_Y \sqrt{1 - r^2} \quad\quad (6.12)$$

where $s_Y = \sqrt{SS/(n-1)}$ \quad (see Chapter 3)

$$= \sqrt{126/8}$$
$$= 3.97$$

and $r = \dfrac{n\Sigma XY - \Sigma X\Sigma Y}{\sqrt{[n\Sigma X^2 - (\Sigma X)^2][n\Sigma Y^2 - (\Sigma Y)^2]}}$

$$= \frac{9(\quad\quad) - (\quad\quad)(\quad\quad)}{\sqrt{[9(\quad\quad) - (\quad\quad)^2][9(\quad\quad) - (\quad\quad)^2]}}$$

$$=$$

Therefore,

$$s_{Y\cdot X} = 3.97\sqrt{1 - (\quad\quad)^2}\sqrt{\quad/\quad} \quad\quad (6.11)$$
$$= (2.53)(1.07)$$
$$=$$

and

$$s_{Y\cdot X} = 3.97\sqrt{1 - (0.770)^2} \quad\quad (6.12)$$
$$=$$

3. For the data in Exercise 2, compute the predicted income ($\hat{Y}$) for each education level (X) and complete the following table.

Subject	Education (X)	Income (× 1,000) (Y)	$\hat{Y}$	e	e^2
1	4	6	9.067	−3.067	9.4065
2	6	12	10.217	1.783	3.1791
3	8	14			
4	11	10			
5	12	17			
6	14	16			
7	16	13			
8	17	16			
9	20	19			
				−0.003*	51.2214

*approximately zero

a. Compute the standard error of prediction using formula 6.10. Compare the answer to the above when formula 6.11 was used.

$$s_{Y \cdot X} = \sqrt{\frac{\Sigma e^2}{n-2}}$$

$$= \sqrt{\underline{\hspace{3cm}}}$$

$$= \underline{\hspace{2cm}}$$

4. Consider the data in Question 2 in Chapter 5 in which the experimental psychologist was investigating the relationship between stimulus and performance. The summary data were

$n = 12$	$\Sigma XY = 2065$
$\Sigma X = 153$	$\Sigma Y = 155$
$\Sigma X^2 = 2075$	$\Sigma Y^2 = 2095$

a. Plot the data in a scatterplot.

b. Determine the regression equation for predicting performance scores (Y) from stimulus scores (X).

$$b = \frac{(\quad)(\quad)-(\quad)(\quad)}{(\quad)(\quad)-(\quad)^2}$$

$$= \frac{\underline{\hspace{3cm}}}{\underline{\hspace{2cm}}}$$

$$= \underline{\hspace{2cm}}$$

$$a = \frac{\underline{\hspace{1cm}}-(\quad)(\quad)}{\underline{\hspace{4cm}}}$$

$$= \underline{\hspace{2cm}}$$

Therefore,

$$\hat{Y} = bX + a = (\quad\quad) X + (\quad\quad)$$

c. Draw the regression line on the scatterplot.

d. For a student who had a stimulus score of 14, predict the performance score.

$$\hat{Y} = bX + a = (\qquad) X + (\qquad)$$
$$= (\qquad)(\quad) + (\qquad)$$
$$=$$

e. Compute the standard error of prediction using formula 6.11 and formula 6.12.

$$s_Y = \sqrt{92.9167/11}$$
$$= 2.906$$

and $r = 0.826$

5. Consider the data in Question 5 in Chapter 5 in which the sociologist was investigating the relationship between education and income. The summary data were

$n = 15$	$\Sigma XY = 3076.8$
$\Sigma X = 193$	$\Sigma Y = 231.6$
$\Sigma X^2 = 2677$	$\Sigma Y^2 = 3654.4$

a. Plot the data in a scatterplot.

b. Determine the regression equation for predicting income (Y) from education (X).

$$b = \frac{(\quad)(\qquad) - (\quad)(\qquad)}{(\quad)(\qquad) - (\quad)^2}$$

$$= \frac{\qquad}{\qquad}$$

$$=$$

$$a = \frac{(\qquad) - (\qquad)(\qquad)}{\qquad}$$

$$=$$

Therefore,

$$\hat{Y} = bX + a = (\qquad) X + (\qquad)$$

c. Draw the regression line on the scatterplot.

d. For an employee who had an education of 14 years, predict the income.

$$\hat{Y} = bX + a = (\qquad) X + (\qquad)$$
$$= (\qquad)(\quad) + (\qquad)$$
$$=$$

e. Compute the standard error of prediction using formula 6.11 and formula 6.12.

$$s_Y = \sqrt{78.496/14}$$
$$= 2.368$$

and $r = 0.786$

Chapter 6 Exercises: Answers

1.

Examinee	Written (X)	Clinical (Y)	X^2	Y^2	XY
1	85	89	7,225	7,921	7,565
2	76	71	5,776	5,041	5,396
3	92	90	8,464	8,100	8,280
4	60	53	3,600	2,809	3,180
5	81	88	6,561	7,744	7,128
6	84	85	7,056	7,225	7,140
7	95	98	9,025	9,604	9,310
8	56	62	3,136	3,844	3,472
9	76	79	5,776	6,241	6,004
10	68	62	4,624	3,844	4,216
11	93	92	8,649	8,464	8,556
12	71	75	5,041	5,625	5,325
13	88	90	7,744	8,100	7,920
14	69	78	4,761	6,084	5,382
15	80	91	6,400	8,281	7,280
Σ	1,174	1,203	93,838	98,927	96,154

b. $b = \dfrac{15(96,154) - (1,174)(1,203)}{15(93,838) - (1,174)^2}$

$= \dfrac{29,988}{29,294}$

$= 1.024$

$a = \dfrac{1,203 - (1.024)(1,174)}{15}$

$= 0.055$

Therefore,

$\hat{Y} = bX + a = (1.024)X + (0.055)$

d. $\hat{Y} = bX + a = (1.024)(77) + (0.055)$

$= 78.903$

e. $s_{Y \cdot X} = s_Y\left(\sqrt{1 - r^2}\right)\left(\sqrt{(n-1)/(n-2)}\right)$ (6.11)

$= \left(\sqrt{1 - (0.915)^2}\right)\left(\sqrt{14/13}\right)$

$= (5.33)(1.04)$

$= 5.54$

$s_{Y \cdot X} = s_Y \sqrt{1 - r^2}$ (6.12)

$= 13.22\sqrt{1 - (0.915)^2}$

$= 5.33$

2.

Subject	Education (X)	Income $(\times 1,000)$ (Y)	X^2	Y^2	XY
1	4	6	16	36	24
2	6	12	36	144	72
3	8	14	64	196	112
4	11	10	121	100	110
5	12	17	144	289	204
6	14	16	196	256	224
7	16	13	256	169	208
8	17	16	289	256	272
9	20	19	400	361	380
Σ	108	123	1522	1807	1606

b. $b = \dfrac{9(1606) - (108)(123)}{9(1522) - (108)^2}$

$= \dfrac{1170}{2034}$

$= 0.575$

$a = \dfrac{123 - (0.575)(108)}{9}$

$= 6.767$

Therefore,

$\hat{Y} = bX + a = (0.575)X + (6.767)$

d. $\hat{Y} = bX + a = (0.575)(13) + (6.767)$

$\qquad = 14.242$

e. $s_{Y \cdot X} = s_Y \left(\sqrt{1 - r^2} \right) \left(\sqrt{(n-1)/(n-2)} \right)$

$\qquad = 3.97 \left(\sqrt{1 - (0.770)^2} \right) \left(\sqrt{8/7} \right)$ $\qquad$ (6.11)

$\qquad = 2.71$

$s_{Y \cdot X} = s_Y \sqrt{1 - r^2}$ $\qquad$ (6.12)

$\qquad = 3.97 \sqrt{1 - (0.770)^2}$

$\qquad = 2.53$

3.

Subject	Education (X)	Income $(\times 1,000)$ (Y)	$\hat{Y}$	e	e^2
1	4	6	9.067	−3.067	9.4065
2	6	12	10.217	1.783	3.1791
3	8	14	11.367	2.633	6.9327
4	11	10	13.092	−3.092	9.5605
5	12	17	13.667	3.333	11.1089
6	14	16	14.817	1.183	1.3995
7	16	13	15.967	−2.967	8.8031

Subject	Education (X)	Income (× 1,000) (Y)	$\hat{Y}$	e	e^2
8	17	16	16.542	−0.542	0.2938
9	20	19	18.267	0.733	0.5373
				−0.003*	51.2214

*approximately zero

a. Compute the standard error of prediction using formula 6.10.

$$s_{Y \cdot X} = \sqrt{\frac{\Sigma e^2}{n-2}}$$

$$= \sqrt{\frac{51.2214}{7}}$$

$$= 2.71$$

4. $n = 12$ $\Sigma XY = 2065$
$\Sigma X = 153$ $\Sigma Y = 155$
$\Sigma X^2 = 2075$ $\Sigma Y^2 = 2095$

b. $b = \dfrac{12(2065) - (153)(155)}{12(2075) - (153)^2}$

$$= \frac{1065}{1491}$$

$$= 0.714$$

$$a = \frac{155 - (0.714)(153)}{12}$$

$$= 3.813$$

Therefore,

$$\hat{Y} = bX + a = (0.714)X + (3.813)$$

d. $\hat{Y} = bX + a = (0.714)X + (3.813)$

$$= (0.714)14 + (3.813)$$

$$= 13.809$$

e. $s_{Y \cdot X} = s_Y \left(\sqrt{1 - r^2} \right) \left(\sqrt{(n-1)/(n-2)} \right)$ (6.11)

$$= 2.906 \left(\sqrt{1 - (0.826)^2} \right) \left(\sqrt{11/10} \right)$$

$$= (1.638)(1.049)$$

$$= 1.718$$

$$s_{Y \cdot X} = s_Y \sqrt{1 - r^2}$$ (6.12)

$$= 2.906 \sqrt{1 - (0.826)^2}$$

$$= 1.638$$

5. $n = 15$ $\Sigma XY = 3076.8$
      $\Sigma X = 193$ $\Sigma Y = 231.6$
     $\Sigma X^2 = 2677$ $\Sigma Y^2 = 3654.4$

b. $b = \dfrac{15(3076.8) - (193)(231.6)}{15(2677) - (193)^2}$

$ = \dfrac{1453.2}{2096}$

$ = 0.500$

$a = \dfrac{231.6 - (0.500)(193)}{15}$

$ = 9.007$

Therefore,

$$\hat{Y} = bX + a = (0.500)X + (9.007)$$

d. $\hat{Y} = bX + a = (0.500)X + (9.007)$

$\phantom{\hat{Y}} = (0.500)14 + (9.007)$

$\phantom{\hat{Y}} = 16.007$

e. $s_{Y \cdot X} = s_Y \left(\sqrt{1 - r^2} \right) \left(\sqrt{(n-1)/(n-2)} \right)$ (6.11)

$\phantom{s_{Y \cdot X}} = 2.368 \left(\sqrt{1 - (0.786)^2} \right) \left(\sqrt{14/13} \right)$

$\phantom{s_{Y \cdot X}} = (1.464)(1.04)$

$\phantom{s_{Y \cdot X}} = 1.522$

$$s_{Y \cdot X} = s_Y \sqrt{1 - r^2}$$ (6.12)

$\phantom{s_{Y \cdot X}} = 2.368 \sqrt{1 - (0.786)^2}$

$\phantom{s_{Y \cdot X}} = 1.464$

CHAPTER 7
Sampling, Probability, and Sampling Distributions

COMPREHENSION CHECK

The following summary reviews the material presented in this chapter. To check your understanding of key concepts, supply the missing words indicated by the numbered blanks.

In previous chapters, we presented ___(1)___ statistics to classify and summarize ___(2)___ , to describe distributions and individual ___(3)___ , and to determine the ___(4)___ between variables. Statistical procedures are also available for ___(5)___ substantive theories, for generalizing those theories to given ___(6)___ , and for ___(7)___ the parameters of a population. The chain of ___(8)___ for inferential statistics allows researchers to make inferences about a population ___(9)___ based on a corresponding sample ___(10)___ .

There are several concepts underlying the application of inferential statistics. A major one is probability. The ___(11)___ of event A is defined as the ___(12)___ of the number of outcomes including the event to the ___(13)___ number of outcomes. Several rules or laws govern the probability of two or more events, defined as ___(14)___ events. For mutually ___(15)___ events, the addition rule is $P(X \text{ or } Y) = $ ___(16)___ . For non-mutually exclusive events, the addition rule is $P(X \text{ or } Y) = $ ___(17)___ . There are also rules for independent and ___(18)___ events. For independent events, the multiplication rule is $P(X \text{ and } Y) = $ ___(19)___ . For non-independent events, the multiplication rule is $P(X \text{ and } Y) = $ ___(20)___ .

A second basic concept involved in inferential statistics is the extension of probability laws to the idea of an ___(21)___ distribution of ___(22)___ possible outcomes of a particular event. The underlying distributions commonly used in statistics are ___(23)___ distributions. They are not recalculated for each analysis, but are contained in tables.

Two other mathematical tools used to develop underlying distributions are the factorial operator and the ___(24)___ operator. A factorial is a number with an ___(25)___ after it, for example 6!; the mathematical operation consists of multiplying the original number, in the present case 6, by each ___(26)___ , down to and including 1. Combinations answer the question, "How many ways can we select a ___(27)___ subset of things or persons from a population?" and are represented symbolically as $_NC_n$. Any combination can be calculated using the factorial operator with this formula: ___(28)___ / ___(29)___ .

Two distributions commonly used as underlying distributions for making statistical inferences are the ___(30)___ and the ___(31)___ distributions. The binomial distribution is generated by taking the binomial ___(32)___ and raising it to the *n*th power. The ___(33)___ distribution is also used as an underlying ___(34)___ . It is most often used for describing the ___(35)___ distribution of a particular statistic, for example the mean. The sampling distribution of the mean is the ___(36)___ distribution of all the possible ___(37)___ ; in this case the outcomes are the sample means. As the number of events or trials increases, the ___(38)___ distribution becomes closer and closer to the ___(39)___ distribution.

Inferential statistics includes hypothesis testing and parameter estimation. The chain of reasoning is intended to help us make informed judgments about __(40)__ parameters based on sample __(41)__ . The three major components include: __(42)__ samples, __(43)__ distributions, and an __(44)__ about one or more parameters. In inferential statistics, three distributions must be kept distinct in your mind:

1. The distribution of __(45)__ in the population
2. The distribution of scores in a __(46)__ from that population
3. The __(47)__ distribution of the mean

Several mathematical theorems define the shape, __(48)__ , and variability of the sampling distribution of the mean. The shape of the sampling distribution is defined by the __(49)__ (2 words) theorem, which states:

As the sample size (*n*) __(50)__ , the sampling distribution of the __(51)__ for simple random samples of *n* cases, taken from a population with a mean of __(52)__ and a finite variance of __(53)__ , approximates the normal distribution.

The __(54)__ tendency and variability of the sampling distribution are defined by using expected __(55)__ . The expected value of the sample mean is __(56)__ , and the expected value of the __(57)__ is σ^2/n where σ^2 is the variance in the __(58)__ and *n* is the sample __(59)__ . Further, the standard deviation of the sampling __(60)__ ($\sigma_{\bar{x}}$) is termed the __(61)__ (2 words) of the mean.

There are two general statements about the sampling distribution of the mean. The first is that as the sample size __(62)__ the standard error decreases. The second is that even when the population is non-normal, the shape of the sampling distribution becomes __(63)__ as the sample size increases.

Sampling is required to study many __(64)__ because researchers do not have the resources to measure everyone of interest. There are __(65)__ plans for sampling from a population, of which __(66)__ techniques are presented in Chapter 7. The first, and most common, is the __(67)__ random sample, which differs depending on whether the sampling procedure is with or without __(68)__ . It is very important to note that samples of __(69)__ are not random and may yield misleading results when inferential statistics are applied. A second type of sampling plan, which involves the use of a sampling fraction (*n/N*, where *n* is the size of the sample and *N* is the size of the population), is called __(70)__ sampling. A potential biasing factor with this procedure is the operation of some __(71)__ factor within the list of population members. When members of a population occur in natural groups or units, for example work groups or classrooms, __(72)__ may be applied; the unit of __(73)__ is the cluster. Following selection, all individuals in the __(74)__ are measured under this procedure. Lastly, __(75)__ random sampling is applicable when the population is heterogeneous and divisible into levels. The levels are called __(76)__ , and the procedure involves taking a __(77)__ (2 words) sample within each level. A variant on this technique is __(78)__ allocation, which means that each of the strata contributes to the total sample proportional to its size in the __(79)__ . A major advantage of a stratified random sampling plan is that the __(80)__ of the sampling distribution will decrease, thus increasing the statistical "precision" of the research design.

Comprehension Check: Answers

1. descriptive
2. data
3. scores
4. relationship
5. testing (evaluating)
6. populations
7. estimating
8. reasoning
9. parameter
10. statistic
11. probability
12. ratio
13. total
14. compound
15. exclusive
16. $P(X) + P(Y)$
17. $P(X) + P(Y) - P(X \text{ and } Y)$
18. nonindependent
19. $P(X) \times P(Y)$
20. $P(X) \times P(Y \mid X)$
21. underlying

22. all	**42.** random	**62.** increases
23. theoretical	**43.** sampling	**63.** normal
24. combination	**44.** inference (judgment)	**64.** populations
25. exclamation point	**45.** scores	**65.** multiple
26. lower number	**46.** sample	**66.** four (4)
27. different	**47.** sampling	**67.** simple
28. $N!$	**48.** location (central tendency)	**68.** replacement
29. $n! (N-n)!$	**49.** central limit	**69.** volunteers
30. binomial	**50.** increases	**70.** systematic
31. normal	**51.** mean	**71.** periodic
32. $(X+Y)$	**52.** μ	**72.** cluster
33. normal	**53.** σ^2	**73.** sampling
34. distribution	**54.** central	**74.** cluster
35. sampling	**55.** values	**75.** stratified
36. underlying	**56.** μ	**76.** strata
37. outcomes	**57.** variance	**77.** simple random
38. binomial	**58.** population	**78.** proportional
39. normal	**59.** size	**79.** population
40. population	**60.** distribution	**80.** variance
41. statistics	**61.** standard error	

CHAPTER 7 EXERCISES

1. Assume that rolling the value of 6 on one roll of a die is considered favorable.

   a. What is the probability of this favorable event occurring?

   $P(A) = 1/? =$

   b. What is the probability of *not* rolling a 6 on one roll of the die?

   $P(\bar{A}) = 1 - P(A) = 1 - \quad =$

2. Assume that each of the following whole numbers is written on a separate slip of paper and placed in a bowl: 1, 2, 3, 4, 5, 6, 7, and 8.

   a. What is the probability of drawing any one number from the bowl?

   $P(A) =$

   b. Define the addition rule for mutually exclusive events.

   $P(A \ or \ B) = P(A) +$

   c. Use the addition rule and determine the probability of drawing either a 3 or 6 from the bowl.

   $P(3 \ or \ 6) = \quad +$
   $\quad =$
   $\quad =$

   d. What is the probability of drawing an odd number from the bowl?

   $P(1 \ or \ 3 \ or \ 5 \ or \ 7) =$
   $\quad =$
   $\quad =$

3. Using the whole numbers 1 through 8, define the following compound events.

Event A = selecting an odd number
Event B = selecting an even number
Event C = selecting a number that is a multiple of 3

a. Use the addition rule and determine P(A *or* B)

P(A *or* B) =
    =

b. Define the addition rule for nonmutually exclusive events.

P(A *or* B) = P(A) +   −

c. Using the addition rule for nonmutually exclusive events with the above compound events, determine P(A *or* C) and P(B *or* C).

P(A *or* C) = P(1 + 3 +   +   ) + P(3 +   ) − P(   )
    =
    =

P(B *or* C) =
    =
    =

4. Define the multiplication rule for statistically independent events.

P(A *and* B) = P(A) · P(B)

a. Assuming sampling with replacement, determine P(2 *and* 5).

P(2 *and* 5) = P(2) ·
    =   ·
    =

b. Define the multiplication rule for statistically dependent events.

P(A *and* B) =   ·

c. Assuming sampling without replacement, determine P(2 *and* 5) (i.e., statistically dependent events).

P(2 *and* 5) =
    =
    =

5. a. Using the concept of the binomial distribution and two unbiased coins, there are four possible outcomes for a single toss of these two coins; they are:

Outcome	First coin	Second coin	Probability
1	H	H	0.25
2	H		
3			
4			

b. Use the binomial expansion and show that outcomes 2 and 3 are the same. (Let X = probability of a head and Y = probability of a tail.)

$P(X + Y)^2 = (X + Y)(X + Y)$
    $= X^2 +$ $+$
    $= (0.50)^2 +$ $+$
    $=$

6. Consider a 6-item true-false test. Use the binomial expansion to determine the probability of getting 5 out of the 6 items correct by chance.

$$P(x) = \frac{n!}{(n-x)!(x)!} p^x q^{(n-x)}$$

$$P(5) = \frac{6!}{(\quad)!(\quad)!} (\quad)^5 (\quad)^{(6-5)}$$

$$= 6 \cdot (\quad)^5 (\quad)$$

$$= 6(\qquad)(\quad)$$

$$=$$

7. Suppose a tire manufacturer knows that 5 percent of a certain brand of tire will fail before the guarantee has expired. If we select three tires at random, what is the probability that all three will fail, two will fail, one will fail, or none will fail?

$$P(x) = \frac{n!}{(n-x)!(x)!} p^x q^{(n-x)}$$

$$P(3) = \frac{!}{(\quad)!(\quad)!} (0.05)^3 (0.95)^{(n-3)}$$

$$=$$

$$=$$

$$P(2) = \frac{3!}{(3-2)!(2)!} (\quad)^2 (\quad)^1$$

$$=$$

$$=$$

$$=$$

$$P(1) =$$

$$=$$

$$=$$

$$=$$

$$P(0) =$$

$$=$$

$$=$$

8. Consider a 10-item multiple-choice test with four choices per item.

a. Use the binomial expansion to determine the probability of getting 7 items correct just by chance.

$$P(x) = \frac{n!}{(n-x)!(x)!} p^x q^{(n-x)}$$

$$P(7) = \frac{10!}{(\quad)!(7)!} (\quad)^7 (0.75)^{(\quad)}$$

$$= (\quad) \cdot (\quad)^7 (\quad)^3$$

$$= 120(\qquad)(\qquad)$$

$$=$$

b. Use the binomial expansion to determine the probability of getting 2 items correct just by chance.

$$P(2) =$$
$$=$$
$$=$$
$$=$$

9. Suppose that the distribution of English achievement scores for all ninth grade students is known to be normal, with mean (μ) equal to 75 and standard deviation (σ) equal to 15. Further, suppose that all these scores have been recorded on small slips of paper and placed in a large container. Using the normal distribution as the underlying distribution of all possible outcomes:

a. Determine the probability of drawing a score from the container that is between 75 and 90.

$$z = \frac{X - \mu}{\sigma} = \frac{90 -}{} =$$

From Table 1, area between $z = 0.0$ and $z = $ is 0.3413. Therefore, the probability of obtaining a score between 75 and 90 is _____ .

b. What is the probability of drawing a score from the container that is between 60 and 75?

$$z = \frac{X -}{} = \frac{-}{} = -1.0$$

From Table 1, area between $z = $ and $z = $ is _____ . Therefore, the probability of obtaining a score between 60 and 75 is _____ .

c. What is the probability of drawing a score from the container that is greater than 90?

From Table 1, area greater than $z = +1.0$ is _____ . Therefore, the probability of obtaining a score greater than 90 is _____ .

d. What is the probability of drawing a score from the container that is less than 45?

$$z =$$

From Table 1, area less than $z = $ is _____ . Therefore, the probability of obtaining a score less than 45 is _____ .

10. Consider a distribution of 15,000 scores that is assumed to be normally distributed, with $\mu = 72$ and $\sigma = 22$. Use the properties of the normal distribution to determine the following probabilities:

a. P(selecting a number less than 60)

$$z = \frac{X - \mu}{\sigma} = \frac{60 -}{} =$$

From Table 1, area less than $z = $ is _____ . Therefore, the probability of obtaining a score less than 60 is _____ .

b. P(selecting a number greater than 85)

$$z = \frac{X -}{\sigma} = \frac{-}{} =$$

From Table 1, area less than $z =$ is   . Therefore, the probability of obtaining a score greater than 85 is   .

c. P(selecting a number between 55 and 90)

$$z = \frac{\quad - \quad}{\quad} =$$

and

$$z =$$

From Table 1, area between $z =$ and $z =$ is   .
From Table 1, area between $z =$ and $z =$ is   .
Therefore, the probability of obtaining a score between 55 and 90 is

   +   =   .

d. P(selecting a number less than 52 or greater than 78)

$$z =$$

$$z =$$

From Table 1, area less than $z =$ is   . From Table 1, area greater than $z =$ is   . Therefore, the probability of obtaining a score less than 52 or greater than 78 is

   +   =   .

11. A college dormitory population is made up of the following numbers of students.

	Male	Female
Freshman	1700	1300
Sophomore	1500	1000
Junior	1400	1100
Senior	1200	800

a. Describe a method of obtaining a 5 percent simple random sample from this population. Assume the sample is to be drawn without replacement.

b. Describe a method of obtaining a 5 percent systematic sample.

c. Describe a method of obtaining a 5 percent stratified random sample.

12. Suppose you are the director of research for a state educational system that is made up of diverse population characteristics. You have been directed to assess the mathematics achievement of all eighth grade students in the state. The achievement test you are to use costs $4.25 per unit. Since you have a budget of $6,800 for purchasing the test, you will be able to test 1,600 students. Assuming an average class size of 32 students in all eighth grades throughout the state, describe the process that you would use to obtain a sample of students to test.

13. For the distribution of scores in Exercises 10, use the central limit theorem to describe the sampling distribution of the mean for samples of size 196 and 625.

a. $n = 196$

1. Distribution of means is _____ _____.

2. Mean of the distribution of means equals $\mu =$

3. Standard error of the mean equals

$$\sigma_{\bar{X}} = \frac{\quad}{\sqrt{n}} = \frac{\quad}{\sqrt{\quad}} =$$

b. $n = 625$

  1. Distribution of means is _____ _____.

  2. Mean of the distribution of means equals μ =

  3. Standard error of the mean equals

  $\sigma_{\bar{X}} =$

14. For the sampling distribution in Exercise 13 for $n = 196$,

  a. What is the probability of selecting a mean greater than 74?

  $$z = \frac{\bar{X} - \mu}{\sigma_{\bar{X}}} = \frac{\quad - \quad}{\quad} =$$

  From Table 1, area greater than $z = $ ____ is ____ . Therefore, the probability of obtaining a mean greater than 74 is ____ .

  b. What is the probability of selecting a mean less than 71?

  $$z = \frac{\quad - \quad}{\sigma_{\bar{X}}} = \frac{\quad - \quad}{\quad} =$$

  From Table 1, area less than $z = $ ____ is ____ . Therefore, the probability of obtaining a mean less than 71 is ____ .

15. For the sampling distribution in Exercise 13 for $n = 625$,

  a. What is the probability of selecting a mean greater than 74?

  $z = $

  From Table 1, area greater than $z = $ ____ is ____ . Therefore, the probability of obtaining a mean greater than 74 is ____ .

  b. What is the probability of selecting a mean less than 71?

  $z = $

  From Table 1, area less than $z = $ ____ is ____ . Therefore, the probability of obtaining a mean less than 71 is ____ .

Chapter 7 Exercises: Answers

  1. a. $P(A) = 1/6 = 0.1667$

  b. $P(A) = 1 - P(A) = 1 - 1/6 = 5/6 = 0.833$

  2. a. $P(A) = 1/8 = 0.125$

  b. $P(A \ or \ B) = P(A) + P(B)$

  c. $P(3 \ or \ 6) = P(3) + P(6)$
    $= 1/8 + 1/8$
    $= 1/4 = 0.25$

d. $P(1 \, or \, 3 \, or \, 5 \, or \, 7) = P(1) + P(3) + P(5) + P(7)$
$= 1/8 + 1/8 + 1/8 + 1/8$
$= 1/2 = 0.50$

3. a. $P(A \, or \, B) = P(1 + 2 + 3 + 4 + 5 + 6 + 7 + 8)$
$= 1.0$

b. $P(A \, or \, B) = P(A) + P(B) - P(A \, and \, B)$

c. $P(A \, or \, C) = P(1 + 3 + 5 + 7) + P(3 + 6) - P(3)$
$= 0.500 + 0.250 - 0.125$
$= 0.625$

$P(B \, or \, C) = P(2 + 4 + 6 + 8) + P(3 + 6) - P(3)$
$= 0.500 + 0.250 - 0.125$
$= 0.625$

4. $P(A \, and \, B) = P(A) \cdot P(B)$

a. $P(2 \, and \, 5) = P(2) \cdot P(5)$
$= 1/8 \cdot 1/8$
$= 1/64 = 0.016$

b. $P(A \, and \, B) = P(A) \cdot P(B|A)$

c. $P(2 \, and \, 5) = P(2) \cdot P(5|2)$
$= 1/8 \cdot 1/7$
$= 1/56 = 0.018$

5. a.

Outcome	First coin	Second coin	Probability
1	H	H	0.25
2	H	T	0.25
3	T	H	0.25
4	T	T	0.25

b. $P(X + Y)^2 = (X + Y)(X + Y)$
$= X^2 + 2XY + Y^2$
$= (0.50)^2 + 2(0.50)(0.50) + (0.50)^2$
$= 0.25 + 0.50 + 0.25$

6. $P(x) = \dfrac{n!}{(n-x)!(x)!} p^x q^{(n-x)}$

$P(5) = \dfrac{6!}{(6-5)!(5)!}(0.50)^5(0.50)^{(6-5)}$

$= 6 \cdot (0.50)^5(0.50)$

$= 6(0.03125)(0.50)$

$= 0.094$

7. $P(3) = \dfrac{3!}{(3-3)!(3)!}(0.05)^3(0.95)^0$

$= 1 \cdot (0.05)^3(0.95)^0$

$= 1(0.000125)$

$= 0.000125$

$$P(2) = \frac{3!}{(3-2)!(2)!}(0.05)^2(0.95)^1$$

$$= 3 \cdot (0.05)^2(0.95)^1$$

$$= 3(0.0025)(0.95)$$

$$= 3(0.002375)$$

$$= 0.007125$$

$$P(1) = \frac{3!}{(3-1)!(1)!}(0.05)^1(0.95)^2$$

$$= 3 \cdot (0.05)^1(0.95)^2$$

$$= 3(0.05)(0.9025)$$

$$= 3(0.045125)$$

$$= 0.135375$$

$$P(0) = \frac{3!}{(3-0)!(0)!}(0.05)^0(0.95)^3$$

$$= 1 \cdot (0.05)^0(0.95)^3$$

$$= 1(0.857375)$$

$$= 0.857375$$

8. a. $P(x) = \dfrac{n!}{(n-x)!(x)!} p^x q^{(n-x)}$

$$P(7) = \frac{10!}{(10-7)!(7)!}(0.25)^7(0.75)^{(10-7)}$$

$$= 120 \cdot (0.25)^7(0.75)^3$$

$$= 120(0.000061)(0.421875)$$

$$= 0.003088$$

b. $P(2) = \dfrac{10!}{(10-2)!(2)!}(0.25)^2(0.75)^{(10-2)}$

$$= 45 \cdot (0.25)^2(0.75)^8$$

$$= 45(0.06250)(0.100113)$$

$$= 0.281568$$

9. a. $z = \dfrac{X - \mu}{\sigma} = \dfrac{90 - 75}{15} = \ +1.0$

From Table 1, the area between $z = 0.0$ and $z = +1.0$ is 0.3413. Therefore, the probability of obtaining a score between 75 and 90 is 0.3413.

b. $z = \dfrac{X - \mu}{\sigma} = \dfrac{60 - 75}{15} = \ -1.0$

From Table 1, the area between $z = -1.0$ and $z = 0.0$ is 0.3413. Therefore, the probability of obtaining a score between 60 and 75 is 0.3413.

c. From Table 1, the area greater than $z = +1.0$ is 0.1587. Therefore, the probability of obtaining a score greater than 90 is 0.1587.

d. $z = \dfrac{X - \mu}{\sigma} = \dfrac{45 - 75}{15} = -2.0$

From Table 1, the area less than $z = -2.0$ is 0.0228. Therefore, the probability of obtaining a score less than 45 is 0.0228.

10. a. $z = \dfrac{X - \mu}{\sigma} = \dfrac{60 - 72}{22} = -0.545$

From Table 1, the area less than $z = -0.545$ is 0.2929. Therefore, the probability of obtaining a score less than 60 is 0.2929.

b. $z = \dfrac{X - \mu}{\sigma} = \dfrac{85 - 72}{22} = +0.591$

From Table 1, the area greater than $z = +0.591$ is 0.2773. Therefore, the probability of obtaining a score greater than 85 is 0.2773.

c. $z = \dfrac{X - \mu}{\sigma} = \dfrac{55 - 72}{22} = -0.773$

$z = \dfrac{X - \mu}{\sigma} = \dfrac{90 - 72}{22} = +0.818$

From Table 1, the area between $z = -0.773$ and $z = 0.0$ is 0.2803, and the area between $z = 0.0$ and $z = +0.818$ is 0.2936. Therefore, the probability of obtaining a score between 55 and 90 is $0.2803 + 0.2936 = 0.5739$.

d. $z = \dfrac{X - \mu}{\sigma} = \dfrac{52 - 72}{22} = -0.909$

$z = \dfrac{X - \mu}{\sigma} = \dfrac{78 - 72}{22} = +0.273$

From Table 1, the area less than $z = -0.909$ is 0.1817, and the area greater than $z = +0.273$ is 0.3924. Therefore, the probability of obtaining a score less than 52 or greater than 78 is $0.1817 + 0.3924 = 0.5741$.

11.

	Male	Female
Freshman	1700	1300
Sophomore	1500	1000
Junior	1400	1100
Senior	1200	800

a. Since the dormitory population equals 10,000, a 5 percent sample would be 500 students. Each student could be coded by number and, with a table of random numbers or computer program, the sample of 500 students could be identified.

b. A list of all the dormitory students could be generated. With a sample size of 500, the sampling fraction would be $500/10,000 = 1/20$. Suppose the researcher would randomly select a number between 1 and 20 and chooses the number 12. The twelfth student on the list would be the first member of the sample selected. The other members of the sample would be identified by adding multiples of 20 to 12. The second number of the sample would be 32, the third would be 52, and so on until 500 students are selected.

    c. The strata or subpopulations are male and female students in each college class, or a total of 8 strata. The researcher would need to take proportional allocations from each stratum, in other words, a 5 percent sample from each stratum. The sample would consist of 85 male and 65 female freshmen, 75 male and 50 female sophomores, 70 male and 55 female juniors, and 60 male and 40 female seniors.

12. Stratified cluster sampling would probably be the best method. The budgeted amount of $6,800 will purchase 1,600 tests, which would be enough for 50 classrooms. Classrooms would be used as clusters to expedite the testing and to reduce the confusion that could result from randomly selecting individual students. The state would be stratified on certain demographic characteristics and the classrooms would be randomly selected from these strata.

13. a. $n = 196$

    1. The distribution of means is normal.

    2. The mean of the distribution of means equals $\mu = 72$.

    3. The standard error of the mean equals

$$\sigma_{\bar{X}} = \frac{\sigma}{\sqrt{n}} = \frac{22}{\sqrt{196}} = 1.57$$

    b. $n = 625$

    1. The distribution of the means is normal.

    2. The mean of the distribution of means equals $\mu = 72$.

    3. The standard error of the mean equals

$$\sigma_{\bar{X}} = \frac{\sigma}{\sqrt{n}} = \frac{22}{\sqrt{625}} = 0.88$$

14. a. $z = \dfrac{\bar{X} - \mu}{\sigma_{\bar{X}}} = \dfrac{74 - 72}{1.57} = +1.274$

From Table 1, the area greater than $z = +1.274$ is 0.1013. Therefore, the probability of obtaining a mean greater than 74 is 0.1013.

    b. $z = \dfrac{\bar{X} - \mu}{\sigma_{\bar{X}}} = \dfrac{71 - 72}{1.57} = -0.637$

From Table 1, the area less than $z = -0.637$ is 0.2621. Therefore, the probability of obtaining a mean less than 71 is 0.2621.

15. a. $z = \dfrac{\bar{X} - \mu}{\sigma_{\bar{X}}} = \dfrac{74 - 72}{0.88} = +2.273$

From Table 1, the area greater than $z = +2.273$ is 0.0115. Therefore, the probability of obtaining a mean greater than 74 is 0.0115.

b. $z = \dfrac{\bar{X} - \mu}{\sigma_{\bar{X}}} = \dfrac{71 - 72}{0.88} = -1.136$

From Table 1, the area less than $z = -1.136$ is 0.1280. Therefore, the probability of obtaining a mean less than 71 is 0.1280.

CHAPTER 8

Hypothesis Testing: One-Sample Case for the Mean

COMPREHENSION CHECK

The following summary reviews the material presented in this chapter. To check your understanding of key concepts, supply the missing words indicated by the numbered blanks.

The logic of testing __(1)__ follows the chain of reasoning for inferential statistics introduced in the last chapter. Basically, this chain involves using observed data from a __(2)__ to determine whether some hypothesized value of the population is tenable. Hypotheses are __(3)__ about population parameters. That is, the hypothesis is stated in terms of a __(4)__ of the population but is tested using a statistic calculated from the __(5)__. For the one-sample situation for the mean, the population parameter is μ and the sample statistic is $\bar{X}$. Note that testing an hypothesis does *not* __(6)__ or __(7)__, but rather supports or refutes, the __(8)__ of the hypothesis. The usual procedure followed is to test the __(9)__ hypothesis against the __(10)__ hypothesis, which specifies the possible outcomes not covered by the null hypothesis.

There are __(11)__ steps in hypothesis testing. The first step is to __(12)__ the hypotheses, which include both the __(13)__ hypothesis and the __(14)__ hypothesis. The null hypothesis associated with the one-sample case for the mean is __(15)__. The second step is to determine the __(16)__ for rejecting the null hypothesis. In this step, researchers must consider __(17)__ types of inferential errors. One of the errors, called the __(18)__ error, is defined a priori by the researcher in setting α or the __(19)__ of significance. A Type I error occurs when the investigator __(20)__ the null hypothesis that was in fact true. The level of significance is used to determine the region of __(21)__ in the sampling distribution. This region contains those values of the sample mean that are __(22)__ if the null hypothesis is actually true.

The other type of inferential error is well known but has attracted less attention. It is the __(23)__ error, defined as __(24)__ to reject the null hypothesis when it is __(25)__ in the population. It is often the case that the __(26)__ of each type of error are different, so careful consideration of both errors is recommended.

The third step is to compute the __(27)__ statistic. This value for testing the null hypothesis ($H_0 : \mu = a$) can be thought of as a standard score indicating how __(28)__ the observed sample mean (__(29)__) is from the hypothesized value of the population mean (__(30)__). A general formula for a test statistic is

$$\text{Test statistic} = \frac{\left(\underline{\quad (31) \quad} \right) - \text{parameter}}{\left(\underline{\quad (32) \quad} \right)}$$

The final step involves comparing the computed value of the test statistic to the __(33)__ value identified in step 2. If the calculated value exceeds the critical value, the null hypothesis is

___(34)___ . By rejecting H_0, we are concluding that the ___(35)___ between the observed sample mean and the hypothesized population mean is too great to attribute to chance ___(36)___ in sampling. If, however, the test statistic does not exceed the critical value, the null hypothesis is not ___(37)___ because the observed sample mean is not sufficiently ___(38)___ from the hypothesized value of the population mean. We therefore attribute the ___(39)___ difference to sampling fluctuations.

We may test the null hypothesis (H_0: $\mu = a$) against either a nondirectional ___(40)___ (H_a: $\mu \neq a$) or a ___(41)___ alternative hypothesis (H_a: $\mu > a$). For the nondirectional alternative, the test is called ___(42)___ because the region of rejection is located in both tails of the sampling distribution. For the ___(43)___ alternative, the test is called one-tailed because the region of rejection is only in ___(44)___ tail of the sampling distribution.

Researchers must use Student's t distribution as the underlying distribution when the population ___(45)___ is unknown. This distribution is actually a ___(46)___ of distributions; the specific distribution to be used depends upon the degrees of ___(47)___ associated with the test. For the one-sample case for the mean, the degrees of freedom are equal to ___(48)___ .

If a researcher rejects the null hypothesis, which establishes the statistical significance of the data, consideration should also be given to the ___(49)___ significance of the test. While the level of significance is preset by the researcher, the statistical ___(50)___ can be increased by increasing the ___(51)___ . However, an important guideline is that practical ___(52)___ is not determined by ___(53)___ significance.

Comprehension Check: Answers

1. hypotheses
2. sample
3. conjectures
4. parameter
5. sample
6. prove
7. disprove
8. tenability
9. null
10. alternative
11. four
12. state
13. null
14. alternative
15. (H_0: $\mu = a$)
16. criterion
17. two
18. Type I

19. level
20. rejects
21. rejection
22. unlikely (improbable)
23. Type II
24. failing
25. false
26. costs (consequences)
27. test
28. different
29. $\bar{X}$
30. μ
31. statistic
32. standard error
33. critical
34. rejected
35. difference
36. fluctuations

37. rejected
38. different
39. observed (obtained)
40. alternative
41. directional
42. two-tailed
43. directional
44. one
45. variance (σ^2)
46. family
47. freedom
48. ($n - 1$)
49. practical
50. significance
51. sample size (n)
52. significance
53. statistical

CHAPTER 8 EXERCISES

1. Determine the null and alternative hypotheses for each of the following statements:

a. The average sixth grader watches television more than 12 hours per week.

H_0: $\mu = 12$
H_a: μ

b. A college placement officer believes that engineering graduates receive higher starting salaries than accounting graduates.

H_0: $\mu_{eng} = \mu_{acc}$
H_a: μ_{eng}

c. Sermons at Protestant and Roman Catholic religious services are of equal length.

H_0: $\mu_{Prot} = \mu_{Cath}$
H_a:

d. A researcher believes that young girls and boys have different growth patterns, and that boys on average are shorter than girls at a certain age. A random sample of 25 boys has a mean height of 32.3 inches, while a random sample of 25 girls has a mean height of 33.1 inches.

H_0: $\mu_f =$
H_a:

e. The levels of self-esteem for urban-dwelling children are lower than those for rural-dwelling children.

H_0:
H_a:

2. State both hypotheses for these situations:

a. A sociologist found that college students consume an average of 48 ounces of beer per week. The sociologist believes that students who are members of certain social organizations drink more beer than their peers.

H_0: $\mu_{exp} = \mu_{con}$
H_a: μ_{exp}

b. Another colleague disagrees with the sociologist in the above example. This person believes that the consumption patterns are identical in the two groups.

H_0: $\mu_{exp} = \mu_{con}$
H_a:

c. A genetic botanist is striving to produce a specific type of miniature apple tree with fruit of normal size. The average height of the original apple tree is 20 feet.

H_0:
H_a:

d. The director of instructional development in a school district has read about declining national test scores for twelfth grade students on a standardized achievement test. This school district has recently adopted new teaching methods, and the director wishes to know whether the methods have in fact improved student performance on the test.
H_0:
H_a:

3. A sociology graduate student doing research believes that a specific population has a mean age of 47 years. A random sample of 150 people drawn from the population has a mean age of 49.4 and a sample standard deviation of 13 years.

a. Define and illustrate the sampling distribution of the means for this example.

1. Distribution = t distribution with ___ df (approximately ___)

2. Mean = μ =

3. Standard error of the mean $= s_{\bar{X}}$

$$= s/\sqrt{n}$$

$$= 13/\sqrt{} =$$

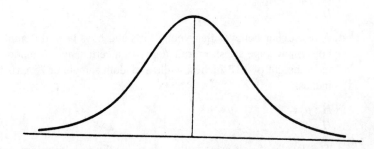

b. Using this distribution, what is the probability of finding a sample of size 150 with a mean age of 49.4 when in fact the true mean of the population is 47?

$$t = \frac{49.4 - }{} =$$

Area beyond = probability =

c. With the above data, use the four steps for hypothesis testing to test the appropriate null hypothesis against the nondirectional alternative (use $\alpha = .05$).

1. State the hypotheses.

$H_0: \mu = 47$
$H_a:$

2. Set the criterion for rejecting H_0.

$t_{cv} = \pm$

3. Compute the test statistic.

$$t = \frac{ - }{} =$$

4. Interpret the results.

H_0

d. With the same data, use the four steps for hypothesis testing to test the appropriate null hypothesis against the directional hypothesis, $H_a: \mu > 47$ (use $\alpha = .05$).

1. State the hypotheses.

$H_0:$
$H_a:$

2. Set the criterion for rejecting H_0:

$t_{cv} =$

3. Compute the test statistic.

$t =$

4. Interpret the results.

H_0

4. Determine whether a Type I or Type II error has been made in each of the following cases:

a. A graduate student hypothesizes that the mean income for a population is $6,800. The population mean income is really $6,800. The student researcher rejects the hypothesis.

b. The graduate student in the above example also hypothesizes that the mean age for the population is 47 years. In fact, the population mean is not 47, and the graduate student rejects the hypothesis.

c. The graduate student further hypothesizes that the average size of a family in the population is 4.3 members. The population mean is actually grossly different, but the hypothesis is retained.

5. a. If the null hypothesis is rejected at the .05 level of significance, what can be said about rejecting or failing to reject at the .01 level of significance?

b. If the null hypothesis is not rejected at the .05 level of significance, what can be said about rejecting or failing to reject at the .01 level of significance?

c. If the null hypothesis is rejected at the .01 level of significance, what can be said about rejecting or failing to reject at the .05 level of significance?

d. If the null hypothesis is not rejected at the .01 level of significance, what can be said about rejecting or failing to reject at the .05 level of significance?

6. A nutrition student has read that people on the average are taller due to better diets. Some literature indicates that the mean height of adult men and women is 67 inches, but the student believes that these data underestimate the true situation. A sample of 30 adults has a mean height of 69 inches and a standard deviation of 6.0 inches.

a. Define and illustrate the sampling distribution of the means for this sample.

1. Distribution = t distirbution with ____ df

2. Mean = μ = ____

3. Standard error of the mean = $s_{\bar{x}}$

$$= s / \sqrt{n}$$

$$= \quad / \sqrt{} \quad =$$

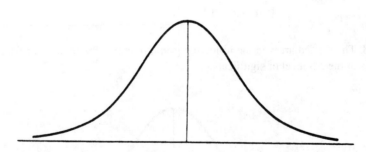

b. With the above data, use the four steps for hypothesis testing to test the appropriate null hypothesis against the nondirectional alternative (use $\alpha = .05$).

1. State the hypotheses.

H_0:
H_a:

2. Set the criterion for rejecting H_0.

$t_{cv} =$

3. Compute the test statistic.

$$t = \frac{-}{} =$$

4. Interpret the results.

$$H_0$$

c. With the same data, use the four steps for hypothesis testing to test the appropriate null hypothesis against the directional hypothesis, $H_a: \mu > 67$ (use $\alpha = .05$).

1. State the hypotheses.

$$H_0:$$
$$H_a:$$

2. Set the criterion for rejecting H_0.

$$t_{cv} =$$

3. Compute the test statistic.

$$t =$$

4. Interpret the results.

$$H_0:$$

7. The two types of errors that arise in hypothesis testing are the Type I error (rejecting a true null hypothesis) and Type II error (retraining a false null hypothesis). In any given hypothesis-testing situation, there are four possible combinations of rejection-retention decisions and the actual truth/falsity of the hypothesis. Complete the following table to indicate whether a correct decision or an error has been made. If an error has been made, indicate which of the two types it is.

		Null hypothesis	
		True	False
Decision	Reject		
	Fail to reject		

8. The shaded areas in the following graph illustrate the region of rejection for a two-tailed test at the .05 level of significance.

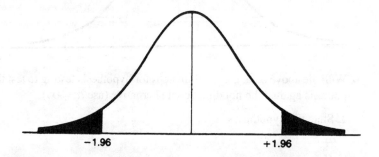

Provide an illustration similar to the one above for each of the following hypotheses and illustrate the critical value(s) for each. Assume that either σ is known or $N > 120$ (to justify using normal distribution).

   a. H_0: $\mu = 47$
     H_a: $\mu \neq 47$
     .10 level of significance

   b. H_0: $\mu = 6800$
     H_a: $\mu > 6800$
     .01 level of significance

   c. H_0: $\mu = 6800$
     H_a: $\mu \neq 6800$
     .02 level of significance

   d. H_0: $\mu = 4.3$
     H_a: $\mu < 4.3$
     .05 level of significance

  9. Suppose that the test statistic (t) were +2.11 for each of the parts of Exercise 8 above. Would you reject or fail to reject the null hypotheses?

   a.

   b.

   c.

   d.

 10. Now suppose that the test statistic (t) is −2.11 in each of the cases. Would you reject or retain the null hypotheses?

   a.

   b.

   c.

   d.

 11. For each of the following levels of significance, indicate the critical value. Use the normal curve as the underlying distribution.

	Critical value	
Level of significance	One-tailed	Two-tailed
.05	+ or −1.645	±1.960
.10		
.01		
.02		
.025		

 12. Using the t distribution as the underlying distribution, state the critical values for each of the following.

		Critical value	
Level of significance	Degrees of freedom	One-tailed	Two-tailed
.05	20	+ or −1.725	±2.086
.05	200		
.01	27		
.01	270		
.10	10		

Chapter 8 Exercises: Answers

1. a. $H_0: \mu = 12$
$H_a: \mu > 12$

b. $H_0: \mu_{eng} = \mu_{acc}$
$H_a: \mu_{eng} > \mu_{acc}$

c. $H_0: \mu_{Prot} = \mu_{Cath}$
$H_a: \mu_{Prot} \neq \mu_{Cath}$

d. $H_0: \mu_f = \mu_m$
$H_a: \mu_f > \mu_m$

e. $H_0: \mu_{urb} = \mu_{rur}$
$H_a: \mu_{urb} < \mu_{rur}$

2. a. $H_0: \mu_{exp} = \mu_{con}$
$H_a: \mu_{exp} > \mu_{con}$

b. $H_0: \mu_{exp} = \mu_{con}$
$H_a: \mu_{exp} \neq \mu_{con}$

c. $H_0: \mu = 20$
$H_a: \mu < 20$

d. $H_0: \mu_{new} = \mu_{old}$
$H_a: \mu_{new} > \mu_{old}$

3. a. 1. Distribution = t distribution with 149 df (approximately normal)

2. Mean = $\mu = 47$

3. Standard error of the mean = $s_{\bar{X}}$
$$= s / \sqrt{150}$$
$$= 13 / \sqrt{150} = 1.061$$

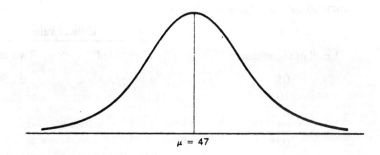

$\mu = 47$

b. $t = \dfrac{49.4 - 47}{1.061} = 2.26$

Area beyond = probability = 0.0119

c. 1. State the hypotheses.

$H_0: \mu = 47$
$H_a: \mu \neq 47$

2. Set the criterion for rejecting H_0.

$t_{cv} = \pm 1.96$

3. Compute the test statistic.

$$t = \frac{49.4 - 47}{1.061} = 2.26$$

4. Interpret the results.

Reject H_0

d. 1. $H_0: \mu = 47$
$H_a: \mu > 47$

2. $t_{cv} = +1.645$

3. $t = 2.26$

4. Reject H_0

4. a. Type I

   b. Correct decision

   c. Type II

5. a. Don't know—depends on value of test statistic

   b. Fail to reject

   c. Reject

   d. Don't know—depends on value of test statistic

6. a. 1. Distribution = t distribution with 29 df

   2. Mean = $\mu = 67$

   3. Standard error of the mean = $s_{\bar{X}}$

$$= s/\sqrt{30}$$

$$= 6/\sqrt{30} = 1.095$$

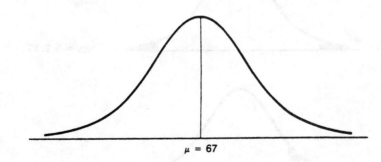

$\mu = 67$

b. 1. $H_0: \mu = 67$

   $H_a: \mu \neq 67$

2. $t_{cv} = \pm 2.045$

3. $t = \dfrac{69 - 67}{1.095} = 1.83$

4. Fail to reject H_0

c. 1. H_0: $\mu = 67$
   H_a: $\mu > 67$

2. $t_{cv} = +1.699$

3. $t = 1.83$

4. Reject H_0

7.

Null hypothesis

		True	False
	Reject	Type I	Correct
Decision			
	Fail to reject	Correct	Type II

8.

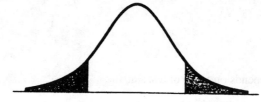

cv = ± 1.645

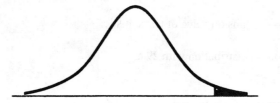

cv = + 2.33

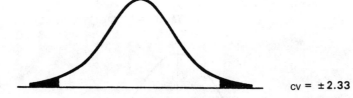

cv = ± 2.33

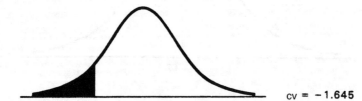

cv = − 1.645

9. a. Reject

    b. Fail to reject

    c. Fail to reject

    d. Fail to reject

10. a. Reject

    b. Fail to reject

    c. Fail to reject

    d. Reject

11.

| | Critical value | |
Level of significance	One-tailed	Two-tailed
.05	+ or −1.645	±1.960
.10	+ or −1.282	±1.645
.01	+ or −2.326	±2.576
.02	+ or −2.055	±2.326
.025	+ or −1.960	±2.24

12.

| | | Critical value | |
Level of significance	Degrees of freedom	One-tailed	Two-tailed
.05	20	+ or −1.725	±2.086
.05	200	+ or −1.645	±1.960
.01	27	+ or −2.473	±2.771
.01	270	+ or −2.326	±2.576
.10	10	+ or −1.372	±1.812

CHAPTER 9

Estimation:
One-Sample Case for the Mean

COMPREHENSION CHECK

The following summary reviews the material presented in this chapter. To check your under-standing of key concepts, supply the missing words indicated by the numbered blanks.

Closely related to testing a hypothesis about a specific value for the population is ___(1)___ the population parameter. This process involves using a statistic computed from data from a ___(2)___ to estimate the corresponding ___(3)___ in the population. A ___(4)___ estimate is a single value that represents the "best" estimate of the population parameter. For example, if we are estimating the population mean (___(5)___), then the ___(6)___ mean ($\bar{X}$) is the point estimate. An ___(7)___ estimate is a range of values around the point estimate. This range of values is given a specified degree of confidence of containing the parameter and is called a ___(8)___ interval.

The general formula for the confidence interval is

$$CI = \underline{\quad (9) \quad} \pm (\underline{\quad (10) \quad})(\underline{\quad (11) \quad})$$

For estimating the population mean when the population ___(12)___ (σ^2) is known, the formula is

$$CI = \underline{\quad (13) \quad} \pm (z_{cv})(\underline{\quad (14) \quad})$$

The level of confidence used in developing confidence intervals is defined as the ___(15)___ of the level of significance, that is, $1 - \alpha$. So if an appropriate null hypothesis is tested at ___(16)___ = .05, the corresponding level of confidence would be ___(17)___.

When the variance in the population (σ^2) is known, the ___(18)___ value is denoted z_{cv} and is found by using the standard ___(19)___ distribution. However, when the variance in the population is ___(20)___ and s^2 is used as the estimate, the formula for the confidence interval is:

$$CI = \bar{X} \pm (\underline{\quad (21) \quad}) (s_{\bar{X}})$$

Note now that the critical ___(22)___ is denoted t_{cv} and is found by using the appropriate ___(23)___ distribution.

There is a relationship between hypothesis ___(24)___ and estimation. For example, if we are testing the null hypothesis $H_0: \mu = a$ and reject it, the corresponding confidence interval ___(25)___ contain the hypothesized value a. On the other hand, if the null hypothesis is ___(26)___ , the interval will contain a.

The accuracy with which a confidence interval can be used to estimate a population parame-ter is a function of the statistical ___(27)___ of the estimate. The smaller the ___(28)___ of the confidence interval, the more __(29)__ the estimate. The width can be decreased by __(30)__ the sample size.

Comprehension Check: Answers

1. estimating	**11.** standard error of the statistic	**21.** t_{cv}
2. sample	**12.** variance	**22.** value
3. parameter	**13.** $\bar{X}$	**23.** t
4. point	**14.** $s_{\bar{X}}$	**24.** testing
5. μ	**15.** complement	**25.** will not
6. sample	**16.** α	**26.** not rejected
7. interval	**17.** $1 - .05 = .95$	**27.** precision
8. confidence	**18.** critical	**28.** width
9. statistic	**19.** normal	**29.** precise
10. critical value	**20.** unknown	**30.** increasing

CHAPTER 9 EXERCISES

1. For each of the following levels of significance, indicate the level of confidence and the critical value. Use the normal distribution as the underlying distribution. (This exercise is related to Exercise 11 from workbook Chapter 8.)

Significance level	Critical value	Confidence level
.05	1.960	.95
.10		
.01		
.02		
.20		

2. Using the t distribution as the underlying distribution, indicate for each of the following the level of confidence and the critical value. (This exercise is related to Exercise 12 from workbook Chapter 8).

Significance level	df	Critical value	Confidence level
.05	20	2.086	.95
.05	200		
.01	27		
.01	270		
.10	10		

3. a. For Exercise 3 from Chapter 8 of this workbook, develop the 95 percent confidence interval.

$$
\begin{aligned}
\text{CI}_{95} &= \bar{X} \pm (t_{cv})(s_{\bar{X}}) \\
&= 49.4 \pm (1.960)(1.061) \\
&= 49.4 \pm \\
&= (47.32, \quad)
\end{aligned}
$$

b. Also compute the 90 percent confidence interval.

$$
\begin{aligned}
\text{CI}_{90} &= \bar{X} \pm (t_{cv})(s_{\bar{X}}) \\
&= 49.4 \pm (\quad)(1.061) \\
&= 49.4 \pm \\
&= (\quad, \quad)
\end{aligned}
$$

4. The dean of the graduate school believes that the mean age of graduate students has changed from five years earlier, when it was 29 years. A sample of 41 entering graduate students has a mean age of 32.6 and a standard deviation of 7.3.

a. With these data, use the four steps for hypothesis testing to test the appropriate null hypothesis against the nondirectional alternative (use $\alpha = .05$).

1. State the hypotheses.

H_0:
H_a:

2. Set the criterion for rejecting H_0.

$t_{cv} = \pm$

3. Compute the test statistic.

$$t = \frac{\quad\overline{\quad}\quad}{\quad\quad} =$$

4. Interpret the results.

H_0

b. Develop the 95 percent confidence interval.

$$\begin{aligned} \mathrm{CI}_{95} &= \bar{X} \pm (t_{cv})(s_{\bar{X}}) \\ &= \quad \pm (\quad\quad)(\quad\quad) \\ &= \quad \pm \\ &= (\quad\quad , \quad\quad) \end{aligned}$$

5. Given: CI_{95} for a population parameter is $(6.24, 18.88)$ and $n > 120$.
Find: CI_{90} and CI_{99}.
[Hint: Determine the mean and half-width of the interval; then determine $(s_{\bar{X}})$.]

6. a. For Exercise 6 from Chapter 8 of this workbook, develop the 95 percent confidence interval.

b. Also compute the 99 percent confidence interval.

7. Given that $\bar{X} = 24.6$ and $s = 2.34$, compare the 95 percent confidence intervals for $n = 150$ and $n = 10$.

for $n = 150$, $\qquad s_{\bar{X}} = \qquad /\sqrt{\quad\quad} =$

for $n = 10$, $\qquad s_{\bar{X}} = \qquad /\sqrt{\quad\quad} =$

for $n = 150$, $\qquad \mathrm{CI}_{95} = \bar{X} \pm (t_{cv})(s_{\bar{X}})$

$$\begin{aligned} &= \quad \pm (\quad)(0.19) \\ &= \quad \pm \\ &= (\quad , \quad) \end{aligned}$$

for $n = 10$, $\qquad \mathrm{CI}_{95} = \bar{X} \pm (t_{cv})(s_{\bar{X}})$

$$\begin{aligned} &= \quad \pm (\quad)(\quad) \\ &= \quad \pm \\ &= (\quad , \quad) \end{aligned}$$

8. Given that the 95 percent confidence interval for the mean of a certain population is $(20.66, 42.88)$, find the 90 and 99 percent confidence intervals.
Assume that $n = 22$.
[Hint: Determine the mean and half-width of the interval; then determine $(s_{\bar{X}})$.]

9. What sample size would we need to estimate the average IQ in a given population to within ±2 points if the 95 percent confidence level is used? Assume that $s = 15$.

[Hint: Since $CI_{90} = \bar{X} \pm (t_{cv})(s_{\bar{X}})$

$\qquad\qquad = \bar{X} \pm$

This implies $(t_{cv})(s_{\bar{X}}) = 2$.]

Chapter 9 Exercises: Answers

1.

Significance level	Critical value	Confidence level
.05	1.960	.95
.10	1.645	.90
.01	2.576	.99
.02	2.326	.98
.20	1.282	.80

2.

Significance level	df	Critical value	Confidence level
.05	20	2.086	.95
.05	200	1.960	.95
.01	27	2.771	.99
.01	270	2.576	.99
.10	10	1.812	.90

3. a. $CI_{95} = \bar{X} \pm (t_{cv})(s_{\bar{X}})$
$\qquad = 49.4 \pm (1.960)(1.061)$
$\qquad = 49.4 \pm 2.08$
$\qquad = (47.32, 51.48)$

b. $CI_{90} = \bar{X} \pm (t_{cv})(s_{\bar{X}})$
$\qquad = 49.4 \pm (1.645)(1.061)$
$\qquad = 49.4 \pm 1.75$
$\qquad = (47.65, 51.15)$

4. a. 1. $H_0: \mu = 29$
$\qquad H_a: \mu \neq 29$

2. $t_{cv} = \pm 2.021$

3. $t = \dfrac{32.6 - 29.0}{7.3/\sqrt{41}} = 3.16$

4. Reject H_0

b. $CI_{95} = \bar{X} \pm (t_{cv})(s_{\bar{X}})$
$\qquad = 32.6 \pm (2.021)(1.14)$
$\qquad = 32.6 \pm 2.30$
$\qquad = (30.30, 34.90)$

5. $CI_{95} = \bar{X} \pm (t_{cv})(s_{\bar{X}})$
$\qquad = (6.24, 18.88)$

$\bar{X} = 12.56 = $ the midpoint of the interval

Therefore, $CI_{95} = 12.56 \pm 6.32$
$= (6.24, 18.88)$

This implies that $(t_{cv})(s_{\bar{X}}) = 6.32$
$(1.960)(s_{\bar{X}}) = 6.32$

Therefore, $s_{\bar{X}} = 3.22$

$CI_{90} = \bar{X} \pm (t_{cv})(s_{\bar{X}})$
$= 12.56 \pm (1.645)(3.22)$
$= 12.56 \pm 5.30$
$= (7.26, 17.86)$

$CI_{99} = \bar{X} \pm (t_{cv})(s_{\bar{X}})$
$= 12.56 \pm (2.576)(3.22)$
$= 12.56 \pm 8.29$
$= (4.27, 20.85)$

6. a. $CI_{95} = \bar{X} \pm (t_{cv})(s_{\bar{X}})$
$= 69 \pm (2.045)(1.095)$
$= 69 \pm 2.24$
$= (66.76, 71.24)$

b. $CI_{99} = \bar{X} \pm (t_{cv})(s_{\bar{X}})$
$= 69 \pm (2.756)(1.095)$
$= 69 \pm 3.02$
$= (65.98, 72.02)$

7. for $n = 150$, $s_{\bar{X}} = 2.34 / \sqrt{150} = 0.19$

for $n = 10$, $s_{\bar{X}} = 2.34 / \sqrt{10} = 0.74$

for $n = 150$, $CI_{95} = \bar{X} \pm (t_{cv})(s_{\bar{X}})$
$= 24.6 \pm (1.960)(0.19)$
$= 24.6 \pm 0.37$
$= (24.23, 24.97)$

for $n = 10$, $CI_{95} = \bar{X} \pm (t_{cv})(s_{\bar{X}})$
$= 24.6 \pm (2.262)(0.74)$
$= 24.6 \pm 1.67$
$= (22.93, 26.27)$

8. $CI_{95} = \bar{X} \pm (t_{cv})(s_{\bar{X}})$
$= (20.66, 42.88)$

$\bar{X} = 31.77 =$ the midpoint of the interval

Therefore, $CI_{95} = 31.77 \pm 11.11$
$= (20.66, 42.88)$

This implies that $(t_{cv})(s_{\bar{X}}) = 11.11$
$$(2.080)(s_{\bar{X}}) = 11.11$$

Therefore, $s_{\bar{X}} = 5.34$

$$CI_{90} = \bar{X} \pm (t_{cv})(s_{\bar{X}})$$
$$= 31.77 \pm (1.721)(5.34)$$
$$= 31.77 \pm 9.19$$
$$= (22.58, 40.96)$$

$$CI_{99} = \bar{X} \pm (t_{cv})(s_{\bar{X}})$$
$$= 31.77 \pm (2.831)(5.34)$$
$$= 31.77 \pm 15.12$$
$$= (16.65, 46.89)$$

9. $CI_{90} = \bar{X} \pm (t_{cv})(s_{\bar{X}})$
$\phantom{CI_{90}} = \bar{X} \pm 2$

This implies $(t_{cv})(s_{\bar{X}}) = 2$

Assume $t_{cv} = 1.960$

And since $s_{\bar{X}} = s / \sqrt{n}$
$$\phantom{And since s_{\bar{X}}} = 15 / \sqrt{n}$$

Therefore

$$(1.960)\left(15 / \sqrt{n}\right) = 2$$
$$\sqrt{n} = (1.960)(15) / 2$$
$$= 14.70$$

$$n = 216.09 \; or \; 217$$

CHAPTER 10
Hypothesis Testing:
One-Sample Case for Other Statistics

COMPREHENSION CHECK

The following summary reviews the material presented in this chapter. To check your understanding of key concepts, supply the missing words indicated by the numbered blanks.

The concepts of ___(1)___ testing and interval estimation can be readily extended to other ___(2)___ : for example, the correlation coefficient, the proportion, and the variance. For each of these statistics, a series of steps for testing hypotheses and developing confidence intervals is proposed; these steps are:

1. State the ___(3)___ .
2. Compute the ___(4)___ statistic.
3. Set the ___(5)___ for rejecting H_0.
4. Construct the ___(6)___ interval.
5. Interpret the ___(7)___ .

The general formula for testing hypotheses is

$$\text{Test statistic} = \frac{\underline{\quad(8)\quad} - \underline{\quad(9)\quad}}{\underline{\quad(10)\quad}}$$

The general formula for the corresponding confidence interval is

$$\text{CI} = \underline{\quad(11)\quad} \pm (\underline{\quad(12)\quad})(\underline{\quad(13)\quad})$$

The shape of sampling distribution of the Pearson correlation coefficient varies with value of ρ, the population parameter. As ρ departs from ___(14)___ , the ___(15)___ distribution becomes exceedingly ___(16)___ . However, if we ___(17)___ the correlation coefficient using Fisher's log transformation, the sampling distribution of the transformed correlation coefficient approximates the ___(18)___ distribution regardless of the value of ___(19)___ and the size of the ___(20)___ . The ___(21)___ of the transformed correlation coefficient is given by $1/\sqrt{(n-3)}$. To construct confidence intervals for the correlation coefficient, the normal distribution should be used as the ___(22)___ distribution. The interval is first constructed for the ___(23)___ values of $r(z_r)$, and then the endpoints of the interval are converted back to ___(24)___ values.

The sampling distribution for a sample proportion is the ___(25)___ distribution. However, the ___(26)___ distribution can be used as an approximation of the binomial distribution for ___(27)___ sample sizes. The rule of thumb for determining whether the sample is sufficiently __(28)__ to use the __(29)__ as the sampling distribution is that the product __(30)__ or $(n)(q)$, whichever is the __(31)__ , must be larger than __(32)__ .

To test the null hypothesis H_0: $\sigma^2 = a$, the appropriate distribution is the __(33)__ for $n - 1$ __(34)__ . Unlike the normal distribution and Student's t distributions, the X^2 distribution is __(35)__ symmetrical. Thus, when testing the null hypothesis against a __(36)__ alternative, there are __(37)__ distinct critical values of the test statistic.

Comprehension Check: Answers

1. hypothesis
2. statistics
3. hypotheses
4. test
5. criterion
6. confidence
7. results
8. statistic
9. parameter
10. standard error of the statistic
11. statistic
12. critical value
13. standard error of the statistic
14. zero
15. sampling
16. skewed
17. transform
18. normal
19. ρ

20. sample
21. standard error
22. underlying
23. transformed
24. r
25. binomial
26. normal
27. large
28. large
29. normal curve
30. $(n)(p)$
31. smaller
32. five
33. χ^2
34. degrees of freedom
35. not
36. nondirectional
37. two

CHAPTER 10 EXERCISES

1. An industrial psychologist at a large corporation believes that there is a positive relationship between selected employee salary levels and the number of years of their professional education. In a random sample of 61 employees the correlation was found to be .64. The psychologist uses the .05 level of significance to test the appropriate null hypothesis.

   a. State the hypotheses.

   H_0: $\rho = 0$
   H_a: $\rho > 0$

   b. Set the criterion for rejecting H_0.

   $z_{cv} = +$

c. Compute the test statistic. (Use both formulas 10.5 and 10.7.)

$$z = \frac{z_r - z_p}{s_{z_r}}$$

for $r = .64$, $z_r =$

$$s_{z_r} = \sqrt{1/(n-3)} = \sqrt{1/(\quad - \quad)} =$$

$$z = \frac{0.758 -}{} =$$

$$t = r\sqrt{\frac{n-2}{1-r^2}}$$

$$= \sqrt{\frac{-2}{1-0.64^2}} =$$

$(t_{cv} = +1.671)$

d. Develop the confidence interval (CI_{95}). (Note that the critical value for the confidence interval will be different from the critical value for testing H_0.)

$$\begin{aligned}
CI_{95} &= z_r \pm (z_{cv})(s_{z_r}) \\
&= \quad\quad \pm (1.960)(\quad\quad) \\
&= \quad\quad \pm \\
&= (\quad , \quad)
\end{aligned}$$

Transforming back to r values

$$= (\quad , \quad)$$

e. Interpret the results.

H_0; 95 percent confident that (0.464, 0.768) contains   .

2. A foreign language teacher believes that the time required to attain a given level of comprehension is inversely related to the age at which the learning process begins. Fifty French students of varying ages participated in the study; a correlation coefficient of $-.45$ was found. Test the appropriate null hypothesis using $\alpha = .10$.

a. State the hypotheses.
   H_0:
   H_a:

b. Set the criterion for rejecting H_0.

   $z_{cv} =$

c. Compute the test statistic. (Use both formulas 10.5 and 10.7.)

for $r =$, $z_r =$

$$s_{z_r} = \sqrt{1/(n-3)} =$$

$$z = \frac{(\quad) -}{} =$$

$$t = \quad \sqrt{\frac{-}{1-(\quad)^2}} =$$

$(t_{cv} = \quad)$

d. Develop the confidence interval (CI_{90}). (Note that the critical value for the confidence interval will be different from the critical value for testing H_0.)

$$CI_{90} = (\quad\quad) \pm (\quad\quad)(\quad\quad)$$
$$= (\quad\quad) \pm$$
$$= (\quad\quad, \quad\quad)$$

Transforming back to *r* values

$$= (\quad\quad, \quad\quad)$$

e. Interpret the results.

H_0; 90 percent confident that $(-0.620, -0.240)$ contains   .

3. Suppose that a state director of certification believes that less than 25 percent of licensed clinical psychologists are female. To test this conjecture, a random sample of 75 clinical psychologists from the state-certified list reveals that 15 are women. Test the appropriate null hypothesis using $\alpha = .01$.

a. State the hypotheses.

$H_0: P =$
$H_a: P < 0.25$

b. Set the criterion for rejecting H_0.

$$z_{cv} =$$

c. Compute the test statistic.

$$z = \frac{p - P}{s_p}$$

$$p = 15/75 =$$

$$s_p \sqrt{PQ/n} = \sqrt{(0.25)(\quad\quad)/75} =$$

$$z = \frac{0.20 -}{\quad\quad} =$$

d. Develop the confidnece interval (CI_{99}). (Note that the critical value for the confidence interval will be different from the critical value for testing H_0.)

$$CI_{99} = p \pm (z_{cv})(s_p)$$
$$= (0.20) \pm (\quad\quad)(\quad\quad)$$
$$= (\quad\quad) \pm$$
$$= (\quad\quad, \quad\quad)$$

e. Interpret the results.

H_0; 99 percent confident that $(0.071, 0.329)$ contains P.

4. Campaign managers for a certain candidate believe that their candidate's views on a controversial issue are supported by more than 75 percent of the district's voters. A survey is conducted using a 500 person sample, and a total of 393 voters express approval. Test the appropriate hypothesis at the .10 level of significance. Construct the 90 percent confidence interval for the population parameter.

a. State the hypotheses.

$H_0: P =$
$H_a: P >$

b. Set the criterion for rejecting H_0.

$z_{cv} =$

c. Compute the test statistic.

$p = \quad / \quad =$

$s_p = \sqrt{PQ/n} = \sqrt{(\quad)(\quad)/\quad} =$

$z = \dfrac{\quad - \quad}{\quad} =$

d. Develop the confidence interval (CI_{90}). (Note that the critical value for the confidence interval will be different from the critical value for testing H_0.)

$CI_{90} = \quad \pm (\quad)(\quad)$
$= (\quad) \pm$
$= (\quad , \quad)$

e. Interpret the results.

H_0; 90 percent confident that ($\quad$, $\quad$) contains P.

5. The director of student housing at a college wants to know if there is a relationship between the scores of freshman students on a quality-of-dorm-life scale and their parents' income level. The dormitory life scale is scored so that higher scores indicate a more positive attitude toward dormitory life. A sample of 57 first year college students is selected randomly and the correlation coefficient is found to be .29. Test the appropriate hypothesis using the .05 level of significance.

a. State the hypotheses.

H_0:
H_a:

b. Set the criterion for rejecting H_0.

$z_{cv} =$

c. Compute the test statistic. (Use both formulas 10.5 and 10.7.)

$z =$
$t =$
$(t_{cv} = \pm 2.02)$

d. Develop the confidence interval (CI_{95}).

$CI_{95} = (\quad , \quad)$

Transforming back to r values
$= (\quad , \quad)$

e. Interpret the results.
H_0; 95 percent confident that ($\quad$, $\quad$) contains $\quad$.

6. A grade school science teacher is concerned about the parental support for a new course, Human Development and Growth, that is scheduled for the next school year. A random sample of 80 parents finds that 44 indicated that they favor the teaching of the course. Test the appropriate null hypothesis using $\alpha = .10$.

a. State the hypotheses.

b. Set the criterion for rejecting H_0.

c. Compute the test statistic.

d. Develop the confidence interval (CI_{90}).

e. Interpret the results.

7. A physical education instructor believes that 64 percent of the variance in student weight can be associated with their variance in height. This instructor randomly selects 50 students and finds the height-weight correlation to be .74. The level of significance is set at .05.

a. State the hypotheses.

b. Set the criterion for rejecting H_0.

c. Compute the test statistic.

d. Develop the confidence interval (CI_{95}).

e. Interpret the results.

Chapter 10 Exercises: Answers

1. a. $H_0: \rho = 0$

$H_a: \rho > 0$

b. $z_{cv} = +1.645$

c. $z = \dfrac{z_r - z_\rho}{s_{z_r}}$

for $r = .64$, $z_r = 0.758$

$s_{z_r} = \sqrt{1/(n-3)} = \sqrt{1/(61-3)} = 0.131$

$z = \dfrac{0.758 - 0}{0.131} = 5.79$

$t = r\sqrt{\dfrac{n-2}{1-r^2}}$

$= 0.64\sqrt{\dfrac{61-2}{1-0.64^2}} = 6.40$

$\left(t_{cv} = +1.671\right)$

d. $CI_{95} = z_r \pm (z_{cv})(s_{z_r})$
$= 0.758 \pm (1.960)(0.131)$
$= 0.758 \pm 0.257$
$= (0.501, 1.015)$

Transforming back to r values

$= (0.464, 0.768)$

e. Reject H_0; 95 percent confident that $(0.464, 0.768)$ contains ρ.

2. a. $H_0: \rho = 0$

$H_a: \rho < 0$

b. $z_{cv} = -1.282$

c. for $r = -.45$, $z_r = -0.485$

$$s_{z_r} = \sqrt{1/(n-3)} = \sqrt{1/(50-3)} = 0.146$$

$$z = \frac{(-0.485)-0}{0.146} = -3.32$$

$$t = -.45\sqrt{\frac{50-2}{1-(-0.45)^2}} = -3.49$$

$$(t_{cv} = -1.30)$$

d. $CI_{90} = (-0.485) \pm (1.645)(0.146)$
$= (-0.485) \pm 0.240$
$= (-0.725, -0.245)$

Transforming back to r values

$= (-0.620, -0.240)$

e. Reject H_0; 90 percent confident that $(-0.620, -0.240)$ contains ρ.

3. a. H_0: $P = 0.25$

H_a: $P < 0.25$

b. $z_{cv} = -2.326$

c. $p = 15/75 = 0.20$

$$s_p\sqrt{PQ/n} = \sqrt{(0.25)(0.75)/75} = 0.050$$

$$z = \frac{0.20-0.25}{0.050} = -1.00$$

d. $CI_{99} = (0.20) \pm (2.576)(0.050)$
$= (0.20) \pm 0.129$
$= (0.071, 0.329)$
(Note that 0.25 is contained in the interval.)

e. Fail to reject H_0; 99 percent confident that $(0.071, 0.329)$ contains P.

4. a. H_0: $P = 0.75$
H_a: $P > 0.75$

b. $z_{cv} = +1.282$

c. $p = 393/500 = 0.786$

$$s_p\sqrt{PQ/n} = \sqrt{(0.75)(0.25)/500} = 0.019$$

$$z = \frac{0.786-0.75}{0.019} = 1.89$$

d. $CI_{90} = (0.786) \pm (1.645)(0.019)$
$= (0.786) \pm 0.031$
$= (0.755, 0.817)$
(Note that 0.75 is not contained in the interval.)

e. Reject H_0; 90 percent confident that $(0.755, 0.817)$ contains P.

5. a. $H_0: \rho = 0$

$H_a: \rho \neq 0$

b. $z_{cv} = \pm 1.960$

c. for $r = .29$, $z_r = 0.299$

$$s_{z_r} = \sqrt{1/(n-3)} = \sqrt{1/(57-3)} = 0.136$$

$$z = \frac{0.299 - 0}{0.136} = 2.20$$

$$t = .29 \sqrt{\frac{57-2}{1-0.29^2}} = 2.25$$

$$\left(t_{cv} = \pm 2.02 \right)$$

d. $CI_{95} = 0.299 \pm (1.960)(0.136)$
$= 0.299 \pm 0.267$
$= (0.032, 0.566)$

Transforming back to r values

$= (0.032, 0.512)$

e. Reject H_0; 95 percent confident that $(0.032, 0.512)$ contains ρ.

6. a. $H_0: P = 0.50$

$H_a: P \neq 0.50$

b. $z_{cv} = \pm 1.645$

c. $p = 44/80 = 0.55$

$$s_p = \sqrt{PQ/n} = \sqrt{(0.50)(0.50)/80} = 0.056$$

$$z = \frac{0.55 - 0.50}{0.056} = 0.893$$

d. $CI_{90} = (0.55) \pm (1.645)(0.056)$
$= (0.55) \pm 0.092$
$= (0.458, 0.642)$
(Note that 0.55 is contained in the interval.)

e. Fail to reject H_0; 90 percent confident that $(0.458, 0.642)$ contains P.

7. a. $H_0: \rho = 0.80$
$H_a: \rho \neq 0.80$

b. $z_{cv} = +1.960$

c. for $r = .74$, $z_r = 0.950$
for $\rho = .80$, $z_\rho = 1.099$

$$s_{z_r} = \sqrt{1/(n-3)} = \sqrt{1/(50-3)} = 0.146$$

$$z = \frac{0.950 - 1.099}{0.146} = -1.021$$

d. $CI_{95} = 0.950 \pm (1.960)(0.146)$
$= 0.950 \pm 0.286$
$= (0.664, 1.236)$

Transforming back to r values

$= (0.581, 0.845)$

(Note that 0.80 is contained in the interval.)

e. Fail to reject H_0; 95 percent confident that $(0.581, 0.845)$ contains ρ.

CHAPTER 11

Hypothesis Testing:
Two-Sample Case for the Mean

COMPREHENSION CHECK

The following summary reviews the material presented in this chapter. To check your understanding of key concepts, supply the missing words indicated by the numbered blanks.

The concepts and procedures for hypothesis testing and interval estimation can be extended to the two-sample case. For the two-sample case, the null hypothesis relates to the __(1)__ between two population parameters. For example, the null hypothesis tested for the two-sample case for the mean is $H_0: \mu_1 = \mu_2$ or $H_0: \mu_1 - \mu_2 = 0$. The steps for testing the __(2)__ and constructing the corresponding confidence __(3)__ are the same as those for the one-sample test for the mean. The concepts underlying these steps involve determining the __(4)__ distribution of the statistic, the level of __(5)__ , and the directional nature of the __(6)__ hypothesis.

To test the null hypothesis for the two-sample case, the assumption of __(7)__ is required. Under this assumption, the subjects in each of the two __(8)__ are first drawn __(9)__ from the __(10)__ and then randomly assigned to the two __(11)__ conditions. For example, the subjects could be randomly assigned to either the __(12)__ group or the __(13)__ group. Random assignment assures that the two groups are __(14)__ before the study begins and that the __(15)__ will not be confounded by __(16)__ differences between the two groups. Testing the null hypothesis under the assumption of independence is called the __(17)__ t test.

A second assumption for the two-sample case is homogeneity of __(18)__ . That is, the variances in two populations are assumed to be __(19)__ , ($\sigma_1^2 = \sigma_2^2$). When the population variance (σ^2) is known, the __(20)__ distribution is used as the underlying distribution. Otherwise, the __(21)__ distribution with __(22)__ degrees of freedom is used. The standard deviation of the sampling distribution of the difference between two means is called the __(23)__ of the __(24)__ .

The formula for the test statistic is the same as for the one-sample case:

$$\text{Test statistic} = \frac{\underline{(25)} - \underline{(26)}}{\underline{(27)}}$$

The statistic is the observed __(28)__ between two sample means ($\bar{X}_1 - \bar{X}_2$), while the __(29)__ is the difference between the two population means ($\mu_1 - \mu_2$), which is zero under the null hypothesis. Similarly, the general formula for the __(30)__ interval is used for the two-sample case:

$$\text{CI} = \underline{(31)} \pm (\underline{(32)})(\underline{(33)})$$

When the null hypothesis is rejected, the confidence interval __(34)__ contain the hypothesized value ($\mu_1 - \mu_2 = 0$). On the other hand, if the null hypothesis is not rejected, zero __(35)__ be in the confidence interval.

There are serious consequences in using the independent *t* test when the assumption of homogeneity of __(36)__ is not met, especially when the __(37)__ of the two samples is not the same ($n_1 \neq n_2$). For these situations, there is an alternate formula for the standard __(38)__ of the difference. In addition, there is a different procedure for determining the degrees of __(39)__ for the *t* test.

There are designs in the behavioral science in which subjects act as their own __(40)__ and are measured under the two __(41)__ conditions. These designs are called repeated measures designs. For such designs, the assumption of __(42)__ cannot be met since the sample data across the two measurements are __(43)__ rather than independent. The null hypothesis for this design would be __(44)__ , where δ is the mean difference in the population, which is hypothesized to be zero. The corresponding __(45)__ is *d*, which is the mean __(46)__ for the sample data. The test of the hypothesis for this design is called the __(47)__ *t* test.

Comprehension Check: Answers

1. difference	**18.** variance	**33.** standard error of
2. hypothesis	**19.** equal	the statistic
3. interval	**20.** normal	**34.** will not
4. sampling	**21.** *t*	**35.** will
5. significance	**22.** $n_1 + n_2 - 2$	**36.** variance
6. alternative	**23.** standard error	**37.** size
7. independence	**24.** mean	**38.** error
8. samples	**25.** statistic	**39.** freedom
9. randomly	**26.** parameter	**40.** controls
10. population	**27.** standard error of	**41.** treatment
11. treatment	the statistic	**42.** independence
12. control	**28.** difference	**43.** dependent
13. experimental	**29.** parameter	**44.** $H_0: \delta = 0$
14. equivalent	**30.** confidence	**45.** statistic
15. treatment	**31.** statistic	**46.** difference
16. initial	**32.** critical value	**47.** dependent
17. independent		

CHAPTER 11 EXERCISES

1. The 23 members of an art appreciation class are asked to evaluate an anonymous painting, giving it a composite score derived from several recently studied measures of quality. Of the class members, 11 are exposed to no initial input, while the other 12 receive some indirect communication suggesting that the painting has been given favorable commentary by outside critics. The researcher suspects that indirect communication will inflate the ratings. Test the appropriate null hypothesis using the .05 level of significance.

No initial input	Indirect communication
22	28
29	26
31	34
25	36
23	31

	28	29
	30	28
	28	33
	24	30
	29	35
	33	31
		36
n	11	12
$\bar{X}$		
ΣX	302	
ΣX^2		11,969

a. State the hypotheses.

$H_0: \mu_1 = \mu_2$
$H_a: \mu_1 < \mu_2$

b. Set the criterion for rejecting H_0.

For df $= n_1 + n_2 - 2 = \qquad$, $t_{cv} = $

c. Compute the test statistic.

$$t = \frac{(\bar{X}_1 - \bar{X}_2) - (\mu_1 - \mu_2)}{s_{\bar{X}_1 - \bar{X}_2}}$$

where

$$s_{\bar{X}_1 - \bar{X}_2} = \sqrt{s^2\left(\frac{1}{n_1} + \frac{1}{n_2}\right)} \quad \text{and} \quad s^2 = \frac{SS_1 + SS_2}{n_1 + n_2 - 2}$$

$$s^2 = \frac{}{11 + 12 - 2}$$

$$= \frac{122.73 +}{} =$$

and

$$s_{\bar{X}_1 - \bar{X}_2} = \sqrt{11.79\left(\frac{1}{11} + \frac{1}{12}\right)} = \sqrt{\quad} =$$

Therefore,

$$t = \frac{(\quad - 31.42) - 0}{} =$$

d. Construct the confidence interval (CI_{95}).
(Note that the critical value for the confidence interval will be different from the critical value for testing H_0.)

$$CI_{95} = (\bar{X}_1 - \bar{X}_2) \pm (t_{cv})(s_{\bar{X}_1 - \bar{X}_2})$$

$$= (27.45 - \quad) \pm (\quad)(1.43)$$

$$= \quad \pm$$

$$= (\quad, -1.00)$$

e. Interpret the results.

H_0; 95% confident that (,) contains $(\mu_1 - \mu_2)$.

2. A psychologist wishes to determine whether the persistence of a child at a learning task is significatly affected by the presence of a parent within the learning environment. Two random samples of 15 children each are chosen. The mean duration of effort among the children with at least one parent present is 27.3 minutes. Among the other children, the average duration of effort is 21.9 minutes. The respective standard deviations are 6.4 and 6.8 minutes. Test the hypothesis of no differences at the .01 level of significance.

a. State the hypotheses.

$H_0: \mu_1 = \mu_2$
$H_a:$

b. Set the criterion for rejecting H_0.

For df =   , $t_{cv} =$

c. Compute the test statistic.

$$t = \frac{(\bar{X}_1 - \bar{X}_2) - (\mu_1 - \mu_2)}{s_{\bar{X}_1 - \bar{X}_2}}$$

where

$$s^2 = \frac{(15-1)6.4^2 + (15-1)6.8^2}{15+15-2}$$

$$= \frac{+}{} =$$

and

$$s_{\bar{X}_1 - \bar{X}_2} = \sqrt{\quad \left(\frac{1}{15} + \frac{1}{15}\right)} = \sqrt{\quad} =$$

Therefore,

$$t = \frac{(\quad - \quad) - 0}{} =$$

d. $CI_{99} = (\quad - \quad) \pm (\quad)(\quad)$

$\quad = \quad \pm$

$\quad = (\quad , \quad)$

e. H_0; 99% confident that (,) contains $(\mu_1 - \mu_2)$.

f. What would the results have been if the researcher had used $\alpha = .05$ and constructed CI_{95}?

$t_{cv} =$

Therefore, H_0.

$CI_{95} = (\quad - \quad) \pm (\quad)(\quad)$

$\quad = \quad \pm$

$\quad = (\quad , \quad)$

95% confident that (,) contains $(\mu_1 - \mu_2)$.

3. A remedial reading teacher is using two methods to improve student reading ability. Method 1 uses taped instructions and a self-paced text, while Method 2 uses a movie projector and

group format. Assuming that samples are independents, text the difference at the .10 level of significance, using the following data:

	Method 1	Method 2
$\bar{X}$	32.8	33.0
n	25	31
s^2	90.9	41.7

a. State the hypotheses.

H_0:

H_a:

b. Set the criterion for rejecting H_0.

Applying the Satterthwaite correction for df

$$df = \frac{(s_1^2/n_1 + s_2^2/n_2)^2}{(s_1^2/n_1)^2/(n_1-1) + (s_2^2/n_2)^2/(n_2-1)}$$

$$= \frac{(\quad /25 + 41.7/\quad)^2}{(90.9/\quad)^2/(25-1) + (\quad/31)^2/(\quad-1)}$$

$$= \frac{(\quad + \quad)^2}{\quad + \quad} =$$

For df= 40.82, t_{cv} =

c. Compute the test statistic.

Applying the Cochran and Cox correction

$$t = \frac{(\bar{X}_1 - \bar{X}_2) - (\mu_1 - \mu_2)}{s_{\bar{X}_1 - \bar{X}_2}}$$

where

$$s_{\bar{X}_1 - \bar{X}_2} = \sqrt{\frac{s_1^2}{n_1} + \frac{s_2^2}{n_2}}$$

$$= \sqrt{\frac{\quad}{\quad} + \frac{\quad}{\quad}} = \sqrt{\quad} =$$

Therefore,

$$t = \frac{(\quad - \quad) - 0}{\quad} =$$

d. Construct the confidence interval (CI_{90})

$$CI_{90} = (\quad - \quad) \pm (\quad)(\quad)$$
$$= (\quad) \pm$$
$$= (\quad , \quad)$$

e. $\qquad$ H_0; 90% confident that (,) contains $(\mu_1 - \mu_2)$.

4. Assume that the 95 percent confidence interval for the difference does not contain the value 0. What can be said, if anything, about rejecting the null hypothesis (H_0: $\mu_1 = \mu_2$) at the .05 level of significance? Consider the alternative hypothesis to be nondirectional.

5. A psychologist administers equivalent forms of a short-term memory test to a sample of 12 individuals before and after their exposure to a stressful situation. Determine whether the results support the conjecture that short-term memory is lessened by such exposure. Test the appropriate null hypothesis using $\alpha = .05$.

Prestress	Poststress	d	d^2
11	10	−1	1
15	13	−2	4
14	15		
19	15		
12	12		
16	14		
13	12		
15	15		
18	16		
20	17		
14	16		
17	14		

Σ

a. State the hypotheses.

$H_0: \delta = 0$
$H_a: \delta < 0$

b. Set the criterion for rejecting H_0.

For df $= n - 1 = 12 - 1 = \quad$, $t_{cv} =$

c. Compute the test statistic.

$$t = \frac{\bar{d} - \delta}{s_{\bar{d}}}$$

where

$$\bar{d} = \Sigma d / n = \quad / 12 =$$

$$s_d = \sqrt{\frac{\Sigma d^2 - (\Sigma d)^2 / n}{n - 1}} = \sqrt{\frac{\quad - (\quad)^2 /}{\quad - 1}}$$

$$= \sqrt{\quad} =$$

$$s_{\bar{d}} = s_d / \sqrt{n}$$

$$= \quad / \sqrt{12} =$$

Therefore,

$$t = \frac{\quad - 0}{\quad} =$$

d. Construct the confidence interval (CI_{95}).

$$\text{CI}_{95} = \bar{d} \pm (t_{cv})(s_{\bar{d}})$$

$$= (\quad) \pm (\quad)(\quad)$$

$$= (\quad) \pm$$

$$= (\quad , \quad)$$

e. Interpet the results.

H_0; 95% confident that ($\quad$, $\quad$) contains δ.

6. The psychologist in Exercise 2 believes that there is a difference between boys and girls in their learning task persistence, girls being more persistent. Assuming that $\sigma_B^2 = \sigma_G^2$, test the appropriate null hypothesis using $\alpha = .05$. For a class of 25 students, the data are as follows:

	Girls	Boys
$\bar{X}$	26.9	21.3
n	13	12
ΣX	350	256
ΣX^2	9,876	6,003

a. State the hypotheses.

H_0:
H_a:

b. Set the criterion for rejecting H_0.

For df =   , t_{cv} =

c. Compute the test statistic.

$$s^2 = \frac{ + }{} = $$

and

$$s_{\bar{X}_1 - \bar{X}_2} = \sqrt{\left(\frac{1}{-} + \frac{1}{-}\right)} = \sqrt{} = $$

Therefore,

$t =$

d. Construct the confidence interval (CI_{95}).

$\text{CI}_{95} = ($, $)$

e. Interpret the results.

H_0; 95% confident that (,   ) contains $(\mu_1 - \mu_2)$.

7. Suppose that a psychologist is interested in performance on a task under sleep-deprived conditions versus rested conditions, as measured by the number of errors made on the task. This researcher, who predicts that more mistakes will be made in the sleep-deprived condition, sets alpha = .01. Use the following information:

$\bar{d}$	5.9
n	10
Σd	59
Σd^2	399

a. State the hypotheses.

H_0:
H_a:

b. Set the criterion for rejecting H_0.

For df =   , t_{cv} =

c. Compute the test statistic.

$$\bar{d} = \Sigma d / n = \quad / \quad =$$

$$s_d = \sqrt{\frac{\Sigma d^2 - (\Sigma d)^2 / n}{n-1}} = \sqrt{\frac{-(\quad)^2 /}{10-1}}$$

$$= \sqrt{\quad} =$$

$$s_{\bar{d}} = \quad / \sqrt{\quad} =$$

Therefore,

$$t =$$

d. Construct the confidence interval (CI_{99}).

$$CI_{99} = (\quad , \quad)$$

e. Interpret the results.

$$H_0; \text{ 99\% confident that } (\quad , \quad) \text{ contains } \delta.$$

8. Given the following data, test the difference between population means using a nondirectional alternative hypothesis and the .10 level of significance.

Sample 1	Sample 2
$n_1 = 25$	$n_2 = 18$
$\bar{X}_1 = 37.38$	$\bar{X}_2 = 42.31$
$s_1^2 = 36.40$	$s_2^2 = 82.15$

a. State the hypotheses.

$$H_0:$$
$$H_a:$$

b. Set the criterion for rejecting H_0.

Applying the Satterthwaite correction for df

$$df = \frac{(\quad / \quad + \quad / \quad)^2}{(\quad / \quad)^2 / (25-1) + (\quad / \quad)^2 / (18-1)}$$

$$= \frac{(\quad + \quad)^2}{\quad + \quad} =$$

For df = $\quad$, $t_{cv} =$

c. Compute the test statistic.

Applying the Cochran and Cox correction

where

$$s_{\bar{X}_1 - \bar{X}_2} = \sqrt{\frac{}{\quad} + \frac{}{\quad}} = \sqrt{\quad} =$$

Therefore,

$$t =$$

d. Construct the confidence interval (CI_{90}).

$$CI_{90} = (\quad , \quad)$$

e. Interpret the results.

$$H_0; \text{ 90\% confident that } (\quad,\quad) \text{ contains } (\mu_1 - \mu_2).$$

Chapter 11 Exercises: Answers

1.

n	11	12
$\bar{X}$	27.45	31.42
ΣX	302	377
ΣX^2	8,414	11,969

a. $H_0: \mu_1 = \mu_2$

$H_a: \mu_1 < \mu_2$

b. For df $= n_1 + n_2 - 2 = 21$, $t_{cv} = -1.721$.

c. $t = \dfrac{(\bar{X}_1 - \bar{X}_2) - (\mu_1 - \mu_2)}{s_{\bar{X}_1 - \bar{X}_2}}$

where

$$s_{\bar{X}_1 - \bar{X}_2} = \sqrt{s^2\left(\frac{1}{n_1} + \frac{1}{n_2}\right)} \text{ and } s^2 = \frac{SS_1 + SS_2}{n_1 + n_2 - 2}$$

$$s^2 = \frac{8,414 - \dfrac{(302)^2}{11} + 11,969 - \dfrac{(377)^2}{12}}{11 + 12 - 2}$$

$$= \frac{122.73 + 124.92}{21} = 11.79$$

and

$$s_{\bar{X}_1 - \bar{X}_2} = \sqrt{11.79\left(\frac{1}{11} + \frac{1}{12}\right)} = \sqrt{2.05} = 1.43$$

Therefore,

$$t = \frac{(27.45 - 31.42) - 0}{1.43} = -2.78$$

d. $CI_{95} = (\bar{X}_1 - \bar{X}_2) \pm (t_{cv})(s_{\bar{x}_1 - \bar{x}_2})$

$= (27.45 - 31.42) \pm (2.080)(1.43)$

$= -3.97 \pm 2.97$

$= (-6.94, -1.00)$

(Note that this interval does not contain the point 0.)

e. Reject H_0; 95% confident that $(-6.94, -1.00)$ contains $(\mu_1 - \mu_2)$.

2. a. $H_0: \mu_1 = \mu_2$

$H_a: \mu_1 \neq \mu_2$

b. For df $= n_1 + n_2 - 2 = 28$, $t_{cv} = \pm 2.763$

c. $s^2 = \dfrac{(15-1)6.4^2 + (15-1)6.8^2}{15+15-2}$

$\qquad = \dfrac{573.44 + 647.36}{28} = 43.60$

and

$$s_{\bar{X}_1 - \bar{X}_2} = \sqrt{43.60\left(\dfrac{1}{15} + \dfrac{1}{15}\right)} = \sqrt{5.81} = 2.41$$

Therefore,

$$t = \dfrac{(27.3 - 21.9) - 0}{2.41} = 2.24$$

d. $CI_{99} = (27.3 - 21.9) \pm (2.763)(2.41)$

$\qquad = 5.40 \pm 6.66$

$\qquad = (-1.26, 12.06)$

(Note that this interval contains the point 0.)

e. Fail to reject H_0; 99% confident that $(-1.26, 12.06)$ contains $(\mu_1 - \mu_2)$.

f. $t_{cv} = \pm 2.048$

Therefore, reject H_0.

$CI_{95} = (27.3 - 21.9) \pm (2.048)(2.41)$

$\qquad = 5.40 \pm 4.94$

$\qquad = (0.46, 10.34)$

95% confident that $(0.46, 10.34)$ contains $(\mu_1 - \mu_2)$.

3.

	Method 1	Method 2
$\bar{X}$	32.8	33.0
n	25	31
s^2	90.9	41.7

a. $H_0: \mu_1 = \mu_2$

$H_a: \mu_1 \neq \mu_2$

b. Applying the Satterthwaite correction for df

$$df = \dfrac{(s_1^2 / n_1 + s_2^2 / n_2)^2}{(s_1^2 / n_1)^2 / (n_1 - 1) + (s_2^2 / n_2)^2 / (n_2 - 1)}$$

$$= \dfrac{(90.9/25 + 41.7/31)^2}{(90.9/25)^2 / (25 - 1) + (41.7/31)^2 / (31 - 1)}$$

$$= \dfrac{(3.64 + 1.35)^2}{0.55 + 0.06} = 40.82$$

For df $= 40.82$, $t_{cv} = \pm 1.684$

c. Applying the Cochran and Cox correction

$$t = \frac{(\bar{X}_1 - \bar{X}_2) - (\mu_1 - \mu_2)}{s_{\bar{X}_1 - \bar{X}_2}}$$

where

$$s_{\bar{X}_1 - \bar{X}_2} = \sqrt{\frac{s_1^2}{n_1} + \frac{s_2^2}{n_2}}$$

$$= \sqrt{\frac{90.9}{25} + \frac{41.7}{31}} = \sqrt{4.97} = 2.23$$

Therefore,

$$t = \frac{(32.8 - 33.0) - 0}{2.23} = -0.09$$

d. $CI_{90} = (32.8 - 33.0) \pm (1.684)(2.23)$

$$= (-0.2) \pm 3.76$$

$$= (-3.96, 3.56)$$

(Note that this interval contains the point 0.)

e. Fail to reject H_0; 90% confident that $(-3.96, 3.56)$ contains $(\mu_1 - \mu_2)$.

4. Since 0 is not in the interval, the observed value of t must exceed the critical value of t. Therefore the null hypothesis ($H_0: \mu_1 = \mu_2$) would be rejected in favor of the nondirectional alternative ($H_a: \mu_1 \neq \mu_2$).

5.

	Prestress	Poststress	d	d^2
	11	10	−1	1
	15	13	−2	4
	14	15	+1	1
	19	15	−4	16
	12	12	0	0
	16	14	−2	4
	13	12	−1	1
	15	15	0	0
	18	16	−2	4
	20	17	−3	9
	14	16	+2	4
	17	14	−3	9
Σ			−15	53

a. $H_0: \delta = 0$

$H_a: \delta < 0$

b. For df $= n - 1 = 12 - 1 = 11$, $t_{cv} = -1.796$

c. $t = \dfrac{\bar{d} - \delta}{s_{\bar{d}}}$

where

$\bar{d} = \Sigma d / n = -15/12 = -1.25$

$s_d = \sqrt{\dfrac{\Sigma d^2 - (\Sigma d)^2 / n}{n-1}} = \sqrt{\dfrac{53 - (-15)^2 / 12}{12 - 1}}$

$\quad = \sqrt{3.11} = 1.76$

$s_{\bar{d}} = s_d / \sqrt{n}$

$\quad = 1.76 / \sqrt{12} = 0.51$

Therefore,

$t \quad = \dfrac{(-1.25) - 0}{0.51} = -2.45$

d. $CI_{95} = \bar{d} \pm (t_{cv})(s_{\bar{d}})$

$\quad = (-1.25) \pm (2.201)(0.51)$

$\quad = (-1.25) \pm 1.12$

$\quad = (-2.37, -0.13)$

e. Reject H_0; 95% confident that $(-2.39, -0.11)$ contains δ.

6.

	Girls	Boys
$\bar{X}$	26.9	21.3
n	13	12
ΣX	350	256
ΣX^2	9,876	6,003

a. $H_0: \mu_G = \mu_B$
$H_a: \mu_G > \mu_B$

b. For df $= n_1 + n_2 - 2 = 23$, $t_{cv} = +1.714$

c. $s^2 = \dfrac{\left[9,876 - (350)^2 / 13\right] + \left[6,003 - (256)^2 / 12\right]}{13 + 12 - 2}$

$\quad = \dfrac{452.92 + 541.67}{23} = 43.24$

and

$s_{\bar{X}_1 - \bar{X}_2} = \sqrt{43.24 \left(\dfrac{1}{13} + \dfrac{1}{12}\right)} = \sqrt{6.93} = 2.63$

Therefore,

$t = \dfrac{(26.9 - 21.3) - 0}{2.63} = 2.13$

d. $CI_{95} = (26.9 - 21.3) \pm (2.069)(2.63)$

$\quad = 5.60 \pm 5.44$

$\quad = (0.16, 11.04)$

(Note that this interval does not contain the point 0.)

e. Reject H_0: 95% confident that $(0.16, 11.04)$ contains $(\mu_1 - \mu_2)$.

7. $\bar{d}$ 5.9
   n 10
   Σd 59
   Σd^2 399

a. $H_0: \delta = 0$
   $H_a: \delta > 0$

b. For df $= n - 1 = 10 - 1 = 9$, $t_{cv} = +2.821$

c. $\bar{d} = \Sigma d/n = 59/10 = 5.9$

$$s_d = \sqrt{\frac{\Sigma d^2 - (\Sigma d)^2 / n}{n-1}} = \sqrt{\frac{399 - (59)^2 / 10}{10-1}}$$

$$= \sqrt{5.66} = 2.38$$

$$s_{\bar{d}} = s_d / \sqrt{n}$$

$$= 2.38 / \sqrt{10} = 0.75$$

Therefore,

$$t = \frac{(5.9) - 0}{0.75} = 7.87$$

d. $\text{CI}_{99} = \bar{d} \pm (t_{cv})(s_{\bar{d}})$

$$= (5.9) \pm (3.250)(0.75)$$

$$= (5.9) \pm 2.44$$

$$= (3.46, 8.34)$$

e. Reject H_0; 99% confident that $(3.46, 8.34)$ contains δ.

8.   Sample 1   Sample 2
       $n_1 = 25$ $n_2 = 18$
       $\bar{X}_1 = 37.38$ $\bar{X}_2 = 42.31$
       $s_1^2 = 36.40$ $s_2^2 = 82.15$

a. $H_0: \mu_1 = \mu_2$
   $H_a: \mu_1 \neq \mu_2$

b. Applying the Satterthwaite correction for df

$$\text{df} = \frac{(36.40/25 + 82.15/18)^2}{(36.40/25)^2 / (25-1) + (82.15/18)^2 / (18-1)}$$

$$= \frac{(1.46 + 4.56)^2}{0.09 + 1.22} = 27.66$$

For df $= 27.66$, $t_{cv} = \pm 2.050$

c. Applying the Cochran and Cox correction

$$s_{\bar{X}_1 - \bar{X}_2} = \sqrt{\frac{36.40}{25} + \frac{82.15}{18}} = \sqrt{6.02} = 2.45$$

Therefore,

$$t = \frac{(37.38 - 42.31) - 0}{2.45} = -2.01$$

d. $CI_{90} = (37.38 - 42.31) \pm (2.050)(2.45)$
$$= (-4.93) \pm 5.02$$
$$= (-9.95, 0.09)$$
(Note that this interval contains the point 0.)

e. Fail to reject H_0; 90% confident that $(-9.95, 0.09)$ contains $(\mu_1 - \mu_2)$.

CHAPTER 12

Hypothesis Testing: Two-Sample Case for Other Statistics

COMPREHENSION CHECK

The two-sample case can be extended to __(1)__ other than means, for example, differences between two proportions, two corelation coefficients, and two variances. As before, the logic and steps for testing __(2)__ and developing __(3)__ intervals remain the same. For these additional two-sample cases, there are tests of hypotheses for independent and __(4)__ samples.

For the two-sample case for proportions, the hypothesis is stated in terms of no __(5)__ in the population between the two proportions, symbolically, $H_0: P_1 = P_2$ or $H_0: P_1 - P_2 = 0$. The __(6)__ distribution for testing this hypothesis is the __(7)__ distribution. The critical values for both __(8)__ testing and developing the __(9)__ confidence interval are found by using the standard __(10)__ distribution. For the case of __(11)__ proportions, the null hypothesis is H_0: $\delta_p = 0$. The underlying distribution for testing this hypothesis is also the __(12)__ distribution.

For testing the null hypothesis for the two-sample case for __(13)__ coefficients ($H_0: \rho_1 = \rho_2$), both sample correlation coefficients must be transformed using Fisher's __(14)__ . With this transformation, the __(15)__ distribution can be used as the underlying distribution for both hypothesis testing and developing confidence intervals. For __(16)__ samples, the actual correlation __(17)__ are used rather than the __(18)__ coefficients and the __(19)__ distribution for testing the hypothesis is the t distribution with __(20)__ degrees of freedom.

To test the null hypothesis $H_0: \sigma_1^2 = \sigma_2^2$ for independent samples, the appropriate underlying distribution is the __(21)__ . The test statistic is the __(22)__ of the two sample __(23)__ . The specific F distribution is determined from two values for __(24)__ , $n_1 - 1$ and $n_2 - 1$. When we test against a nondirectional __(25)__ and the F ratio is *greater* than 1.0, the critical value of the __(26)__ is determined from the F distribution table for $\alpha/2$. When the F ratio is *less* than 1.0, the critical value is the __(27)__ of the tabled value for $\alpha/2$ and __(28)__ , respectively. For testing the null hypothesis of no difference between population variances for __(29)__ samples, the underlying distribution of the test statistic is the __(30)__ with __(31)__ degrees of freedom.

Comprehension Check: Answers

1. statistics	**9.** corresponding	**17.** coefficients
2. hypotheses	**10.** normal	**18.** transformed
3. confidence	**11.** dependent	**19.** underlying
4. dependent	**12.** normal	**20.** $n - 3$
5. difference	**13.** correlation	**21.** F distribution
6. underlying	**14.** log transformation	**22.** ratio
7. normal	**15.** normal	**23.** variances
8. hypothesis	**16.** dependent	**24.** degrees of freedom

25. alternative
26. test statistic
27. reciprocal

28. df_2 and df_1
29. dependent

30. t distribution
31. $n - 2$

CHAPTER 12 EXERCISES

1. A college administrator believes the retention rate to be higher among work-study students than among other students. Two random samples of size 300 are selected for participation in a two-year study. Over that period, 225 of the work-study participants and 201 of the nonwork-study sample remain in school. Test the appropriate null hypothesis against the directional alternative hypothesis using $\alpha = .05$.

   a. State the hypotheses.
   $H_0\colon P_{WS} = P_{CON}$
   $H_a\colon$

   b. Set the criterion for rejecting H_0.
   $z_{cv} =$

   c. Compute the test statistic.
   $$z = \frac{(p_1 - p_2) - (P_1 - P_2)}{s_{p_1} - s_{p_2}}$$
   where
   $p_1 = 225 / 300 = \qquad$ and $p_2 = 201 / 300 =$

   $$s_{p_1 - p_2} = \sqrt{pq \left(\frac{1}{n_1} + \frac{1}{n_2} \right)} \text{ and } p = \frac{f_1 + f_2}{n_1 + n_2} \text{ and } q = 1 - p$$

   $$p = \frac{225 +}{ + 300} = \qquad \text{and } q = (1 -) =$$

   and

   $$s_{p_1 - p_2} = \sqrt{(.710)()\left(\frac{1}{300} + \frac{1}{} \right)} =$$

   Therefore,

   $$z = \frac{(-) - 0}{} =$$

   d. Construct the confidence interval (CI_{95}). (Note that the critical value for the confidence interval will be different from the critical value for testing H_0.)

   $CI_{95} = (p_1 - p_2) \pm (z_{cv})(s_{p_1} - s_{p_2})$
   $\phantom{CI_{95}} = (- .670) \pm ()(^2)$
   $\phantom{CI_{95}} = \pm$
   $\phantom{CI_{95}} = (.007,)$

   e. Interpret the results.
   H_0: 95% confident that (,) contains ($P_1 - P_2$).

2. Suppose that a teacher education program has a requirement that all students take a course in identifying deficient readers. After their first year of teaching, a random sample of 80 mathematics and 70 science teachers were asked how helpful the required course had been to them.

Forty math teachers and 45 science teachers indicated that the course had been helpful. Is there a difference in the perceptions of helpfulness for the two groups of teachers? Test the appropriate null hypothesis using $\alpha = .10$.

a. State the hypotheses.

H_0:

H_a:

b. Set the criterion for rejecting H_0.

$z_{cv} =$

c. Compute the test statistic.

$$p_1 = \quad / \quad = \quad \text{and } p_2 = \quad / \quad =$$

$$p = \frac{+}{+} = \quad \text{and } q = (1 - \quad) =$$

and

$$s_{p_1 - p_2} = \sqrt{(\quad)(\quad)\left(\frac{1}{\quad} + \frac{1}{\quad}\right)} =$$

Therefore,

$$z = \frac{(\quad - \quad) - 0}{} =$$

d. Construct the confidence interval (CI_{90}).

$$CI_{90} = (\quad - \quad) \pm (\quad)(\quad)$$
$$= (\quad) \pm$$
$$= (\quad , \quad)$$

e. Interpret the results.

$\qquad H_0$: 90% confident that $(\quad , \quad)$ contains $(P_1 - P_2)$.

3. A psychologist wishes to determine whether teenagers state similar attitudes when interviewed alone and in the presence of peers. Under each situation, 150 youths are asked to indicate whether or not they favor a relaxation of current drug regulations. When interviewed alone, 70 express agreement with relaxation of drug regulations; when in the presence of peers, 85 teenagers express agreement. The data are tabulated below. Determine (at the .05 level of significance) if a significant difference exists.

		Alone	
		Favor	Disfavor
Peers present	Disfavor	2	63
	Favor	68	17

150

a. State the hypotheses.

H_0: $\delta = 0$

H_a:

b. Set the criterion for rejecting H_0.

$z_{cv} =$

c. Compute the test statistic.

$$z = \frac{(p_1 - p_2) - (\delta_p)}{s_{\delta_p}}$$

where

$$p_1 = (2 + 68)/150 = \qquad \text{and } p_2 = (68 + 17)/150 =$$

$$s_{\delta_p} = \sqrt{\frac{a+d}{n}} \qquad\qquad a = A/n \quad \text{and } d = D/n$$
$$= 2/150 \qquad = 17/150$$
$$= \sqrt{\qquad + \qquad} \qquad = \qquad\qquad =$$
$$=$$

Therefore,

$$z = \frac{(\quad - \quad) - 0}{} =$$

d. Construct the confidence interval (CI_{95}).
$$CI_{95} = (\quad - \quad) \pm (1.96)(.0291)$$
$$= (\quad) \pm$$
$$= (\quad , \quad)$$

e. Interpret the results.
$$H_0: \text{95\% confident that } (\quad , \quad) \text{ contains } (\delta_p).$$

4. A personnel administrator received numerical ratings of job performance from both employees and their supervisors. An analysis is to be conducted to determine whether the consistency is greater in the case of salaried or unsalaried workers. Data were collected and compiled for 100 salaried and 100 unsalaried workers; the correlation coefficients computed were .72 and .64, respectively. Do these correlation coefficients differ significantly at the .05 level of significance?

a. State the hypotheses.
$$H_0: \rho_S = \rho_U$$
$$H_a:$$

b. Set the criterion for rejecting H_0.
$$z_{cv} =$$

c. Compute the test statistic.

$$z = \frac{(z_{r_1} - z_{r_2}) - (z_{\rho_1} - z_{\rho_2})}{s_{z_{r_1} - z_{r_2}}}$$

For $r_1 = .72 \qquad z_{r_1} =$
$r_2 = .64 \qquad z_{r_2} =$

$$s_{z_{r_1} - z_{r_2}} = \sqrt{\frac{1}{n_1 - 3} + \frac{1}{n_2 - 3}} = \sqrt{\frac{1}{100 - 3} + \frac{1}{100 - 3}} =$$

Therefore,

$$z = \frac{(\quad - \quad) - 0}{} =$$

d. Construct the confidence interval (CI_{95}). (Note that the critical value for the confidence interval will be different from the critical value for testing H_0.)

$$\begin{aligned}
\text{CI}_{95} &= (z_{r_1} = z_{r_2}) \pm (z_{cv})(s_{z_{r_1}} - s_{z_{r_2}}) \\
&= (\quad - \quad) \pm (\quad)(\quad) \\
&= \quad \pm \\
&= (\quad, \quad)
\end{aligned}$$

Transforming back to r values

$$= (\quad, \quad)$$

e. Interpret the results.

      H_0: 95% confident that $(\quad, \quad)$ contains $(\rho_1 - \rho_2)$.

5. The director of graduate education in a statistics department feels that there is a relationship between GRE scores and statistics final examination scores. Two graduate-level classes of 37 and 28 students have .315 and .645 correlations between the two scores. Is there a difference between the two coefficients at the .10 level of significance?

a. State the hypotheses.

    H_0:

    H_a:

b. Set the criterion for rejecting H_0.

    $z_{cv} =$

c. Compute the test statistic.

    For $r_1 = .315$ $z_{r_1} =$

         $r_2 = .645$ $z_{r_2} =$

$$= \sqrt{\frac{1}{\quad - 3} + \frac{1}{\quad - 3}} =$$

Therefore,

$$z = \frac{(\quad - \quad) - 0}{} =$$

d. Construct the confidence interval (CI_{90}).

$$\begin{aligned}
\text{CI}_{90} &= (\quad - \quad) \pm (\quad)(\quad) \\
&= \quad \pm \\
&= (\quad, \quad)
\end{aligned}$$

Transforming back to r values

$$= (\quad, \quad)$$

e. Interpret the results.

      H_0: 90% confident that $(\quad, \quad)$ contains $(\rho_1 - \rho_2)$.

6. A remedial reading specialist is using two methods to improve the reading ability of her students. Method 1 uses taped instructions and a self-paced text; Method 2 employs movies in a group format. The specialist is concerned with the difference in the variances of two classes using two methods. For the data given below, first test the equality of means under the assumption that the variances are equal; next, test the assumption by comparing the variances using the .10 level of significance; finally, retest the difference between means using the Satterthwaite correction to the degrees of freedom. Use alpha = .05 for each of the tests on means.

	Method 1	*Method 2*
n	25	31
s^2	90.9	41.7
$\bar{X}$	32.8	35.9

Pooled Test

a. State the hypotheses.

$H_0: \mu_1 = \mu_2$

$H_a:$

b. Set the criterion for rejecting H_0.

For df $= n_1 + n_2 - 2 = \quad$, $t_{cv} = \pm$

c. Compute the test statistic.

$$t = \frac{(X_1 - X_2) - (\mu_1 - \mu_2)}{s_{\bar{X}_1 - \bar{X}_2}}$$

where

$$s_{\bar{X}_1 - \bar{X}_2} = \sqrt{s^2 \left(\frac{1}{n_1} + \frac{1}{n_2} \right)} \text{ and } s^2 = \frac{SS_1 + SS_2}{n_1 + n_2 - 2}$$

$$s^2 = \frac{(25-1) \quad + (31-1)}{\quad + \quad - 2}$$

$$= \frac{\quad + \quad}{\quad} = \frac{\quad}{\quad} =$$

and

$$s_{\bar{X}_1 - \bar{X}_2} = \sqrt{\quad \left(\frac{1}{25} + \frac{1}{31} \right)} = \sqrt{\quad} =$$

Therefore,

$$t = \frac{(\quad - \quad) - 0}{\quad} =$$

d. $\qquad H_0$

Test of Homogeneity of Variance

a. State the hypotheses.

$H_0: \sigma_1^2 = \sigma_2^2$

$H_a:$

b. Set the criterion for rejecting H_0.

For df $= n_1 - 1 = 25 - 1 = \quad$ and $n_2 - 1 = 31 - 1 = \quad$, $F_{cv} =$

c. Compute the test statistic.

$F = s_1^2 / s_2^2 = \quad / \quad =$

d. Interpret the results.

$\qquad H_0.$

Satterthwaite Procedure

a. State the hypotheses.

$H_0:$

$H_a:$

b. Applying the Satterthwaite correction for df

$$df = \frac{(s_1^2 / n_1 + s_2^2 / n_2)^2}{(s_1^2 / n_1)^2 / (n_1 - 1) + (s_2^2 / n_2)^2 / (n_2 - 1)}$$

$$= \frac{(\quad / 25 + \quad / 31)^2}{(\quad / 25)^2 / (25 - 1) + (\quad / 31)^2 / (31 - 1)}$$

$$= \frac{(\quad + \quad)^2}{\quad + \quad} =$$

For df = ____, t_{cv} =

c. Applying the Cochran and Cox correction

$$s_{\bar{X}_1 - \bar{X}_2} = \sqrt{\frac{s_1^2}{n_1} + \frac{s_2^2}{n_2}}$$

$$= \sqrt{\frac{\quad}{25} + \frac{\quad}{31}} = \sqrt{\quad} =$$

Therefore,

$$t = \frac{(\quad - \quad) - 0}{\quad} =$$

d. Construct the confidence interval (CI_{95}).

$$CI_{95} = (\quad - \quad) \pm (\quad)(\quad)$$
$$= (\quad) \pm$$
$$= (\quad , \quad)$$

e. Interpret the results.

$$H_0: \text{95\% confident that } (\quad , \quad) \text{ contains } (\mu_1 - \mu_2).$$

7. A researcher wishes to test the assumption of homogeneity of variance before testing for differences between means. Given the following data, make this decision at the .10 level of significance.

	Sample A	Sample B
n	31	66
s^2	22.5	35.3

a. State the hypotheses.
H_0:
H_a:

b. Set the criterion for rejecting H_0.
For df = $n_1 - 1 = 66 - 1 =$ ____ and $n_2 - 1 = 31 - 1 =$ ____ , F_{cv} =

c. Compute the test statistic.
$F = s_1^2 / s_2^2 =$ ____ / ____ =

d. Interpret the results.
H_0 (apply the pooled test).

Chapter 12 Exercises: Answers

1. a. H_0: $P_{WS} = P_{CON}$
H_a: $P_{WS} > P_{CON}$

b. $z_{cv} = +1.645$

c. $z = \dfrac{(p_1 - p_2) - (P_1 - P_2)}{s_{p_1 - p_2}}$

where

$p_1 = 225 / 300 = .750$

and

$p_2 = 201 / 300 = .670$

$p = \dfrac{225 + 201}{300 + 300} = .710$

and

$q = (1 - .710) = .290$

and

$s_{p_1 - p_2} = \sqrt{(.710)(.290)\left(\dfrac{1}{300} + \dfrac{1}{300}\right)} = .037$

Therefore,

$z = \dfrac{(.750 - .670) - 0}{.037} = 2.162$

d. $CI_{95} = (p_1 - p_2) \pm (z_{cv})(s_{p_1} - s_{p_2})$

$= (.750 - .670) \pm (1.96)(.037)$

$= .080 \pm .073$

$= (.007, .153)$

e. Reject H_0: 95% confident that $(.007, .153)$ contains $(P_1 - P_2)$.

2. a. H_0: $P_M = P_S$
H_a: $P_M \neq P_S$

b. $z_{cv} = \pm 1.645$

c. $p_1 = 40 / 80 = .500$

and

$p_2 = 45 / 70 = .643$

$p = \dfrac{40 + 45}{80 + 70} = .567$

and

$q = (1 - .567) = .433$

and

$$s_{p_1 - p_2} = \sqrt{(.567)(.433)\left(\frac{1}{80} + \frac{1}{70}\right)} = .081$$

Therefore,

$$z = \frac{(.500 - .643) - 0}{.081} = -1.765$$

d. $CI_{90} = (.500 - .643) \pm (1.645)(.081)$

$$= (-.143) \pm .133$$

$$= (-.276, \ -.010)$$

e. Reject H_0: 90% confident that $(-.276, -.010)$ contains $(P_1 - P_2)$.

3. a. H_0: $\delta_p = 0$
H_a: $\delta_p \neq 0$

b. $z_{cv} = +1.96$

c. $p_1 = (2 + 68)/150 = .467$ and $p_2 = (68 + 17)/150 = .567$

$$s_{\delta_p} = \sqrt{\frac{a + d}{n}}$$

$$= \sqrt{\frac{.0133 + .1133}{150}}$$

$$= .0291$$

$a = A/n \quad$ and $d = D/n$
$\quad = 2/150 \qquad = 17/150$
$\quad = .0133 \qquad = .1133$

Therefore,

$$z = \frac{(.467 - .567) - 0}{.0291} = -3.436$$

d. $CI_{95} = (.467 - .567) \pm (1.96)(.0291)$

$$= (-.100) \pm .057$$

$$= (-.157, -.043)$$

e. Reject H_0: 95% confident that $(-.157, -.043)$ contains (δ_ρ).

4. a. H_0: $\rho_S = \rho_U$
H_a: $\rho_S > \rho_U$

b. $z_{cv} = +1.645$

c. $z = \dfrac{(z_{r_1} - z_{r_2}) - (z_{\rho_1} - z_{\rho_2})}{s_{z_{r_1} - z_{r_2}}}$

For $r_1 = .72$ $z_{r_1} = .908$

$r_2 = .64$ $z_{r_2} = .758$

$$s_{z_{r_1} - z_{r_2}} = \sqrt{\frac{1}{n_1 - 3} + \frac{1}{n_2 - 3}} = \sqrt{\frac{1}{100 - 3} + \frac{1}{100 - 3}} = .1436$$

Therefore,

$$z = \frac{(.908 - .758) - 0}{.1436} = 1.045$$

d. $\begin{aligned} \text{CI}_{95} &= (z_{r_1} - z_{r_2}) \pm (z_{cv})(s_{z_{r_1}} - s_{z_{r_2}}) \\ &= (.908 - .758) \pm (1.96)(.1436) \\ &= .150 \pm .282 \\ &= (-.132, .432) \end{aligned}$

Transforming back to r values
$$= (-.131, .407)$$

e. Fail to reject H_0: 95% confident that $(-.131, .407)$ contains $(\rho_1 - \rho_2)$.

5. a. $H_0: \rho_1 = \rho_2$
$H_a: \rho_1 \neq \rho_2$

b. $z_{cv} = +1.645$

c. For $r_1 = .315$ $z_{r_1} = .326$

$r_2 = .645$ $z_{r_2} = .767$

$$s_{z_{r_1} - z_{r_2}} = \sqrt{\frac{1}{n_1 - 3} + \frac{1}{n_2 - 3}} = \sqrt{\frac{1}{37 - 3} + \frac{1}{28 - 3}} = .2635$$

Therefore,

$$z = \frac{(.326 - .767) - 0}{.2635} = -1.674$$

d. $\begin{aligned} \text{CI}_{90} &= (.326 - .767) \pm (1.645)(.2635) \\ &= -.441 \pm .433 \\ &= (-.874, \; -.008) \end{aligned}$

Transforming back to r values.
$$= (-.704, -.008)$$

e. Reject H_0: 90% confident that $(-.704, -.008,)$ contains $(\rho_1 - \rho_2)$.

6. *Pooled Test*

a. $H_0: \mu_1 = \mu_2$
$H_a: \mu_1 \neq \mu_2$

b. For df $= n_1 + n_2 - 2 = 54$, $t_{cv} = \pm 2.01$

c. $s^2 = \dfrac{(25-1)\,90.9 + (31-1)\,41.7}{25+31-2}$

$$= \frac{2181.60 + 1251.00}{54} = \frac{3432.60}{54} = 63.57$$

and

$$s_{\bar{X}_1 - \bar{X}_2} = \sqrt{63.57\left(\frac{1}{25} + \frac{1}{31}\right)} = \sqrt{4.59} = 2.14$$

Therefore,

$$t = \frac{(32.8 - 35.9) - 0}{2.14} = -1.45$$

d. Fail to reject H_0.

Test of Homogeneity of Variance

a. $H_0: \sigma_1^2 = \sigma_2^2$
   $H_a: \sigma_1^2 \neq \sigma_2^2$

b. For df $n_1 - 1 = 25 - 1 = 24$ and $n_2 - 1 = 31 - 1 = 30$, $F_{cv} = 1.89$.

c. $F = s_1^2/s_2^2 = 90.9/41.7 = 2.18$

d. Reject H_0.

Satterthwaite Procedure

a. $H_0: \mu_1 = \mu_2$
   $H_a: \mu_1 \neq \mu_2$

b. Applying the Satterthwaite correction

$$df = \frac{(90.9 / 25 + 41.7 / 31)^2}{(90.9 / 25)^2 / (25 - 1) + (41.7 / 31)^2 / (31 - 1)}$$

$$= \frac{(3.64 + 1.35)^2}{0.55 + 0.06} = 40.82$$

For df $= 40.82$, $t_{cv} = \pm 2.02$

c. Applying the Cochran and Cox correction

$$s_{\bar{X}_1 - \bar{X}_2} = \sqrt{\frac{90.9}{25} + \frac{41.7}{31}} = \sqrt{4.98} = 2.23$$

Therefore,

$$t = \frac{(32.8 - 35.9) - 0}{2.23} = -1.39$$

d. $CI_{95} = (32.8 - 35.9) \pm (2.02)(2.23)$
   $= (-3.1) \pm 4.50$
   $= (-7.60, 1.40)$

(Note that this interval contains the point 0.)

e. Fail to reject H_0: 95% confident that $(-7.60, 1.40)$ contains $(\mu_1 - \mu_2)$.

7. a. $H_0: \sigma_1^2 = \sigma_2^2$
$H_a: \sigma_1^2 \neq \sigma_2^2$

b. For df $= n_1 - 1 = 66 - 1 = 65$ and $n_2 - 1 = 31 - 1 = 30$, $F_{cv} = 1.73$.

c. $F = s_1^2/s_2^2 = 35.3/22.5 = 1.57$

d. Fail to reject H_0 (apply the pooled test).

CHAPTER 13
Determining Power and Sample Size

COMPREHENSION CHECK

Two concepts that are integral to designing research studies and interpreting statistical results are the appropriate ___(1)___ size for the design and the ___(2)___ of the statistical test. In determining the appropriate sample size, the following four factors must be considered:

1. The level of ___(3)___ (α).
2. The ___(4)___ of the test ($1 - \beta$).
3. The population error ___(5)___ (σ^2).
4. The ___(6)___ size (ES).

The ___(7)___ of making a Type I error (rejecting H_0 when it is ___(8)___) is called the ___(9)___ of significance and denoted as ___(10)___. The probability of making a ___(11)___ error (failing to reject H_0 when it is ___(12)___) is denoted as ___(13)___. While α is set ___(14)___ by the researcher, determining β requires specifying a value for the ___(15)___ hypothesis (H_a). Once a value for H_a is specified, it is possible to determine both β and power, which is defined as ___(16)___.

There is an ___(17)___ relationship between α and β, that is, as α increases, β ___(18)___. Thus in order to minimize both the probability of making both Type I and Type II errors, certain trade-offs must be made. One consideration is the ___(19)___ of making a Type I error. When the ___(20)___ is not too great, a higher α-level can be used which will result in a ___(21)___ β-level.

Several factors affect power; they are: the directional nature of the ___(22)___ hypothesis, the level of ___(23)___, the ___(24)___ size, and the effect size. For example, when all other factors are held constant, a ___(25)___ alternative hypothesis is more powerful than a ___(26)___ alternative hypothesis. Secondly, as α ___(27)___, power increases. Thirdly, as the sample size increases, the standard error ___(28)___ and power ___(29)___. Finally, the effect size, which is defined as the degree to which a phenomenon exists in the population, influences power in that as the effect size ___(30)___ (the value for H_a departs from the value for H_0), so does the power.

In the chapter, formulas are provided for determining both the power of the statistical test and the appropriate sample size. Both values should be determined ___(31)___ a study is conducted. In determining the ___(32)___ sample size, the four factors listed above must be considered. The level of ___(33)___ (α) is determined ___(34)___ by the researcher. For determining the power, β should be set at ___(35)___ times α ($4 \times \alpha$). The population error variance (σ^2) can be established from previous studies or a ___(36)___ effect sizes (ES) can be used.

While each of these factors can be considered important in determining the appropriate sample size, the argument is made that the ___(37)___ is the most critical. Further, it is argued that the question of the appropriate sample size ___(38)___ be answered without considering the complex issue of determining the effect size.

Comprehension Check: Answers

1. sample	**14.** a priori	**27.** increases
2. power	**15.** alternative	**28.** decreases
3. significance	**16.** $1 - \beta$	**29.** increases
4. power	**17.** inverse	**30.** increases
5. variance	**18.** decreases	**31.** before
6. effect	**19.** seriousness	**32.** appropriate
7. probability	**20.** consequence	**33.** significance
8. true	**21.** lower	**34.** a priori
9. level	**22.** H_a	**35.** four
10. α	**23.** significance	**36.** standardized
11. Type II	**24.** sample	**37.** effect size
12. false	**25.** directional	**38.** cannot
13. β	**26.** nondirectional	

CHAPTER 13 EXERCISES

1. In a program for assisting high school graduates from disadvantaged families to succeed in college, the director of admissions of Southwest State College decides to test the null hypothesis that the mean verbal SAT score for this population equals 440, that is, H_0: $\mu = 440$. The director is only concerned with making a Type II error if the mean verbal SAT score is *less* than 10 points *above* this hypothesized value. That is, the effect size is 10 and the alternative hypothesis is H_a: $\mu = 450$. Assume the population standard deviation (σ) equals 100. The standard error of the mean is determined as follows assuming that $N = 225$:

$$\sigma_{\bar{X}} = \sigma/\sqrt{n} =$$

a. For $\alpha = .05$ and $n = 225$, determine the power of *both* a one-tailed and two-tailed test of the null hypothesis (H_0: $\mu = 440$) against the alternative hypothesis (H_a: $\mu = 450$).

One-tailed test

$$\mu + 1.645\, \sigma_{\bar{X}} = 440 + (\quad)(\quad)$$
$$= 440 +$$
$$=$$

$$z = \frac{\qquad - 450}{\qquad} =$$

Power = area beyond = .5000 −
$$=$$

Two-tailed test

$$\mu + 1.96\, \sigma_{\bar{X}} = 440 \pm (\quad)(\quad)$$
$$= 440 \pm$$
$$=$$

(Left-hand tail of H_a)

$$z = \frac{\qquad 450}{\qquad} =$$

Area beyond =

(Right-hand tail of H_a)

$$z = \frac{-450}{} =$$

Area beyond $= .5000 -$

$$=$$

Power $= 0 +$ $=$

b. For the above example, consider only a one-tailed test. For $n = 225$, determine the power of the test of H_0: $\mu = 440$ against H_a: $\mu = 450$ for $\alpha = .01$ and $\alpha = .10$.

For $\alpha = .01$

$$\mu + 2.326\, \sigma_{\bar{X}} = 440 + (\quad)(\quad)$$
$$= 440 +$$
$$=$$

$$z = \frac{-}{} =$$

Power $=$ area beyond $= .5000 -$
$$=$$

For $\alpha = .10$
$$\mu + 1.282\, \sigma_{\bar{X}} =$$
$$=$$
$$=$$

$z =$

Power $=$
$$=$$

c. For a one-tailed test and $\alpha = 0.5$, determine the power of the test of H_0: $\mu = 440$ using an effect size of 20, that is, H_a: $\mu = 460$.
$$\mu + 1.645\, \sigma_{\bar{X}} =$$
$$=$$
$$=$$

$z =$

Power $=$
$$=$$

d. For $n = 400$, determine the standard error of the mean and the power of the test of H_0: $\mu = 440$ against H_a: $\mu = 450$ using a one-tailed test at $\alpha = .05$.

$$\sigma_{\bar{X}} = \sigma/\sqrt{n} =$$

$$\mu + 1.645\, \sigma_{\bar{X}} = 440 + (\quad)(\quad)$$
$$=$$
$$=$$

$z =$

Power $=$
$$=$$

2. Consider testing the null hypothesis H_0: $\mu = 100$ using a one-tailed test at $\alpha = .05$. Assume $\sigma = 30$ and $n = 225$.

a. What is the alternative hypothesis if the effect size is one standard error *above* the value specified in the H_0?

$$\sigma_{\bar{X}} = \sigma/\sqrt{n} =$$

$$H_a : \mu =$$

b. What is the power of the test of H_0: $\mu = 100$ against this alternative hypothesis?

$$\mu + 1.645\,\sigma_{\bar{X}} = 100 + (\quad)(\quad)$$
$$=$$
$$=$$
$$z =$$

Power = area beyond = $.5000 - .2422$
$$= .2578$$

c. For the example, what is the alternative hypothesis if the effect size is two standard errors *above* the value specified in the H_0?

$$H_a : \mu =$$

d. What is the power of the test of H_0: $\mu = 100$ against this alternative hypothesis?

$$\mu + 1.645\sigma_{\bar{X}} =$$
$$=$$
$$=$$

$$z =$$

Power =
$$=$$

3. Two researchers are conducting separate experiments and both test the null hypothesis H_0: $\mu = 24.4$ against the alternative hypothesis H_a: $\mu = 24.8$ using $\alpha = .05$ for the one-tailed test. Researcher A uses a sample size of 144 while Researcher B uses a sample size of 225. Assume the population variance (σ) equals 3. For each researcher, compute the power of the test of H_0 against H_a.

Researcher A

$$\sigma_{\bar{X}} = \sigma/\sqrt{n} =$$

$$\mu + 1.645\sigma_{\bar{X}} =$$
$$=$$
$$=$$

$$z =$$

Power =
$$=$$

Researcher B

$$\sigma_{\bar{X}} = \sigma/\sqrt{n} =$$

$$\mu + 1.645\,\sigma_{\bar{X}} =$$
$$=$$
$$=$$

$$z =$$

Power =
$$=$$

4. For Exercise 3, what sample size is necessary to test the null hypothesis (H_0: $\mu = 24.4$) against the alternative hypothesis (H_a: $\mu = 24.8$) with power equal to .95?

a. For a one-tailed test using $\alpha = .05$ and $\alpha = .01$.

$$n = \frac{\sigma^2 (z_\beta - z_\alpha)^2}{(ES)^2}$$

For $\alpha = .05$

$$n = \frac{3^2(-1.645 - \quad)^2}{(\quad)^2} = \frac{3^2(\quad)^2}{(\quad)^2}$$

$$=$$

For $\alpha = .01$

$$n = \frac{^2(-1.645 \quad)^2}{(\quad)^2} = \frac{^2(\quad)^2}{(\quad)^2}$$

$$=$$

b. For a two-tailed test using $\alpha = .05$ and $\alpha = .01$.

$$n = \frac{\sigma^2 (z_\beta - z_{\alpha/2})^2}{(ES)^2}$$

For $\alpha = .05$

$$n = \frac{^2(\quad - \quad)^2}{(\quad)^2} = \frac{^2(\quad)^2}{(\quad)^2}$$

$$=$$

For $\alpha = .01$

$$n = \frac{\quad\quad\quad\quad\quad}{} = \frac{\quad\quad\quad}{}$$

$$=$$

5. Potential salespersons for a textbook company are being offered a new training program as part of a human resources improvement program. This new program was the result of a year-long study that compared the productivity of salespersons trained under this new program and those trained under the traditional one. In this study, there were 120 trainees in each program and the pooled estimate of the population variance (s^2) was found to be 150. Thus, the standard error of the difference was

$$= \sqrt{150 \left(\frac{1}{120} + \frac{1}{120} \right)} =$$

a. For $\alpha = .05$ and effect size equal to 3.0, determine the power for both a one-tailed and two-tailed test of the null hypothesis:

$$H_0: \mu_1 - \mu_2 = 0$$
$$H_a: \mu_1 - \mu_2 = 3.0$$

One-tailed test

$$(\mu_1 - \mu_2) + 1.645\, s_{\bar{X}_1 - \bar{X}_2} = 0 + (\quad)(\quad)$$
$$= 0 +$$
$$=$$

$$z = \frac{-3.0}{} =$$

Power $= .5000 +$
$$=$$

Two-tailed test

$$(\mu_1 - \mu_2) + 1.96\, s_{\bar{X}_1 - \bar{X}_2} = 0 + (\quad)(\quad)$$
$$=$$
$$=$$

$$z = \frac{-}{} =$$

Power $= .5000 -$
$$=$$

b. For an effect size equal to 3.0 and a one-tailed test, determine the power for $\alpha = .01$ and $\alpha = .10$.

For $\alpha = .01$

$$(\mu_1 - \mu_2) + 2.326\, s_{\bar{X}_1 - \bar{X}_2} = 0 + (\quad)(\quad)$$
$$=$$
$$=$$

$$z =$$
Power $=$
$$=$$

For $\alpha = .10$

$$(\mu_1 - \mu_2) + 1.282\, s_{\bar{X}_1 - \bar{X}_2} =$$
$$=$$
$$=$$

$$z =$$

Power $=$
$$=$$

c. For effect size equal to 4.2, find the power for $\alpha = .05$ and a one-tailed test.

$$(\mu_1 - \mu_2) + 1.645\, s_{\bar{X}_1 - \bar{X}_2} =$$
$$=$$
$$=$$

$$z =$$

Power $=$
$$=$$

d. Now let $n_1 = n_2 = 200$. Determine the standard error of the difference and then determine the power of a one-tailed test using $\alpha = .05$ and ES = 3.0.

$$= \sqrt{150 \left(\frac{1}{200} + \frac{1}{200} \right)} = 1.23$$

$$(\mu_1 - \mu_2) + 1.645 \, s_{\bar{X}_1 - \bar{X}_2} =$$

$$=$$

$$=$$

$$z =$$

Power $=$

$$=$$

6. For Exercise 5, what sample would be necessary for both groups to test $H_0: \mu_1 - \mu_2 = 0$ against $H_a: \mu_1 - \mu_2 = 3.0$ with power = .90?

a. For a one-tailed test using $\alpha = .05$ and $\alpha = .01$.

$$n = \frac{2s^2 (z_\beta - z_\alpha)^2}{(ES)^2}$$

For $\alpha = .05$

$$n = \frac{2(\quad)(\quad -1.645)^2}{(3.0)^2} = \frac{2(\quad)(\quad)^2}{(\quad)^2}$$

$$=$$

For $\alpha = .01$

$$n = \frac{(\quad)(\quad - \quad)^2}{(\quad)^2} = \frac{(\quad)(\quad)^2}{(\quad)^2}$$

$$=$$

b. For a two-tailed test using $\alpha = .05$ and $\alpha = .01$.

$$n = \frac{2s^2 (z_\beta - z_{\alpha/2})^2}{(ES)^2}$$

For $\alpha = .05$

$$n = \frac{(\quad)(\quad - \quad)^2}{(\quad)^2} = \frac{(\quad)(\quad)^2}{(\quad)^2}$$

$$=$$

For $\alpha = .01$

$$n = \frac{}{} = $$

$$=$$

7. A hospital administrator is conducting time and motion studies of how much time per day is spent on the average by individual employees in the performance of emergency duties: the unit of analysis is the mean time spent per day. The research literature suggests that the mean (μ) is 12 and the standard deviation (σ) is 3.8. Given the following conditions, determine the appropriate sample size:

a. $\alpha = .05$, $\beta = .20$, ES = 1.20, one-tailed *and* two-tailed tests.

For one-tailed test.

$$n = \underline{\hspace{4cm}} = \underline{\hspace{4cm}}$$

$$= $$

For two-tailed test.

$$n = \underline{\hspace{4cm}} = \underline{\hspace{4cm}}$$

$$= $$

b. $\alpha = .05$, $\beta = .20$, ES = 1.00, one-tailed test only.

$$n = \underline{\hspace{4cm}} = \underline{\hspace{4cm}}$$

$$= $$

c. $\alpha = .01$, $\beta = .05$, ES = 1.20, one-tailed *and* two-tailed tests.

For one-tailed test.

$$n = \underline{\hspace{4cm}} = \underline{\hspace{4cm}}$$

$$= $$

For two-tailed test.

$$n = \underline{\hspace{4cm}} = \underline{\hspace{4cm}}$$

$$= $$

d. $\alpha = .01$, $\beta = .05$, ES = 1.00, one-tailed test only.

$$n = \underline{\hspace{4cm}} = \underline{\hspace{4cm}}$$

$$= $$

8. For Exercise 7, determine the appropriate sample size for the following standardized effect sizes and conditions:

a. $\alpha = .05$, $\beta = .20$, $d = .30$, one-tailed *and* two-tailed tests.

For one-tailed test.

$$n = \frac{(z_\beta - z_\alpha)^2}{(d)^2}$$

$$n = \frac{(\quad -1.645)^2}{(.30)^2} = \frac{(\quad)^2}{(\quad)^2}$$

$$= $$

For two-tailed test.

$$n = \frac{(z_\beta - z_{\alpha/2})^2}{(d)^2}$$

$$n = \frac{(\quad -1.96)^2}{(\quad)^2} = \frac{(\quad)^2}{(\quad)}$$

$$= $$

b. $\alpha = .05$, $\beta = .20$, $d = .20$, one-tailed test only.

$$n = \frac{(-0.842 - 1.645)^2}{(.20)^2} = \frac{(-2.487)^2}{(.20)^2}$$
$$=$$

c. $\alpha = .01$, $\beta = .05$, $d = .30$, one-tailed *and* two-tailed tests.

For one-tailed test.

$$n = \underline{\hspace{3cm}} = \underline{\hspace{3cm}}$$
$$=$$

For two-tailed test.

$$n = \underline{\hspace{3cm}} = \underline{\hspace{3cm}}$$
$$=$$

d. $\alpha = .01$, $\beta = .05$, $d = .20$, one-tailed test only.

$$n = \underline{\hspace{3cm}} = \underline{\hspace{3cm}}$$
$$=$$

9. A sociologist is investigating juvenile deviance in Western Europe and in a Third World country. The standardized measure used in this study has a standard deviation (σ) of 22.6. Given the following conditions, determine the appropriate sample size for both groups when testing the null hypothesis H_0: $\mu_1 - \mu_2 = 0$.

a. $\alpha = .05$, $\beta = .20$, ES = 10, one-tailed *and* two-tailed tests.

For one-tailed test.

$$n = \underline{\hspace{3cm}} = \underline{\hspace{3cm}}$$
$$=$$

For two-tailed test.

$$n = \underline{\hspace{3cm}} = \underline{\hspace{3cm}}$$
$$=$$

b. $\alpha = .05$, $\beta = .20$, ES = 6, one-tailed test only.

$$n = \underline{\hspace{3cm}} = \underline{\hspace{3cm}}$$
$$=$$

c. $\alpha = .01$, $\beta = .05$, ES = 10, one-tailed *and* two-tailed tests.

For one-tailed test.

$$n = \underline{\hspace{3cm}} = \underline{\hspace{3cm}}$$
$$=$$

For two-tailed test.

$$n = \underline{\hspace{3cm}} = \underline{\hspace{3cm}}$$
$$=$$

d. $\alpha = .01$, $\beta = .05$, ES = 6, one-tailed test only.

$$n = \frac{}{} = \frac{}{}$$

$$= $$

10. For Exercise 9, determine the appropriate sample size for the following standardized effect sizes and conditions:

a. $\alpha = .05$, $\beta = .20$, $d = .30$, one-tailed *and* two-tailed tests.

For one-tailed test.

$$n = \frac{2(z_\beta - z_\alpha)^2}{(d)^2}$$

$$n = \frac{2(-0.842 -)^2}{(.30)^2} = \frac{2()^2}{()^2}$$

$$= $$

For one-tailed test.

$$n = \frac{2(z_\beta - z_{\alpha/2})^2}{(d)^2}$$

$$n = \frac{2(- 1.96)^2}{()^2} = \frac{2()^2}{()^2}$$

$$= $$

b. $\alpha = .05$, $\beta = .20$, $d = .40$, one-tailed test only.

$$n = \frac{}{} = \frac{}{}$$

$$= $$

c. $\alpha = .01$, $\beta = .05$, $d = .30$, one-tailed *and* two-tailed tests.

For one-tailed test.

$$n = \frac{}{} = \frac{}{}$$

$$= $$

For two-tailed test.

$$n = \frac{}{} = \frac{}{}$$

$$= $$

d. $\alpha = .01$, $\beta = .05$, $d = .40$, one-tailed test only.

$$n = \frac{}{} = \frac{}{}$$

$$= $$

Chapter 13 Exercises: Answers

1. $\sigma_{\bar{X}} = \sigma/\sqrt{n} = 100/15 = 6.67$

a. One-tailed test

$$\mu + 1.645\,\sigma_{\bar{X}} \;=\; 440 + (1.645)(6.67)$$
$$= 440 + 10.97$$
$$= 450.97$$
$$z = \frac{450.97 - 450}{6.67} = 0.15$$
$$\text{Power} = \text{area beyond} = .5000 - .0596$$
$$= .4404$$

Two-tailed test.

$$\mu + 1.96\,\sigma_{\bar{X}} \;=\; 440 \pm (1.96)(6.67)$$
$$= 440 \pm 13.07$$
$$= (426.93,\;\; 453.07)$$
$$z = \frac{426.93 - 450}{6.67} = -3.46$$
$$\text{Area beyond} = 0$$
$$z = \frac{453.07 - 450}{6.67} = 0.46$$
$$\text{Area beyond} = .5000 - .1772$$
$$= .3228$$
$$\text{Power} = 0 + .3228 = .3228$$

b. For $\alpha = .01$

$$\mu + 2.326\,\sigma_{\bar{X}} \;=\; 440 + (2.326)(6.67)$$
$$= 440 + 15.51$$
$$= 455.51$$
$$z = \frac{455.51 - 450}{6.67} = 0.83$$
$$\text{Power} = \text{area beyond} = .5000 - .2967$$
$$= .2033$$

For $\alpha = .10$

$$\mu + 1.282\,\sigma_{\bar{X}} \;=\; 440 + (1.282)(6.67)$$
$$= 440 + 8.55$$
$$= 448.55$$
$$z = \frac{448.55 - 450}{6.67} = -0.22$$
$$\text{Power} = .5000 + .0871$$
$$= .5871$$

c. $\mu + 1.645\,\sigma_{\bar{X}} = 440 + (1.645)(6.67)$
$$= 440 + 10.97$$
$$= 450.97$$
$$z = \frac{450.97 - 460}{6.67} = -1.35$$
$$\text{Power} = .5000 + .4115$$
$$= .9115$$

    d. $\sigma_{\bar{X}} = \sigma/\sqrt{n} = 100/20 = 5.00$

$$\mu + 1.645\,\sigma_{\bar{X}} = 440 + (1.645)(5.00)$$
$$= 440 + 8.23$$
$$= 448.23$$

$$z = \frac{448.23 - 450}{5.00} = -0.35$$

$$\text{Power} = .5000 + .1368$$
$$= .6368$$

2. a. $\sigma_{\bar{X}} = \sigma/\sqrt{n} = 30/15 = 2.00$

      $H_a : \mu = 102$

  b. $\mu + 1.645\,\sigma_{\bar{X}} = 100 + (1.645)(2.00)$
$$= 100 + 3.29$$
$$= 103.29$$

$$z = \frac{103.29 - 102}{2.00} = 0.65$$

$$\text{Power} = \text{area beyond} = .5000 - .2422$$
$$= .2578$$

  c. $H_a : \mu = 104$

  d. $\mu + 1.645\,\sigma_{\bar{X}} = 100 + (1.645)(2.00)$
$$= 100 + 3.29$$
$$= 103.29$$

$$z = \frac{103.29 - 104}{2.00} = -0.36$$

$$\text{Power} = .5000 - .1406$$
$$= .6406$$

3. Researcher A

$$\sigma_{\bar{X}} = \sigma/\sqrt{n} = 3/12 = 0.25$$
$$\mu + 1.645\,\sigma_{\bar{X}} = 24.4 + (1.645)(0.25)$$
$$= 24.4 + 0.41$$
$$= 24.81$$
$$z = \frac{24.81 - 24.80}{0.25} = 0.04$$
$$\text{Power} = \text{area beyond} = .5000 - .0160$$
$$= .4840$$

Researcher B

$$\sigma_{\bar{X}} = \sigma/\sqrt{n} = 3/15 = 0.20$$

$$\mu + 1.645\,\sigma_{\bar{X}} = 24.4 + (1.645)(0.20)$$

$$= 24.4 + 0.33$$

$$= 24.73$$

$$z = \frac{24.73 - 24.80}{0.20} = -0.35$$

$$\text{Power} = .5000 - .1368$$

$$= .6368$$

4. a.
$$n = \frac{\sigma^2 (z_\beta - z_\alpha)^2}{(ES)^2}$$

For $\alpha = .05$

$$n = \frac{3^2(-1.645 - 1.645)^2}{(.4)^2} = \frac{3^2(-3.290)^2}{(.4)^2}$$

$$= 608.86 \text{ or } 609$$

For $\alpha = .01$

$$n = \frac{3^2(-1.645 - 2.326)^2}{(.4)^2} = \frac{3^2(-3.971)^2}{(.4)^2}$$

$$= 886.99 \text{ or } 887$$

b.
$$n = \frac{\sigma^2 (z_\beta - z_{\alpha/2})^2}{(ES)^2}$$

For $\alpha = .05$

$$n = \frac{3^2(-1.645 - 1.96)^2}{(.4)^2} = \frac{3^2(-3.605)^2}{(.4)^2}$$

$$= 731.03 \text{ or } 732$$

For $\alpha = .01$

$$n = \frac{3^2(-1.645 - 2.576)^2}{(.4)^2} = \frac{3^2(-4.221)^2}{(.4)^2}$$

$$= 1002.20 \text{ or } 1003$$

5. a. One-tailed test.

$$(\mu_1 - \mu_2) + 1.645\,s_{\bar{X}_1 - \bar{X}_2} = 0 + (1.645)(1.58)$$

$$= 0 + 2.5991$$

$$= 2.5991$$

$$z = \frac{2.5991 - 3.0}{1.58} = -0.25$$

$$\text{Power} = .5000 + .0987$$

$$= .5987$$

Two-tailed test

$$(\mu_1 - \mu_2) + 1.96\, s_{\bar{X}_1 - \bar{X}_2} = 0 + (1.96)(1.58)$$
$$= 0 + 3.0968$$
$$= 3.0968$$

$$z = \frac{3.0968 - 3.0}{1.58} = 0.06$$
$$\text{Power} = .5000 - .0239$$
$$= .4761$$

b. For $\alpha = .01$

$$(\mu_1 - \mu_2) + 2.326\, s_{\bar{X}_1 - \bar{X}_2} = 0 + (2.326)(1.58)$$
$$= 0 + 3.6751$$
$$= 3.6751$$

$$z = \frac{3.6751 - 3.0}{1.58} = 0.43$$
$$\text{Power} = .5000 - .1664$$
$$= .3336$$

For $\alpha = .10$

$$(\mu_1 - \mu_2) + 1.282\, s_{\bar{X}_1 - \bar{X}_2} = 0 + (1.282)(1.58)$$
$$= 0 + 2.0256$$
$$= 2.0256$$

$$z = \frac{2.0256 - 3.0}{1.58} = -0.62$$
$$\text{Power} = .5000 + .2324$$
$$= .7324$$

c. $(\mu_1 - \mu_2) + 1.645\, s_{\bar{X}_1 - \bar{X}_2} = 0 + (1.645)(1.58)$
$$= 0 + 2.5991$$
$$= 2.5991$$

$$z = \frac{2.5991 - 4.2}{1.58} = -1.01$$
$$\text{Power} = .5000 + .3438$$
$$= .8438$$

d. $(\mu_1 - \mu_2) + 1.645\, s_{\bar{X}_1 - \bar{X}_2} = 0 + (1.645)(1.23)$
$$= 0 + 2.0234$$
$$= 2.0234$$

$$z = \frac{2.0234 - 3.0}{1.23} = -0.79$$
$$\text{Power} = .5000 + .2852$$
$$= .7852$$

6. a.
$$n = \frac{2s^2(z_\beta - z_\alpha)^2}{(ES)^2}$$

For $\alpha = .05$

$$n = \frac{2(150)(-1.282 - 1.645)^2}{(3.0)^2} = \frac{2(150)(-2.927)^2}{(3.0)^2}$$
$$= 285.58 \text{ or } 286$$

For $\alpha = .01$

$$n = \frac{2(150)(-1.282 - 2.326)^2}{(3.0)^2} = \frac{2(150)(-3.608)^2}{(3.0)^2}$$
$$= 433.92 \text{ or } 434$$

b.
$$n = \frac{2s^2(z_\beta - z_{\alpha/2})^2}{(ES)^2}$$

For $\alpha = .05$

$$n = \frac{2(150)(-1.282 - 1.96)^2}{(3.0)^2} = \frac{2(150)(-3.242)^2}{(3.0)^2}$$
$$= 350.35 \text{ or } 351$$

$$n = \frac{2(150)(-1.282 - 2.576)^2}{(3.0)^2} = \frac{2(150)(-3.858)^2}{(3.0)^2}$$
$$= 496.14 \text{ or } 497$$

7. a. For one-tailed test.

$$n = \frac{(3.8)^2(-0.842 - 1.645)^2}{(1.2)^2} = \frac{(3.8)^2(-2.487)^2}{(1.2)^2}$$
$$= 62.02 \text{ or } 63$$

For two-tailed test.

$$n = \frac{(3.8)^2(-0.842 - 1.96)^2}{(1.2)^2} = \frac{(3.8)^2(-2.802)^2}{(1.2)^2}$$
$$= 78.73 \text{ or } 79$$

b.
$$n = \frac{(3.8)^2(-0.842 - 1.645)^2}{(1.0)^2} = \frac{(3.8)^2(-2.487)^2}{(1.0)^2}$$
$$= 89.31 \text{ or } 90$$

c. For one-tailed test.
$$n = \frac{(3.8)^2(-1.645 - 2.326)^2}{(1.2)^2} = \frac{(3.8)^2(-3.971)^2}{(1.2)^2}$$
$$= 158.13 \text{ or } 159$$

For two-tailed test.
$$n = \frac{(3.8)^2(-1.645 - 2.576)^2}{(1.2)^2} = \frac{(3.8)^2(-4.221)^2}{(1.2)^2}$$
$$= 178.66 \text{ or } 179$$

d. $n = \dfrac{(3.8)^2(-1.645-2.326)^2}{(1.0)^2} = \dfrac{(3.8)^2(-3.971)^2}{(1.0)^2}$

$= 227.70$ or 228

8. a. For one-tailed test.

$$n = \frac{(z_\beta - z_\alpha)^2}{(d)^2}$$

$$n = \frac{(-0.842-1.645)^2}{(.30)^2} = \frac{(-2.487)^2}{(.30)^2}$$

$= 68.72$ or 69

For two-tailed test.

$$n = \frac{(z_\beta - z_{\alpha/2})^2}{(d)^2}$$

$$n = \frac{(-0.842-1.96)^2}{(.30)^2} = \frac{(-2.802)^2}{(.30)^2}$$

$= 87.24$ or 88

b.

$$n = \frac{(-0.842-1.645)^2}{(.20)^2} = \frac{(-2.487)^2}{(.20)^2}$$

$= 154.63$ or 155

c. For one-tailed test.

$$n = \frac{(-1.645-2.326)^2}{(.30)^2} = \frac{(-3.971)^2}{(.30)^2}$$

$= 175.21$ or 176

For two-tailed test.

$$n = \frac{(-1.645-2.576)^2}{(.30)^2} = \frac{(-4.221)^2}{(.30)^2}$$

$= 197.96$ or 198

d. $n = \dfrac{(-1.645-2.326)^2}{(.20)^2} = \dfrac{(-3.971)^2}{(.20)^2}$

$= 394.22$ or 395

9. a. For one-tailed test.

$$n = \frac{2(22.6)^2(-0.842-1.645)^2}{(10)^2} = \frac{2(22.6)^2(-2.487)^2}{(10)^2}$$

$= 63.18$ or 64

For two-tailed test.

$$n = \frac{2(22.6)^2(-0.842-1.96)^2}{(10)^2} = \frac{2(22.6)^2(-2.802)^2}{(10)^2}$$

$= 80.20$ or 81

b. $$n = \frac{2(22.6)^2(-0.842-1.645)^2}{(6)^2} = \frac{2(22.6)^2(-2.487)^2}{(6)^2}$$

$$= 175.51 \text{ or } 176$$

c. For one-tailed test.

$$n = \frac{2(22.6)^2(-1.645-2.326)^2}{(10)^2} = \frac{2(22.6)^2(-3.971)^2}{(10)^2}$$

$$= 161.08 \text{ or } 162$$

For two-tailed test.

$$n = \frac{2(22.6)^2(-1.645-2.576)^2}{(10)^2} = \frac{2(22.6)^2(-4.221)^2}{(10)^2}$$

$$= 182$$

d. $$n = \frac{2(22.6)^2(-1.645-2.326)^2}{(6)^2} = \frac{2(22.6)^2(-3.971)^2}{(6)^2}$$

$$= 447.52 \text{ or } 448$$

10. a. For one-tailed test.

$$n = \frac{2(z_\beta - z_\alpha)^2}{(d)^2}$$

$$n = \frac{2(-0.842-1.645)^2}{(.30)^2} = \frac{2(-2.487)^2}{(.30)^2}$$

$$= 137.45 \text{ or } 138$$

For two-tailed test.

$$n = \frac{2(z_\beta - z_\alpha)^2}{(d)^2}$$

$$n = \frac{2(-0.842-1.96)^2}{(.30)^2} = \frac{2(-2.802)^2}{(.30)^2}$$

$$= 174.47 \text{ or } 175$$

b. $$n = \frac{2(-0.842-1.645)^2}{(.40)^2} = \frac{2(-2.487)^2}{(.40)^2}$$

$$= 77.31 \text{ or } 78$$

c. For one-tailed test.

$$n = \frac{2(-1.645-2.326)^2}{(.30)^2} = \frac{2(-3.971)^2}{(.30)^2}$$

$$= 350.42 \text{ or } 351$$

For two-tailed test.

$$n = \frac{2(-1.645-2.576)^2}{(.30)^2} = \frac{2(-4.221)^2}{(.30)^2}$$

$$= 395.93 \text{ or } 396$$

d. $$n = \frac{2(-1.645-2.326)^2}{(.40)^2} = \frac{2(-3.971)^2}{(.40)^2}$$

$$= 197.11 \text{ or } 198$$

CHAPTER 14

Hypothesis Testing, *K*-Sample Case, Analysis of Variance, One-Way Classification

COMPREHENSION CHECK

The null hypothesis in the analysis of variance, one-way classification, is that the population __(1)__ from which the __(2)__ samples were selected are __(3)__ . That is H_0: __(4)__ . The alternative hypothesis is that at least one population mean differs from the rest, H_a: __(5)__ for some *i, k*. If multiple *t* tests were used to test the above null hypothesis by comparing all possible combinations of the *K* sample means, the Type I __(6)__ rate for the entire set of comparisons __(7)__ dramatically beyond the __(8)__ α level. However, by using ANOVA to test the null hypothesis, we were able to __(9)__ the Type I error rate at alpha.

In ANOVA, the total __(10)__ of the scores on the __(11)__ variable is partitioned into two __(12)__ , which are the __(13)__ groups variation and the __(14)__ groups variation. The variation within groups (s_W^2) is defined as the inherent or natural __(15)__ due to individual __(16)__ observed among the subjects in each of the *K* groups. This variation is attributed to __(17)__ fluctuation and is used to estimate the __(18)__ variance or the __(19)__ variance (σ_e^2). The between groups variation (s_B^2) reflects both the variation due to __(20)__ sampling fluctuation and the variation due to __(21)__ treatment effects.

If the null hypothesis is __(22)__ , that is, if there is __(23)__ treatment effect, both s_B^2 and s_W^2 would be __(24)__ of the population error variance and we would expect the ratio s_B^2/s_W^2 to be approximately __(25)__ . However, if the null hypothesis is __(26)__ , then we would expect s_B^2 to be larger than s_W^2 and the ratio s_B^2/s_W^2 would be __(27)__ than 1.0.

The actual calculation of an ANOVA begins with partitioning the __(28)__ of __(29)__ deviations around the grand mean (SS_T) into two components: the sum of __(30)__ groups (SS_W) and the sum of __(31)__ groups (SS_B). Dividing SS_B and SS_W by their associated degrees of freedom gives __(32)__ estimates for __(33)__ groups and __(34)__ groups, called __(35)__ , and symbolized MS_B and MS_W. The number of degrees of freedom associated with MS_B is __(36)__ and with MS_W is __(37)__ . The test statistic for ANOVA is the __(38)__ of the two variance estimates __(39)__ .

The __(40)__ distribution of the test statistic in ANOVA, the *F* ratio, is the *F* distribution. The *F* distribution is like the __(41)__ in that it is a family of distributions, each a function of the __(42)__ of __(43)__ for the two variance estimates. To test the null hypothesis, the observed __(44)__ is compared with the critical value of __(45)__ . If *F* exceeds F_{cv}, we __(46)__ the null hypothesis and conclude that at least __(47)__ , or a __(48)__ , of the population means differ.

There are three assumptions relevant to ANOVA interpretation. These assumptions are that the observations are __(49)__ and __(50)__ samples from populations __(51)__ distributed with __(52)__ variances. The most important assumption is that the observations are independent; violations of the other assumptions have __(53)__ effect on ANOVA results except in the case of unequal __(54)__ and unequal __(55)__ sizes.

Since statistical significance can be easily manipulated by the researcher with increases in

__(56)__ size, a measure of the __(57)__ of association between the independent and dependent variables, similar to the correlation coefficient, is needed. One such measure is omega squared, symbolized __(58)__ , which is interpreted in the same way as r^2; that is, the __(59)__ of variance in the __(60)__ variable that is accounted for by the levels of the __(61)__ variable.

Comprehension Check: Answers

1. means	**22.** true	**42.** degrees
2. K	**23.** no	**43.** freedom
3. equal	**24.** estimates	**44.** F ratio
4. $\mu_1 = \mu_2 = \ldots = \mu_k$	**25.** 1.00	**45.** F
5. $\mu_i \neq \mu_k$	**26.** false	**46.** reject
6. error	**27.** greater	**47.** one pair
7. increases	**28.** sum	**48.** combination
8. a priori	**29.** squared	**49.** random
9. maintain	**30.** squares within	**50.** independent
10. variation	**31.** squares between	**51.** normally
11. dependent	**32.** variance	**52.** equal
12. components	**33.** between	**53.** little
13. within	**34.** within	**54.** variances
14. between	**35.** mean squares	**55.** sample
15. variation	**36.** $K - 1$	**56.** sample
16. differences	**37.** $N - K$	**57.** degree
17. random sampling	**38.** F ratio	**58.** ω^2
18. population	**39.** MS_B/MS_W	**59.** proportion
19. error	**40.** underlying	**60.** dependent
20. random	**41.** t distribution	**61.** independent
21. differential		

CHAPTER 14 EXERCISES

1. The director of a regional training consortium examined the success of five participating agencies relative to their retention of disadvantaged youths in special, 15-week training programs. The following data, obtained from randomly selected samples of program participants, represent the numbers of weeks of meaningful involvement in the programs for the participants. Set the level of significance at .05.

	Agency				
	A	**B**	**C**	**D**	**E**
	15	6	12	8	15
	8	9	14	12	10
	6	8	6	9	12
	11	7	15	14	11
	10	13	9	7	9
	4	5	10	10	15

$$n_k = 6 \qquad\qquad N =$$
$$T_k = 54 \qquad\qquad \Sigma T_k = 300$$
$$\bar{X}_k = 9 \qquad\qquad T^2/N =$$
$$\Sigma X_{ik}^2 = 562 \qquad\qquad \Sigma\Sigma X_{ik}^2 =$$
$$T_k^2/n_k = 486 \qquad\qquad \Sigma(T_k^2/n_k) = 3060$$

a. What hypothesis is being tested?

$H_0: \mu_1 = \mu_2 = \mu_3 = \mu_4 = \mu_5$
$H_a:$

b. What is the critical value of the test statistic?

For $K - 1 = \qquad$ and $N - K = \qquad$ degrees of freedom,

$F_{cv} = $

c. What is the value of the test statistic?

$$SS_B = \sum_{k=1}^{K} (T_k^2/n_k) - T^2/N \qquad = \qquad - \qquad = $$

$$SS_W = \sum_{k=1}^{K} \sum_{i=1}^{n_k} X_{ik}^2 - \sum_{k=1}^{k} (T_k^2/n_k) = \qquad - \qquad = $$

$$SS_T = \sum_{k=1}^{K} \sum_{i=1}^{n_k} X_{ik}^2 - T^2/N \qquad = \qquad - \qquad = $$

Summary ANOVA

Source	SS	df	MS	F	F_{cv}
Between	60				
Within		25			
Total					

d. What is the conclusion?

H_0

2. A social psychologist wants to investigate the influence that other children in a family may have on the number of child-to-child interactions that kindergartners make on their first day at school. The data below represent the number of interactions made per child from varying family backgrounds. Set the level of significance at .10.

Number of siblings in family unit

0	1	2	3+
4	5	3	4
5	2	5	5
3	0	6	8
2	1	7	3
0	4	5	6
1	3	2	
2	6		

$n_k = \qquad\qquad\qquad\qquad\qquad N = $
$T_k = \qquad\qquad\qquad\qquad\qquad \Sigma T_k = $
$\bar{X}_k = \qquad\qquad\qquad\qquad\qquad T^2/N = $
$\Sigma X_{ik}^2 = \qquad\qquad\qquad\qquad \Sigma\Sigma X_{ik}^2 = $
$T_k^2/n_k = \qquad\qquad\qquad\qquad \Sigma(T_k^2/n_k) = $

a. What hypothesis is being tested?

$H_0:$
$H_a:$

b. What is the critical value of the test statistic?

For $K - 1 =$ and $N - K =$ degrees of freedom,

$F_{cv} =$

c. What is the value of the test statistic?

$$SS_B = \sum_{k=1}^{K} (T_k^2/n_k) - T^2/N \quad =$$

$$SS_W = \sum_{k=1}^{K} \sum_{i=1}^{n_k} X_{ik}^2 - \sum_{k=1}^{k} (T_k^2/n_k) \quad =$$

$$SS_T = \sum_{k=1}^{K} \sum_{i=1}^{n_k} X_{ik}^2 - T^2/N \quad =$$

Summary ANOVA

Source	SS	df	MS	F	F_{cv}
Between					
Within					
Total					

d. What is the conclusion?

H_0

3. A research psychologist wishes to compare the effectiveness of two reinforcement schedules in teaching a desired behavior. The following are the number of times that the desired behavior is demonstrated within a specified interval following a certain phase of the study. Use ANOVA procedures to test for a difference between schedule means using the .01 level of significance.

Reinforcement schedule

A	B
8	6
6	7
5	4
10	7
4	5
7	5
8	10
9	11
12	9
10	8

$n_k =$ $\qquad$ $N =$

$T_k =$ $\qquad$ $\Sigma T_k =$

$\bar{X}_k =$ $\qquad$ $T^2/N =$

$\Sigma X_{ik}^2 =$ $\qquad$ $\Sigma\Sigma X_{ik}^2 =$

$T_k^2/n_k =$ $\qquad$ $\Sigma(T_k^2/n_k) =$

a. What hypothesis is being tested?

H_0:

H_a:

b. What is the critical value of the test statistic?

For $K - 1 =$ _____ and $N - K =$ _____ degrees of freedom,

$F_{cv} =$

c. What is the value of the test statistic?

$SS_B =$

$SS_W =$

$SS_T =$

Summary ANOVA

Source	SS	df	MS	F	F_{cv}
Between					
Within					
Total					

d. What is the conclusion?

H_0.

4. Referring to the data presented in Exercise 3, calculate an independent groups t test to determine whether or not the schedule means differ significantly at the .01 level of significance. For your convenience, the same data are presented below.

Reinforcement schedule

A	B
8	6
6	7
5	4
10	7
4	5
7	5
8	10
9	11
12	9
10	8
$\bar{X} = 7.90$	7.20
$s = 2.47$	2.30

a. State the hypotheses.

H_0:
H_a:

b. Set the criterion for rejecting H_0.

For df = _____ , t_{cv}

c. Compute the test statistic.

$$t = \frac{(\bar{X}_1 - \bar{X}_2) - (\mu_1 - \mu_2)}{s_{\bar{X}_1 - \bar{X}_2}}$$

where

$$s^2 = \frac{(10-1)()^2 + (10-1)()^2}{ + - 2}$$

$$= \frac{ + }{} =$$

and

$$s_{\bar{X}_1 - \bar{X}_2} = \sqrt{\left(\frac{1}{10} + \frac{1}{10}\right)} = \sqrt{} =$$

Therefore,

$$t = \frac{(-) - 0}{} =$$

d. What is the conclusion?

$$H_0.$$

e. Can you state the relationship between the value of the *t* statistic and the value of the *F* statistic for Exercise 3?

$$=$$

5. Find the values for a, b, c, d, e, and f in the following summary ANOVA table (use $\alpha = .05$).

Summary ANOVA

Source	SS	df	MS	F	F_{cv}
Between	a	b	c	7.00	f
Within	240	d	16		
Total	e	19			

6. The difficulty with computing multiple *t* tests on data from several samples is that doing so increases the risk of the Type I error rate beyond the intended alpha level. For example, suppose that a researcher has three groups with mean results from each group, such as

Group 1	Group 2	Group 3
$\bar{X}_1$	$\bar{X}_2$	$\bar{X}_3$

a. If the researcher were to conduct all possible *t* tests, there would be how many total *t* tests?

$$(K)(K-1)/2 =$$

b. If this researcher had established the level of significance at .05, would the Type I error rate be maintained at .05?

$$\alpha_E = 1 - (1 - \alpha)^c$$

where

α = level of significance for each test
c = number of tests conducted

$$.05 = 1 - (1 - \alpha)^3$$
$$(1 - \alpha)^3 = 1 - .05$$
$$(1 - \alpha)^3 =$$
$$1 - \alpha =$$
$$\alpha =$$

or

$$\alpha = \alpha_E/c$$
$$= \quad /$$
$$=$$

7. A music teacher is interested in a comparison of teaching methods for music appreciation skills. Three groups of students are randomly selected and randomly assigned to groups that are instructed by different methods. The data layout for this study, using as dependent variable the scores on a 50-item music appreciation scale, are as follows. Use $\alpha = .05$.

Teaching method

I	II	III
21	35	42
27	31	39
25	26	40
32	24	33
20		32
		30

$n_k =$ $N =$
$T_k =$ $\Sigma T_k =$
$\bar{X}_k =$ $T^2/N =$
$\Sigma X_{ik}^2 =$ $\Sigma\Sigma X_{ik}^2 =$
$T_k^2/n_k =$ $\Sigma(T_k^2/n_k) =$

a. What hypothesis is being tested?

$H_0:$
$H_a:$

b. What is the critical value of the test statistic?
For $K - 1 =$ and $N - K =$ degrees of freedom,
$F_{cv} =$

d. What is the value of the test statistic?

$SS_B =$

$SS_W =$

$SS_T =$

Summary ANOVA

Source	SS	df	MS	F	F_{cv}
Between					
Within					
Total					

d. What is the conclusion?

$$H_0.$$

8. Suppose a psychologist wants to know whether an individual's reaction time (RT) to a given stimulus is a function of the time of day. Four groups are randomly selected and tested at the following times. The mean reaction times and group sizes are given below. The level of significance is set at .05.

	9 AM	1 PM	5 PM	9 PM
$\bar{X}_k =$	22.13	24.09	18.21	17.58
$n_k =$	8	11	6	13

a. Complete the following ANOVA summary table.

Summary ANOVA

Source	SS	df	MS	F	F_{cv}
Between	281.67				
Within			7.44		
Total	534.41				

b. The researcher, based on the results of the analysis above, would _____ the null hypothesis and conclude that at least one _____ is different from the others.

Chapter 14 Exercises: Answers

1.

$n_k =$	6	6	6	6	6	$N =$	30
$T_k =$	54	48	66	60	72	$\Sigma T_k =$	300
$\bar{X}_k =$	9	8	11	10	12	$T^2/N =$	3000
$\Sigma X_{ik}^2 =$	562	424	782	634	896	$\Sigma\Sigma X_{ik}^2 =$	3298
$T_k^2/n_k =$	486	384	726	600	864	$\Sigma(T_k^2/n_k) =$	3060

a. $H_0: \mu_1 = \mu_2 = \mu_3 = \mu_4 = \mu_5$
$H_a: \mu_i \neq \mu_k$ for some i, k

b. For $K - 1 = 5 - 1 = 4$ and $N - K = 30 - 5 = 25$ degrees of freedom,
$F_{cv} = 2.76.$

c.

$$SS_B = \sum_{k=1}^{K}(T_k^2/n_k) - T^2/N \qquad = 3060 - 3000 = 60$$

$$SS_W = \sum_{k=1}^{K}\sum_{i=1}^{n_k} X_{ik}^2 - \sum_{k=1}^{k}(T_k^2/n_k) = 3298 - 3060 = 238$$

$$SS_T = \sum_{k=1}^{K}\sum_{i=1}^{n_k} X_{ik}^2 - T^2/N \qquad = 3298 - 3000 = 298$$

Summary ANOVA

Source	SS	df	MS	F	F_{cv}
Between	60	4	15	1.58	2.76
Within	238	25	9.52		
Total	298	29			

d. Fail to reject H_0.

2.

$n_k =$	7	7	6	5	$N = 25$
$T_k =$	17	21	28	26	$\Sigma T_k = 92$
$\bar{X}_k =$	2.43	3.00	4.67	5.20	$T^2/N = 338.56$
$\Sigma X_{ik}^2 =$	59	91	148	150	$\Sigma\Sigma X_{ik}^2 = 448$
$T_k^2/n_k =$	41.29	63.00	130.67	135.20	$\Sigma(T_k^2/n_k) = 370.16$

a. $H_0: \mu_1 = \mu_2 = \mu_3 = \mu_4$
    $H_a: \mu_i \neq \mu_k$ for some i, k

b. For $K - 1 = 4 - 1 = 3$ and $N - K = 25 - 4 = 21$ degrees of freedom,
    $F_{cv} = 2.47$.

c.

$$SS_B = \sum_{k=1}^{K}(T_k^2/n_k) - T^2/N \qquad = 370.16 - 338.56 = 31.60$$

$$SS_W = \sum_{k=1}^{K}\sum_{i=1}^{n_k} X_{ik}^2 - \sum_{k=1}^{k}(T_k^2/n_k) = 448.00 - 370.16 = 77.84$$

$$SS_T = \sum_{k=1}^{K}\sum_{i=1}^{n_k} X_{ik}^2 - T^2/N \qquad = 448.00 - 338.56 = 109.44$$

Summary ANOVA

Source	SS	df	MS	F	F_{cv}
Between	31.60	3	10.53	2.84	2.47
Within	77.84	21	3.71		
Total	109.44	24			

d. Reject H_0.

3.

$n_k = 10$	10	$N = 20$
$T_k = 79$	72	$\Sigma T_k = 151$
$\bar{X}_k = 7.9$	7.2	$T^2/N = 1140.05$
$\Sigma X_{ik}^2 = 679$	566	$\Sigma\Sigma X_{ik}^2 = 1245$
$T_k^2/n_k = 624.1$	518.4	$\Sigma(T_k^2/n_k) = 1142.5$

a. $H_0: \mu_1 = \mu_2$
$H_a: \mu_1 \neq \mu_2$

b. For $K - 1 = 2 - 1 = 1$ and $N - K = 20 - 2 = 18$ degrees of freedom,
$F_{cv} = 8.29$.

c. $SS_B = \sum_{k=1}^{K} (T_k^2/n_k) - T^2/N \qquad = 1142.50 - 1140.05 = \quad 2.45$

$SS_W = \sum_{k=1}^{K} \sum_{i=1}^{n_k} X_{ik}^2 - \sum_{k=1}^{k} (T_k^2/n_k) \quad = 1245.00 - 1142.50 = 102.50$

$SS_T = \sum_{k=1}^{K} \sum_{i=1}^{n_k} X_{ik}^2 - T^2/N \qquad = 1245.00 - 1140.05 = 104.95$

Summary ANOVA

Source	SS	df	MS	F	F_{cv}
Between	2.45	1	2.45	0.43	8.29
Within	102.50	18	5.69		
Total	104.95	19			

d. Fail to reject H_0.

4. $\bar{X} = 7.90 \qquad 7.20$
$s = 2.47 \qquad 2.30$

a. $H_0: \mu_1 = \mu_2$
$H_a: \mu_1 \neq \mu_2$

b. For df $= 18$, $t_{cv} = 2.878$.

c. $t = \dfrac{(X_1 - X_2) - (\mu_1 - \mu_2)}{s_{\bar{X}_1 - \bar{X}_2}}$

where

$s^2 = \dfrac{(10 - 1)2.47^2 + (10 - 1)2.30^2}{10 + 10 - 2}$

$= \dfrac{54.91 + 47.61}{18} = 5.70$

and

$s_{\bar{X}_1 - \bar{X}_2} = \sqrt{5.70 \left(\dfrac{1}{10} + \dfrac{1}{10} \right)} = \sqrt{1.14} = 1.07$

Therefore,

$t = \dfrac{(7.90 - 7.20) - 0}{1.07} = 0.65$

d. Fail to reject H_0.

e. $t^2 = F$

5.

Summary ANOVA

Source	SS	df	MS	F	F_{cv}
Between	448	4	112	7.00	3.06
Within	240	15	16		
Total	688	19			

6. a. $(K)(K-1)/2 = (3)(2)/2 = 3$

b. $\alpha_E = 1 - (1-\alpha)^c$

where

α = level of significance of each test
c = number of tests conducted

$$.05 = 1 - (1-\alpha)^3$$
$$(1-\alpha)^3 = 1 - .05$$
$$(1-\alpha)^3 = .95$$
$$1-\alpha = .983$$
$$\alpha = .017$$

or

$$\alpha = \alpha_E/c$$
$$= .05/3$$
$$= .017$$

7.

$n_k =$	5	4	6	$N =$	15
$T_k =$	125	116	216	$\Sigma T_k =$	457
$\bar{X}_k =$	25.00	29.00	36.00	$T^2/N =$	13,923.27
$\Sigma X_{ik}^2 =$	3,219	3,438	7,898	$\Sigma\Sigma X_{ik}^2 =$	14,555
$T_k^2/n_k =$	3,125.00	3,364.00	7,776.00	$\Sigma(T_k^2/n_k) =$	14,265.00

a. $H_0: \mu_1 = \mu_2 = \mu_3$
   $H_a: \mu_i \neq \mu_k$ for some i, k

b. For $K - 1 = 3 - 1 = 2$ and $N - K = 15 - 3 = 12$ degrees of freedom,
   $F_{cv} = 3.89$.

c. $SS_B = \Sigma(T_k^2/n_k) - T^2/N = 14,265.00 - 13,923.27 = 341.73$
   $SS_W = \Sigma\Sigma X_{ik}^2 - \Sigma(T_k^2/n_k) = 14,555 - 14,265.00 = 290.00$
   $SS_T = \Sigma\Sigma X_{ik}^2 - T^2/N = 14,555 - 13,923.27 = 631.73$

Summary ANOVA

Source	SS	df	MS	F	F_{cv}
Between	341.73	2	170.87	7.07	3.89
Within	290.00	12	24.17		
Total	631.73	14			

d. Reject H_0.

8. a.

Source	SS	df	MS	F	F_{cv}
Summary ANOVA					
Between	281.67	3	93.89	12.62	2.89
Within	252.74	34	7.44		
Total	534.41	37			

b. The researcher, based on the results of the analysis above, would *reject* the null hypothesis and conclude that at least one *mean* is different from the others.

CHAPTER 15
Multiple-Comparison Procedures

COMPREHENSION CHECK

The null hypothesis in one-way ANOVA states that the K __(1)__ means from which samples were selected are __(2)__ equal. This null hypothesis is __(3)__ if the observed F ratio exceeds the __(4)__ of F. Rejecting the null hypothesis indicates that at least one __(5)__ differs from another or that a __(6)__ of sample means differs. Post hoc __(7)__ procedures must then be used to determine which of the __(8)__ differ significantly.

Post hoc multiple comparisons were developed to __(9)__ the Type I error rate at the a priori __(10)__ . With these tests, we need to differentiate the concepts of __(11)__ and __(12)__ Type I error rates. The comparisonwise error rate is defined as __(13)__ , the level of significance, for __(14)__ comparison. The __(15)__ error rate is the probability of making a Type I error for the set of __(16)__ __(17)__ comparisons. To maintain the experimentwise error rate at a specified α level, each comparison can be tested at a __(18)__ α level or one of the __(19)__ procedures can be used. However, testing each comparison at the smaller alpha level is an extremely __(20)__ procedure, which means that sometimes no comparisons will be significant.

Three post hoc multiple comparison tests that can be used when __(21)__ comparisons are of interest are the __(22)__ , the __(23)__ , and the __(24)__ procedures. All three procedures use the studentized range distribution, or __(25)__ distribution. The Tukey/Kramer method is recommended when group sample sizes are __(26)__ . The Tukey procedure maintains the experimentwise error rate at the priori α level by using the __(27)__ range distributions. The Newman-Keuls procedure also uses the __(28)__ distributions as the underlying distribution in such a way that the Type I error rate is somewhat __(29)__ than α_E, but it is still substantially __(30)__ than the comparisonwise error rate for all possible pairwise comparisons. In comparing the Tukey and Newman-Keuls procedures, the Newman-Keuls method is __(31)__ powerful in the statistical sense, but the Tukey procedure provides better control of __(32)__ error rates. If sample sizes are only slightly different, the Tukey and Newman-Keuls procedures could be modified by substituting the __(33)__ n for n in the __(34)__ of the Q statistic.

If __(35)__ comparisons between more than two means are of interest, the recommended procedure is the __(36)__ method, which uses the F distribution as the __(37)__ distribution. With the Scheffé procedure, each hypothesis is stated in terms of a __(38)__ combination of __(39)__ and means that are called __(40)__ . For each hypothesis, the sum of the coefficients must equal __(41)__ . The critical value of F with the Scheffé method is determined by __(42)__ the tabled value of F by __(43)__ , which inflates the critical value. The Scheffé method is the most __(44)__ and, at the same time, the most __(45)__ post hoc multiple comparison procedure.

Specific sets of hypotheses may be tested by a priori or __(46)__ comparisons. These tests are performed __(47)__ of the overall test of the null hypothesis of ANOVA. Two such comparison methods are planned __(48)__ contrasts and __(49)__ analysis. The test statistic for both procedures is __(50)__ , and it is computed in the same way as the Scheffé method. However, the critical value is not __(51)__ by multiplying by $K - 1$. For two contrasts to be orthogonal, the sum of the coefficients for each contrast must be equal to __(52)__ . In addition, the sum of the __(53)__ products for the corresponding coefficients for the two contrasts must be __(54)__ . If the contrasts are orthogonal, the hypotheses tested by these contrasts are __(55)__ and the experimentwise Type I error rate is maintained at α.

If the independent variable in the ANOVA is __(56)__ , the __(57)__ relationship between the levels of the independent variable and the dependent variable can be examined with a __(58)__ analysis. The purpose of this method is to determine whether the relationship departs significantly from __(59)__ , and if so, whether the trend is __(60)__ , __(61)__ , and so on. Trend analysis is a special case of __(62)__ contrasts that uses a set of specific coefficients, called coefficients of orthogonal __(63)__ . The number of possible trends that can be tested is __(64)__ . Tests for trends are made __(65)__ , that is, first for a linear trend, then for a __(66)__ , and so on. If the test for a linear trend is not statistically significant, we conclude that the trend __(67)__ from linearity. More than one __(68)__ can be statistically significant in the same trend analysis.

Comprehension Check: Answers

1. population
2. simultaneously
3. rejected
4. critical value
5. sample mean
6. combination
7. multiple comparison
8. sample means
9. maintain
10. α level
11. comparisonwise
12. experimentwise
13. α
14. each
15. experimentwise
16. all
17. possible
18. smaller
19. post hoc
20. conservative
21. pairwise
22. Tukey/Kramer
23. Tukey

24. Newman-Keuls
25. Q
26. unequal
27. Q
28. Q
29. greater
30. less
31. more
32. Type I
33. harmonic
34. denominator
35. complex
36. Scheffé
37. underlying
38. linear
39. coefficients
40. contrasts
41. zero
42. multiplying
43. $K - 1$
44. versatile
45. conservative
46. planned

47. instead
48. orthogonal
49. trend
50. F
51. inflated
52. zero
53. cross
54. zero
55. independent
56. quantitative
57. functional
58. trend
59. linearity
60. quadratic
61. cubic
62. orthogonal
63. polynomials
64. $K - 1$
65. sequentially
66. quadratic
67. departs
68. contrast

CHAPTER 15 EXERCISES

1. In preparing a planning report, the director of a community continuing education program classifies course requests as (1) job related, (2) consumer related, (3) health related, (4) recreational, or (5) other. Over five registration periods, the following numbers of special requests were received. Use one-way ANOVA procedures to determine whether or not the registration data suggest differences in overall community interest. Use the .05 level of significance.

Course request classifications

	1	2	3	4	5
	18	28	23	30	25
	25	40	30	35	29
	20	26	24	29	22
	16	31	25	24	16
	11	20	18	22	18

$n_k =$	5	5			$N =$
$T_k =$	90	145			$\Sigma T_k =$
$\bar{X}_k =$	18.0	29.0			$T^2/N =$
$\Sigma X_{ik}^2 =$	1726	4421			$\Sigma\Sigma X_{ik}^2 =$
$T_k^2/n_k =$	1620.0	4205.0			$\Sigma(T_k^2/n_k) =$

a. What hypothesis is being tested?

$H_0: \mu_1 = \mu_2 = \mu_3 = \mu_4 = \mu_5$

$H_a: \mu_i \neq \mu_k$ for some i, k

b. What is the critical value of the test statistic?

For $K - 1 = 4$ and $N - K = 20$ degrees of freedom, $F_{cv} =$

c. What is the value of the test statistic?

$$SS_B = \sum_{k=1}^{K}(T_k^2/n_k) - T^2/N \qquad = 15045 - 14641 =$$

$$SS_W = \sum_{k=1}^{K}\sum_{i=1}^{n_k} X_{ik}^2 - \sum_{k=1}^{k}(T_k^2/n_k) \; = 15657 - 15045 =$$

$$SS_T = \sum_{k=1}^{K}\sum_{i=1}^{n_k} X_{ik}^2 - T^2/N \qquad = 15657 - 14641 =$$

Summary ANOVA

Source	SS	df	MS	F	F_{cv}
Between					
Within					
Total					

d. What is the conclusion?

H_0.

2. For the results of the one-way ANOVA presented in Exercise 1, use the Tukey method to test for pairwise differences among the population means at the .05 level of significance. (Although not required for the Tukey or Tukey/Kramer procedures, the means are ranked from low to high.)

	$\bar{X}_i$	$(\bar{X}_i - \bar{X}_k)$	Q
$\bar{X}_1$	18		
$\bar{X}_5$	22	4	1.62
$\bar{X}_3$	24	6	2.43
$\bar{X}_4$	28		
$\bar{X}_2$	29		

$\sqrt{MS_W/n} = \sqrt{30.60/5} =$

What is the conclusion?

For $r = 5$ and $df_W = 20$, $Q_{cv} =$

Therefore $\mu_1 \neq$; all other pairwise comparisons are not statistically significant.

3. Again referring to the data used in Exercises 1 and 2, perform the Newman-Keuls procedure to test for pairwise differences between means. Use .05 as your level of significance.

	$\bar{X}_i$	$(\bar{X}_i - \bar{X}_j)$	Q	Q_{cv}
$\bar{X}_1$	18			
$\bar{X}_5$	22			2.95
$\bar{X}_3$	24			3.58
$\bar{X}_4$	28			
$\bar{X}_2$	29			

$\sqrt{MS_W/n} =$

What are your conclusions?

$\mu_1 \neq$ and $\mu_1 \neq$; all other pairwise comparisons are not statistically significant.

4. A teacher wants to compare the effectiveness of four different learning environments for a class. Students are randomly assigned to four groups: (1) self-directed, (2) self-directed with weekly meetings, (3) teacher-led small group discussions, and (4) student-led small group discussions. Attrition during the school year results in slightly different group sizes. The following are the end-of-year exam scores. Use the .05 level of significance for the test.

	Learning environment			
	1	*2*	*3*	*4*
	70	69	89	77
	80	71	71	84
	72	88	83	98
	69	66	82	88
	73	73	85	96
	68	74		91
		70		

$n_k =$ $\qquad\qquad\qquad$ $N =$

$T_k =$ $\qquad\qquad\qquad$ $\Sigma T_k =$

$\bar{X}_k =$ $\qquad\qquad\qquad$ $T^2/N =$

$\Sigma X_{ik}^2 =$ $\qquad\qquad$ $\Sigma\Sigma X_{ik}^2 =$

$T_k^2/n_k =$ $\qquad\qquad$ $\Sigma(T_k^2/n_k) =$

a. What hypothesis is being tested?

H_0:

H_a:

b. What is the critical value of the test statistic?

For $K - 1 =$ and $N - K =$ degrees of freedom, $F_{cv} =$

c. What is the value of the test statistic?

$$SS_B =$$

$$SS_W =$$

$$SS_T =$$

Summary ANOVA

Source	SS	df	MS	F	F_{cv}
Between					
Within					
Total					

d. What is the conclusion?

$$H_0.$$

e. Perform the Tukey/Kramer procedure to test for pairwise mean differences at the .05 level of significance. What are your conclusions?

	$\bar{X}_i$	n_k	$(\bar{X}_i - \bar{X}_k)$	denominator	Q
$\bar{X}_1$	72	6			
$\bar{X}_2$	73	7		2.61	0.38
$\bar{X}_3$	82	5		2.84	3.52
$\bar{X}_4$	89	6			

$$\text{denominator} = \sqrt{MS_W / n_k'} \quad \text{where} \quad n_k' = \frac{k}{\frac{1}{n_1} + \frac{1}{n_2} + \quad +}$$

$$=$$

f. What is the conclusion?
For $r =$ and $df_W =$, $Q_{cv} =$
Therefore,

---

5. For the data in Exercise 7 of Chapter 14, perform the Tukey/Kramer procedure to test for pairwise mean differences. Set the level of significance at .05.

		Method		
	I	*II*	*III*	
n_k	5	4	6	N = 15
$\bar{X}_k$	25.00	29.00	36.00	

Summary ANOVA

Source	SS	df	MS	F	F_{cv}
Between	341.73	2	170.87	7.07	3.89
Within	290.00	12	24.17		
Total	631.73	14			

	$\bar{X}_i$	n_k	$(\bar{X}_i - \bar{X}_k)$	Q
$\bar{X}_1$	25.0	5		
$\bar{X}_2$	29.0	4		
$\bar{X}_3$	36.0	6		

$$\text{denominator} = \sqrt{MS_W / n_k'} \quad \text{where } n_k' = \underline{\hspace{3cm}}$$
$$= \underline{\hspace{1cm}}$$

What is the conclusion?
For $r = \underline{\hspace{1cm}}$ and $df_W = \underline{\hspace{1cm}}$, $Q_{cv} = \underline{\hspace{1cm}}$
Therefore,

6. A pharmacologist wants to investigate the effects of different drug dosages on the symptoms of the common cold. Forty people are randomly selected and randomly assigned to one of four groups. Group 1 receives 1 unit of the drug, Group 2 receives 2 units, Group 3 receives 3 units, and Group 4 receives 4 units. Subjects in this investigation are asked to record the number of days that they experience cold symptoms during a three-month period. Test the following null hypotheses at the .05 level of significance using the data below.

$H_{0_1}: \mu_1 = \mu_4$

$H_{0_2}: \mu_2 = \mu_3$

$H_{0_3}: \mu_1 + \mu_4 = \mu_2 + \mu_3$

Summary ANOVA

Source	SS	df	MS	F
Between	331.87	3	110.62	30.06
Within	132.50	36	3.68	
Total	464.37	39		

Group	1	2	3	4
$\bar{X}$	15	12	7.5	9
n	10	10	10	10

a. What are the contrast coefficients for these hypotheses?

C_1:

C_2:

C_3:

b. Compute the test statistic for each hypothesis.

$$F = \frac{(\Sigma C\bar{X})^2}{(MS_W)(\Sigma(C^2/n))}$$

$$F_1 = \frac{(\quad\quad)^2}{\quad + \quad} = \frac{}{} = $$

$$F_2 = \frac{(\quad\quad)^2}{\quad + \quad} = \frac{}{} = $$

$$F_3 = \frac{(\quad - \quad - \quad + \quad)^2}{\quad + \quad + \quad + \quad} = \frac{}{} = $$

$$F_{cv\,(.05)} = $$

c. What are your conclusions?

7. Assume that in Exercise 6 the drug dosages were measured on a ratio scale and that the drug dosages increase from Group 1 and Group 4. Use orthogonal polynomial contrasts to test for linear, quadratic, and cubic trends at the .05 level of significance. Also, graph your results.

Group	1	2	3	4
$\bar{X}$	15	12	7.5	9
n	10	10	10	10

a. What are the orthogonal polynomials for these three trends?

Linear	−3	−1	1	3
Quadratic				
Cubic				

b. Compute the test statistic for each trend.

$$F = \frac{(\Sigma C\bar{X})^2}{(MS_W)(\Sigma(C^2/n))}$$

c. What are your conclusions?

Chapter 15 Exercises: Answers

1.

Course request classifications

	1	2	3	4	5		
	18	28	23	30	25		
	25	40	30	35	29		
	20	26	24	29	22		
	16	31	25	24	16		
	11	20	18	22	18		
$n_k =$	5	5	5	5	5	$N =$	25
$T_k =$	90	145	120	140	110	$\Sigma T_k =$	605
$\bar{X}_k =$	18.0	29.0	24.0	28.0	22.0	$T^2/N =$	14641
$\Sigma X_{ik}^2 =$	1726	4421	2954	4026	2530	$\Sigma\Sigma X_{ik}^2 =$	15657
$T_k^2/n_k =$	1620.0	4205.0	2880.0	3920.0	2420.0	$\Sigma(T_k^2/n_k) =$	15045

a. $H_0: \mu_1 = \mu_2 = \mu_3 = \mu_4 = \mu_5$
$H_a: \mu_i \neq \mu_k$ for some i, k

b. For $K - 1 = 4$ and $N - K = 20$ degrees of freedom, $F_{cv} = 2.87$.

c.

$$SS_B = \sum_{k=1}^{K}(T_k^2/n_k) - T^2/N \qquad = 15045 - 14641 = 404$$

$$SS_W = \sum_{k=1}^{K}\sum_{i=1}^{n_k} X_{ik}^2 - \sum_{k=1}^{k}(T_k^2/n_k) \quad = 15657 - 15045 = 612$$

$$SS_T = \sum_{k=1}^{K}\sum_{i=1}^{n_k} X_{ik}^2 - T^2/N \qquad = 15657 - 14641 = 1016$$

Summary ANOVA

Source	SS	df	MS	F	F_{cv}
Between	404	4	101	3.30	2.87
Within	612	20	30.60		
Total	1016	24			

d. Reject H_0.

2.

	$\bar{X}_i$	$(\bar{X}_i - \bar{X}_k)$				Q			
$\bar{X}_1$	18								
$\bar{X}_5$	22	4				1.62			
$\bar{X}_3$	24	6	2			2.43	0.81		
$\bar{X}_4$	28	10	6	4		4.05	2.43	1.62	
$\bar{X}_2$	29	11	7	5	1	4.45*	2.83	2.02	0.40

$\sqrt{MS_W/n} = \sqrt{30.60/5} = 2.47$; $*p < .05$

For $r = 5$ and $df_W = 20$, $Q_{cv} = 4.23$
Therefore $\mu_1 \neq \mu_2$; all other pairwise comparisons are not statistically significant.

3.

	$\bar{X}_i$	$(\bar{X}_i - \bar{X}_k)$				Q				Q_{cv}			
$\bar{X}_1$	18												
$\bar{X}_5$	22	4				1.62				2.95			
$\bar{X}_3$	24	6	2			2.43	0.81			3.58	2.95		
$\bar{X}_4$	28	10	6	4		4.05**	2.43	1.62		3.96	3.58	2.95	
$\bar{X}_2$	29	11	7	5	1	4.45**	2.83	2.02	0.40	4.23	3.96	3.58	2.95

$\sqrt{MS_W/n} = \sqrt{30.60/5} = 2.47$; $**p < .01$

$\mu_1 \neq \mu_4$ and $\mu_1 \neq \mu_4$; all other pairwise comparisons are not statistically significant.

4.

Learning environment

	1	2	3	4
	70	69	89	77
	80	71	71	84
	72	88	83	98
	69	66	82	88
	73	73	85	96
	68	74		91
	70			

	1	2	3	4		
$n_k =$	6	7	5	6	$N =$	24
$T_k =$	432	511	410	534	$\Sigma T_k =$	1887
$\bar{X}_k =$	72.0	73.0	82.0	89.0	$T^2/N =$	148365.38
$\Sigma X_{ik}^2 =$	31198	37607	33800	47830	$\Sigma\Sigma X_{ik}^2 =$	150435
$T_k^2/n_k =$	31104.0	37303.0	33620.0	47526.0	$\Sigma(T_k^2/n_k) =$	149553

a. $H_0: \mu_1 = \mu_2 = \mu_3 = \mu_4$
$H_a: \mu_i \neq \mu_k$ for some i,k

b. For $K - 1 = 3$ and $N - K = 20$ degrees of freedom, $F_{cv} = 3.10$.

c.
$$SS_B = \sum_{k=1}^{K} (T_k^2/n_k) - T^2/N \qquad = 149,553 - 148,365.38 \qquad = 1,187.62$$

$$SS_W = \sum_{k=1}^{K} \sum_{i=1}^{n_k} X_{ik}^2 - \sum_{k=1}^{k} (T_k^2/n_k) \quad = 150,435 - 149,553 \qquad = \quad 882.00$$

$$SS_T = \sum_{k=1}^{K} \sum_{i=1}^{n_k} X_{ik}^2 - T^2/N \qquad = 150,435 - 148,365.38 \quad = 2,069.62$$

Summary ANOVA

Source	SS	df	MS	F	F_{cv}
Between	1187.62	3	395.87	8.98	3.10
Within	882.00	20	44.10		
Total	2069.62	23			

d. Reject H_0.

e.

	$\bar{X}_i$	n_k		$(\bar{X}_i - \bar{X}_k)$			Q		
$\bar{X}_1$	72	6							
$\bar{X}_2$	73	7	1			0.37			
$\bar{X}_3$	82	5	10	9		3.66	3.30		
$\bar{X}_4$	89	6	17	16	7	6.23*	5.86*	2.56	

$\sqrt{MS_W / n_n'} = \sqrt{44.10/5.915} = 2.73$; $*p < .05$

f. For $r = 4$ and $df_w = 20$, $Q_{cv} = 3.96$.

Therefore, $\mu_1 \neq \mu_4$ and $\mu_2 \neq \mu_4$; all other pairwise comparisons are not statistically significant.

5.

	Method		
	I	**II**	**III**
n_k	5	4	6	$N = 15$
$\bar{X}_k$	25.00	29.00	36.00	

Summary ANOVA

Source	SS	df	MS	F	F_{cv}
Between	341.73	2	170.87	7.07	3.89
Within	290.00	12	24.17		
Total	631.73	14			

	$\bar{X}_i$	n_k	$(\bar{X}_i - \bar{X}_k)$		Q	
$\bar{X}_1$	25.0	5				
$\bar{X}_2$	29.0	4	4		1.79	
$\bar{X}_3$	36.0	6	11	7	4.93*	3.14

$$\sqrt{MS_W / n_n'} = \sqrt{24.17 / 4.865} = 2.23; \ *p < .05$$

For $r = 3$ and $df_w = 12$, $Q_{cv} = 3.77$.

Therefore, $\mu_1 \neq \mu_3$; all other pairwise comparisons are not statistically significant.

6. $H_{0_1}: \mu_1 = \mu_4$

$H_{0_2}: \mu_2 = \mu_3$

$H_{0_3}: \mu_1 + \mu_4 = \mu_2 + \mu_3$

a. $C_1: \quad 1 \quad 0 \quad 0 \quad -1$

$\quad C_2: \quad 0 \quad 1 \quad -1 \quad 0$

$\quad C_3: \quad 1 \quad -1 \quad -1 \quad 1$

b. $F_1 = \dfrac{(15-9)^2}{3.68\left(\dfrac{1}{10} + \dfrac{1}{10}\right)} = \dfrac{36}{0.736} = 48.91*$

$F_2 = \dfrac{(12-7.5)^2}{3.68\left(\dfrac{1}{10} + \dfrac{1}{10}\right)} = \dfrac{20.25}{0.736} = 27.51*$

$F_3 = \dfrac{(15-12-7.5+9)^2}{3.68\left(\dfrac{1}{10} + \dfrac{1}{10} + \dfrac{1}{10} + \dfrac{1}{10}\right)} = \dfrac{20.25}{1.472} = 13.76*$

$*p < .05; \ F_{cv(.05)} = 4.11$ for $df = 1, \ 36$

c. What are your conclusions?

All three null hypotheses are rejected. The researcher would conclude that $\mu_1 \neq \mu_4$, $\mu_2 \neq \mu_3$, and $\mu_1 + \mu_4 \neq \mu_2 + \mu_3$.

7. a.
Linear	−3	−1	1	3
Quadratic	1	−1	−1	1
Cubic	−1	3	−3	1

b.
$$F_{\text{linear}} = \frac{[(-3)(15)+(-1)(12)+(1)(7.5)+(3)(9)]^2}{3.68\left(\dfrac{9}{10}+\dfrac{1}{10}+\dfrac{1}{10}+\dfrac{9}{10}\right)}$$

$$= \frac{(-22.5)^2}{7.36} = 68.78$$

$$F_{\text{quadratic}} = \frac{[(1)(15)+(-1)(12)+(-1)(7.5)+(1)(9)]^2}{3.68\left(\dfrac{1}{10}+\dfrac{1}{10}+\dfrac{1}{10}+\dfrac{1}{10}\right)}$$

$$= \frac{(4.5)^2}{1.472} = 13.76$$

$$F_{\text{cubic}} = \frac{[(-1)(15)+(3)(12)+(-3)(7.5)+(1)(9)]^2}{3.68\left(\dfrac{1}{10}+\dfrac{9}{10}+\dfrac{9}{10}+\dfrac{1}{10}\right)}$$

$$= \frac{(7.5)^2}{7.36} = 7.64$$

$F_{\text{cv}(.05)} = 4.11$ for df $= 1,\ 36$

c. What are your conclusions?

All three contrasts are significant; the linear, quadratic, and cubic trends are all significant. The researcher would want to describe all three, but concentrate on the cubic trend.

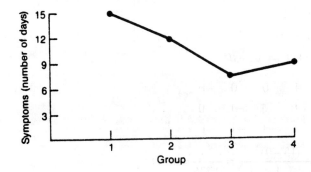

CHAPTER 16
Analysis of Variance, Two-Way Classification

COMPREHENSION CHECK

The two-way classification or two-way ANOVA is the procedure for testing the __(1)__ hypothesis when two __(2)__ variables are considered __(3)__ . This arrangement is called a __(4)__ design, and it has several advantages. The simultaneous analysis of two independent variables is __(5)__ , since, in essence, we are carrying out two separate research studies concurrently. The two-way ANOVA provides __(6)__ over more than one __(7)__ variable or factor. Factorial designs allow us to examine the __(8)__ among the independent variables.

The total variation of scores on the __(9)__ variable can be partitioned into __(10)__ components. The first component is the __(11)__ variance (s_W^2), which is the variation due to __(12)__ fluctuation and considered an estimate of the __(13)__ variance (σ_e^2). The other components are the variation among __(14)__ means (s_J^2), the variation among __(15)__ means (s_K^2), and the variation due to the __(16)__ between the two independent variables (s_{JK}^2).

In two-way ANOVA the different __(17)__ effects for the two independent variables in the __(18)__ and __(19)__ can be interpreted in the same way as treatment effects in __(20)__ ANOVA. The __(21)__ hypotheses for both row and column means state that there is __(22)__ difference between the respective population __(23)__ . If both of the null hypotheses are true, that is, that the different __(24)__ effects for the two __(25)__ variables have no effect on the __(26)__ variable, we would expect s_J^2 to be equal to __(27)__ and __(28)__ to be equal to s_W^2. Thus the ratios s_J^2/s_W^2 and s_K^2/s_W^2 will be approximately equal to __(29)__ . Should there be differential treatment effects associated with the __(30)__ or __(31)__ , s_J^2/s_W^2 and s_K^2/s_W^2 would be __(32)__ than 1.00. The null hypothesis for the interaction is that there is no __(33)__ among either the __(34)__ means, the __(35)__ means, or both. If the null hypothesis is false, the ratio s_{JK}^2/s_W^2 will be __(36)__ than 1.00.

In two-way ANOVA we partition the total sum of squares into four components: (1) __(37)__ sum of squares (SS_W), (2) the row sum of squares (SS_J), (3) the column sum of squares (SS_K), and (4) the __(38)__ sum of squares (SS_{JK}). The variance estimates, called __(39)__ (MS), are obtained by __(40)__ the component sums of squares by the __(41)__ associated with each variance estimate.

In two-way ANOVA there are __(42)__ null hypotheses to be tested. Tests of the hypotheses on the two independent __(43)__ , the row population __(44)__ and the column population __(45)__ , are called tests of the __(46)__ of the investigation. The third null hypothesis, referred to as the __(47)__ , is that there are no differences in cell population means that cannot be attributed to the population means of the __(48)__ , __(49)__ , or __(50)__ . The test statistic for each of these hypotheses is the __(51)__ , which is obtained by dividing the respective mean square by the __(52)__ . The underlying distribution for all test statistics is the F distribution, with the __(53)__ degrees of freedom.

The __(54)__ of either of the two __(55)__ variables in two-way ANOVA are __(56)__ if they represent the levels that are of __(57)__ to the researcher. If, however, the levels of either independent variable are randomly selected from a __(58)__ of levels, the levels are said to be __(59)__ . If both independent variables have fixed levels, the model for the two-way ANOVA is referred to as a ___(60)___ model. If both variables have random levels, the model is said to be a ___(61)___ model. If one of the variables has fixed levels and the other has random levels, the model is a ___(62)___ model. Most research in the behavioral sciences involves ___(63)___ or ___(64)___ effects models.

Interpretation of the tests of hypotheses for each of the independent ___(65)___ is the same as in one-way ANOVA. The hypothesis for interaction is tested in the conventional manner using the ___(66)___ ; however, the most effective way to examine interaction is to ___(67)___ the ___(68)___ means. The scale of the ___(69)___ variable is placed on the ___(70)___ axis and levels of one ___(71)___ variable on the ___(72)___ axis. If there is no interaction between the two independent variables, the lines that connect the cell ___(73)___ are essentially ___(74)___ . A significant interaction is illustrated by ___(75)___ lines. An interaction is ___(76)___ when the lines do not intersect within the plot, and is ___(77)___ when they do intersect.

The assumptions for two-way ANOVA are the same as for one-way ANOVA. That is, the observations must be ___(78)___ , and ___(79)___ samples from populations are ___(80)___ distributed with ___(81)___ variances. In addition, it is assumed that the ___(82)___ variable is measured on at least an interval scale. Another extension from the one-way ANOVA to the two-way classification is the use of ___(83)___ comparison procedures to follow up a significant overall effect if there are more than ___(84)___ levels of the factor and the factor has ___(85)___ levels. The procedures are extremely similar in the one-way and two-way cases, with the only difference being the use of the ___(86)___ sizes for the respective factors. To follow up a significant interaction effect, however, a procedure called the analysis of ___(87)___ effects is used.

Comprehension Check: Answers

1. null
2. independent
3. simultaneously
4. factorial
5. efficient
6. control
7. independent
8. interaction
9. dependent
10. four
11. within-cell
12. random sampling
13. population
14. row
15. column
16. interaction
17. treatment
18. rows
19. columns
20. one-way
21. null
22. no
23. means
24. treatment
25. independent
26. dependent
27. s_W^2
28. s_K^2
29. 1.00

30. rows
31. columns
32. greater
33. difference
34. row
35. column
36. greater
37. within-cell
38. interaction
39. mean squares
40. dividing
41. degrees of freedom
42. three
43. variables
44. means
45. means
46. main effects
47. interaction
48. rows
49. columns
50. both
51. *F* ratio
52. MS_W
53. appropriate
54. levels
55. independent
56. fixed
57. interest
58. population

59. random
60. fixed-effects
61. random-effects
62. mixed-effects
63. fixed-
64. mixed-
65. variables
66. *F* ratio
67. plot
68. cell
69. dependent
70. vertical (Y)
71. independent
72. horizontal (X)
73. means
74. parallel
75. nonparallel
76. ordinal
77. disordinal
78. random
79. independent
80. normally
81. equal
82. dependent
83. post hoc
84. two
85. fixed
86. sample
87. simple

CHAPTER 16 EXERCISES

1. The director of a counseling agency asks a random sample of clients to specify their perceptions of counselor effectiveness. Numerical ratings are derived, and these are examined in relationship to (1) age difference between counselor and client, and (2) the counseling approach. Given the following data, use analysis of variance procedures to test for differences among population means at the .01 level of significance.

		Age Difference					
		Younger client		*Same-age client*		*Older client*	
Counseling approach	Directive	22	30	25	28	33	28
		28	25	31	22	30	34
		24	27	23	24	35	32
	Nondirective	36	31	29	31	24	27
		34	35	32	25	28	21
		29	32	26	28	23	25
	Combined	35	30	36	32	33	34
		29	34	35	34	30	28
		32	28	38	36	32	36

		Age Difference			
		Younger client	*Same-age client*	*Older client*	
Counseling approach	Directive	$T_{11} = 156$ $\bar{X}_{11} = 26.00$ $\Sigma X_i^2 = 4{,}098$	$T_{12} =$ $\bar{X}_{12} =$ $\Sigma X_i^2 =$	$T_{13} =$ $\bar{X}_{13} =$ $\Sigma X_i^2 =$	$T_{1.} = 501$ $\bar{X}_{1.} = 27.83$ $\Sigma X_i^2 = 14{,}235$
	Nondirective	$T_{21} =$ $\bar{X}_{21} =$ $\Sigma X_i^2 =$	$T_{22} =$ $\bar{X}_{22} =$ $\Sigma X_i^2 =$	$T_{23} =$ $\bar{X}_{23} =$ $\Sigma X_i^2 =$	$T_{2.} =$ $\bar{X}_{2.} =$ $\Sigma X_i^2 =$
	Combined	$T_{31} =$ $\bar{X}_{31} =$ $\Sigma X_i^2 =$	$T_{32} =$ $\bar{X}_{32} =$ $\Sigma X_i^2 =$	$T_{33} =$ $\bar{X}_{33} =$ $\Sigma X_i^2 =$	$T_{3.} =$ $\bar{X}_{3.} =$ $\Sigma X_i^2 =$
		$T_{.1} = 541$ $\bar{X}_{.1} = 30.06$ $\Sigma X_i^2 = 16{,}531$	$T_{.2} =$ $\bar{X}_{.2} =$ $\Sigma X_i^2 =$	$T_{.3} =$ $\bar{X}_{.3} =$ $\Sigma X_i^2 =$	$T =$ $\bar{X} =$ $\Sigma\Sigma\Sigma X_{ijk}^2 = 48{,}953$

a. State the hypotheses.

$H_{0_1}: \mu_{1.} = \quad =$

$H_{a_1}: \mu_i \neq$

$H_{0_2}: \mu_{.1} = \quad =$

$H_{a_2}:$

$H_{0_3}:$ all $(\mu_{jk} - \mu_{j.} - \mu_{.k} + \mu) = 0$

$H_{a_3}:$

b. Set the criterion for rejecting each H_0.

F_{cv} for rows =

F_{cv} for columns =

F_{cv} for interaction =

c. Complete the ANOVA and compute the test statistics.

$$\Sigma T_{j.}^2 = (501)^2 + (\quad)^2 + (\quad)^2 =$$

$$\Sigma T_{.k}^2 = (541)^2 + (\quad)^2 + (\quad)^2 =$$

$$\Sigma\Sigma T_{jk}^2 = (156)^2 + (\quad)^2 + (\quad)^2 + (\quad)^2 + (\quad)^2 + (\quad)^2$$
$$+ (\quad)^2 + (\quad)^2 + (\quad)^2 =$$

$$SS_J = \frac{1}{nK} \sum_{j=1}^{J} T_{j.}^2 - \frac{T^2}{N} = \frac{1}{(6)(3)}(\qquad) - \frac{(1,609)^2}{54}$$
$$= \qquad - \qquad$$
$$=$$

$$SS_K = \frac{1}{nJ} \sum_{k=1}^{K} T_{.k}^2 - \frac{T^2}{N} = \frac{1}{(\ )(\ )}(\qquad) - \frac{(\quad)^2}{\qquad}$$
$$= \qquad - \qquad$$
$$=$$

$$SS_{JK} = \frac{1}{n} \sum_{k=1}^{K} \sum_{j=1}^{J} T_{jk}^2 - \frac{1}{nK} \sum_{j=1}^{J} T_{j.}^2 - \frac{1}{nJ} \sum_{k=1}^{K} T_{.k}^2 + \frac{T^2}{N}$$
$$= \frac{1}{6}(\qquad) - \frac{1}{(6)(3)}(\qquad)$$
$$- \frac{1}{(\ )(\ )}(\qquad) + \frac{(\quad)^2}{\qquad}$$
$$= \qquad - \qquad - \qquad + \qquad$$
$$=$$

$$SS_W = \sum_{k=1}^{K} \sum_{j=1}^{J} \sum_{i=1}^{n} X_{ijk}^2 - \frac{1}{n} \sum_{k=1}^{K} \sum_{j=1}^{J} T_{jk}^2$$
$$= 48,953 - \frac{1}{6}(\qquad)$$
$$= \qquad - \qquad$$
$$=$$

$$SS_T = \sum_{k=1}^{K} \sum_{j=1}^{J} \sum_{i=1}^{n} X_{ijk}^2 - \frac{T^2}{N} = \qquad - \frac{(\quad)^2}{\qquad}$$
$$= \qquad - \qquad$$

Summary ANOVA

Source	SS	df	MS	F	F_{cv}
Rows	264.48	2	132.24	17.49	
Columns					
Interaction					
Within	———	——			
Total	1,010.76	53			

d. Compute the ω^2 for the main effects and the interaction.

$$\omega^2 = \frac{SS_{\text{effect}} - (df_{\text{effect}})(MS_W)}{SS_T + MS_W}$$

For the row main effect

$$\omega^2 = \frac{SS_J - (J-1)(MS_W)}{SS_T + MS_W}$$

$$= \frac{264.48 - (\ )(\quad)}{1{,}010.76 +}$$

$$=$$

For the column main effect

$$\omega^2 = \frac{SS_K - (K-1)(MS_W)}{SS_T + MS_W}$$

$$= \frac{-(2)(\quad)}{+7.559}$$

$$=$$

For the interaction

$$\omega^2 = \frac{SS_{JK} - (J-1)(K-1)(MS_W)}{SS_T + MS_W}$$

$$= \frac{-(\ )(\ )(\quad)}{+}$$

$$=$$

e. Compute the Tukey procedure for the Method main effect.

	$\bar{X}_i$	$(\bar{X}_i - \bar{X}_k)$	Q
$\bar{X}_1$	27.83		
$\bar{X}_2$	28.67	0.84	1.30
$\bar{X}_3$			

$$Q = \frac{-}{\sqrt{\rule{2em}{0pt}}} \qquad Q_{cv(.01)} =$$

f. Plot the interaction.

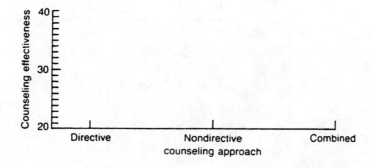

g. Compute the simple effects.

$$\text{SS}_J \text{ at column } k = \sum_{j=1}^{J} \frac{(T_{jk})^2}{n} - \frac{T_{\cdot k}^2}{nJ}$$

$$\text{SS}_J \text{ at column } 1 = \frac{(156)^2}{6} + \frac{(197)^2}{6} + \frac{(\quad)^2}{\rule{1cm}{0.4pt}} - \frac{(541)^2}{18}$$

$$=$$

$$\text{SS}_J \text{ at column } 2 = \frac{(153)^2}{6} + \frac{(\quad)^2}{\rule{1cm}{0.4pt}} + \frac{(\quad)^2}{\rule{1cm}{0.4pt}} - \frac{(535)^2}{\rule{1cm}{0.4pt}}$$

$$=$$

$$\text{SS}_J \text{ at column } 3 = \frac{(\quad)^2}{\rule{1cm}{0.4pt}} + \frac{(\quad)^2}{\rule{1cm}{0.4pt}} + \frac{(\quad)^2}{\rule{1cm}{0.4pt}} - \frac{(\quad)^2}{\rule{1cm}{0.4pt}}$$

$$=$$

$$\text{SS}_K \text{ at row } j = \sum_{k=1}^{K} \frac{(T_{jk})^2}{n} - \frac{T_{j\cdot}^2}{nK}$$

$$\text{SS}_K \text{ at row } 1 = \frac{(156)^2}{6} + \frac{(153)^2}{6} + \frac{(\quad)^2}{\rule{1cm}{0.4pt}} - \frac{(501)^2}{18}$$

$$=$$

$$\text{SS}_K \text{ at row } 2 = \frac{(197)^2}{6} + \frac{(\quad)^2}{\rule{1cm}{0.4pt}} + \frac{(\quad)^2}{\rule{1cm}{0.4pt}} - \frac{(516)^2}{\rule{1cm}{0.4pt}}$$

$$=$$

$$\text{SS}_K \text{ at row } 3 = \frac{(\quad)^2}{\rule{1cm}{0.4pt}} + \frac{(\quad)^2}{\rule{1cm}{0.4pt}} + \frac{(\quad)^2}{\rule{1cm}{0.4pt}} - \frac{(\quad)^2}{\rule{1cm}{0.4pt}}$$

$$=$$

2. A horticulturist is conducting an experiment in growing zinnias and wants to determine the influence of sunlight and soil nitrogen content. The heights in inches of mature plants grown in three sunlight conditions and two soil conditions are as follows:

		Sunlight					
		Shade		Half sun		Full sun	
	Low	10	11	12	14	11	17
Soil		12	13	16	15	18	20
nitrogen content	High	12	14	18	22	16	13
		11	13	24	26	14	11

		Sunlight			
		Shade	Half sun	Full sun	
Soil nitrogen content	Low	$T_{11} = \ \ 46$ $\bar{X}_{11} = \ \ 11.5$ $\Sigma X_i^2 = \ \ 534$			
	High	$T_{21} =$ $\bar{X}_{21} =$ $\Sigma X_i^2 =$			$T_{2.} = \ \ 194$ $\bar{X}_{2.} = \ 16.17$ $\Sigma X_i^2 = 3{,}432$
		$T_{.1} = \ \ 96$ $\bar{X}_{1} = \ \ 12$ $\Sigma X_i^2 = 1{,}164$			$T =$ $\bar{X} =$ $\Sigma\Sigma\Sigma X_{ijk}^2 =$

a. State the hypotheses.

$H_{0_1}: \mu_{.1} = \qquad$ for rows

$H_{a_1}:$

$H_{0_2}: \mu_{.1} = \quad = \quad$ for columns

$H_{a_2}:$

$H_{0_3}:$ all $\qquad$ for interaction

$H_{a_3}:$ all

b. Set the criterion for rejecting each hypothesis (use $\alpha = .05$).

F_{cv} for rows $=$

F_{cv} for columns $=$

F_{cv} for interaction $=$

c. Complete the ANOVA and compute the test statistics.

$$\Sigma T_{j.}^2 = (169)^2 + \qquad =$$

$$\Sigma T_{.k}^2 = (96)^2 + (\quad)^2 + \qquad =$$

$$\Sigma T_{jk}^2 = (46)^2 + (\quad)^2 + \qquad + \qquad + \qquad +$$

$$=$$

$$T = \Sigma\Sigma\Sigma X_{ijk} =$$

$$\Sigma\Sigma\Sigma X_{ijk}^2 =$$

$$SS_J = \frac{1}{nK} \sum_{j=1}^{J} T_{j.}^2 - \frac{T^2}{N}$$

$$= \frac{1}{(\ \ )(\ \ )}(\qquad) - \frac{(363)^2}{}$$

$$= \qquad - \qquad =$$

$$SS_K = \frac{}{nJ} \quad - \frac{}{}$$

$$= \frac{}{(\quad)(2)}(45,225) - \frac{(\quad)^2}{}$$

$$= \quad - \quad =$$

$$SS_{JK} = \frac{1}{n} \quad - \quad - \quad +$$

$$= \frac{}{} - \frac{}{(\quad)(\quad)} - \frac{}{} +$$

$$= \quad - \quad - \quad +$$

$$SS_W = \quad -$$

$$= \quad - \quad =$$

$$SS_T =$$

Summary ANOVA

Source	SS	df	MS	F	F_{cv}
Fertilizer	26.04				
Sun		2			
Interaction			65.4		
Within	_____	__			
Total					

d. Compute the ω^2 for the main effects and the interaction.

$$\omega^2 = \frac{SS_{effect} - (df_{effect})(MS_W)}{SS_T + MS_W}$$

For the row main effect

$$\omega^2 = \frac{SS_J - (J-1)(MS_W)}{SS_T + MS_W}$$

$$= \frac{26.04 - (\quad)(\quad)}{430.62 +} =$$

For the column main effect

$$\omega^2 = \frac{SS_K - (K-1)(MS_W)}{SS_T + MS_W}$$

$$= \frac{-(2)(\quad)}{+6.21} =$$

For the interaction

$$\omega^2 = \frac{SS_{JK} - (J-1)(K-1)(MS_W)}{SS_T + MS_W}$$

$$= \frac{-(\quad)(\quad)(\quad)}{+} =$$

e. Compute the Tukey procedure for the Sun main effect.

	$\bar{X}_i$	$(\bar{X}_i - \bar{X}_k)$	Q
Shade	12.00		
Full sun	15.00		
Half sun	18.38		

f. Plot the interaction.

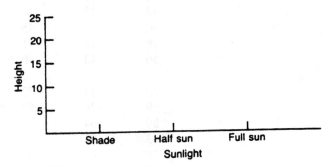

g. Compute the simple effects.

$$\text{SS}_J \text{ at column } k = \sum_{j=1}^{J} \frac{(T_{jk})^2}{n} - \frac{T_{.k}^2}{nJ}$$

$$\text{SS}_J \text{ at column } 1 = \frac{(46)^2}{4} + \frac{(50)^2}{} - \frac{(\quad)}{8}$$

$$=$$

$$\text{SS}_J \text{ at column } 2 = \frac{(57)^2}{} + \frac{(\quad)^2}{} - \frac{(\quad)^2}{}$$

$$=$$

$$\text{SS}_J \text{ at column } 3 = \frac{(\quad)^2}{} + \frac{(\quad)^2}{} - \frac{(\quad)^2}{}$$

$$=$$

$$\text{SS}_K \text{ at row } j = \sum_{k=1}^{K} \frac{(T_{jk})^2}{n} - \frac{T_{j.}^2}{nK}$$

$$\text{SS}_K \text{ at row } 1 = \frac{(46)^2}{4} + \frac{(57)^2}{} + \frac{(\quad)^2}{} - \frac{(169)^2}{12}$$

$$=$$

$$\text{SS}_K \text{ at row } 2 = \frac{(50)^2}{4} + \frac{(\quad)^2}{} + \frac{(\quad)^2}{} - \frac{(\quad)^2}{}$$

$$=$$

3. Consider the following data from an experiment that involved the effects of three different dosages of two drugs in alleviating migraine headache pain. The measure of effectiveness of the drug was a clinical measure of the level of headache pain experienced by the patient. Complete the analysis of variance, using the .05 level of significance.

		Drug dosage					
		Low		Moderate		High	
		76	43	36	43	37	27
		66	42	45	54	22	23
	A	43	60	47	45	22	24
		62	78	23	41	25	25
		65	66	43	40	11	31
Drug							
		94	80	74	72	67	55
		85	69	74	62	64	57
	B	80	80	64	64	70	66
		81	63	86	78	65	79
		80	58	68	61	60	80

		Drug dosage			
		Level 1 Low	Level 2 Moderate	Level 3 High	
Drug	A	$T_{11} = 601$ $\bar{X}_{11} = 60.1$ $\Sigma X_i^2 = 37{,}703$	$T_{12} =$ $\bar{X}_{12} =$ $\Sigma X_i^2 =$	$T_{13} =$ $\bar{X}_{13} =$ $\Sigma X_i^2 =$	$T_{1.} = 1{,}265$ $\bar{X}_{1.} = 42.17$ $\Sigma X_i^2 = 62{,}185$
	B	$T_{21} =$ $\bar{X}_{21} =$ $\Sigma X_i^2 =$	$T_{22} =$ $\bar{X}_{22} =$ $\Sigma X_i^2 =$	$T_{23} =$ $\bar{X}_{23} =$ $\Sigma X_i^2 =$	$T_{2.} =$ $\bar{X}_{2.} =$ $\Sigma X_i^2 =$
		$T_{.1} = 1{,}371$ $\bar{X}_{.1} = 68.55$ $\Sigma X_i^2 = 98{,}019$	$T_{.2} =$ $\bar{X}_{.2} =$ $\Sigma X_i^2 =$	$T_{.3} =$ $\bar{X}_{.3} =$ $\Sigma X_i^2 =$	$T = 3{,}401$ $\bar{X} = 56.68$ $\Sigma\Sigma\Sigma X_{ijk}^2 = 217{,}079$

$$\Sigma T_{j.}^2 = (1265)^2 + (\quad)^2 =$$

$$\Sigma T_{.k}^2 = (1371)^2 + (\quad)^2 + (\quad)^2 =$$

$$\Sigma\Sigma T_{jk}^2 = (601)^2 + (\quad)^2 + (\quad)^2 + (\quad)^2 + (\quad)^2 + (\quad)^2$$

$$=$$

a. State the hypotheses.

b. Set the criterion for rejecting each H_0.

c. Complete the ANOVA and compute the test statistics.

d. Compute the ω^2 for the main effects and the interaction.

e. Compute the Tukey procedure for the Dosage main effect.

f. Plot the interaction.

g. Compute the simple effects.

4. An exercise physiologist is interested in whether weight training is effective in enhancing the recovery of cardiac patients. Sixty patients are randomly assigned either to a weight-training program (*A1*) or to a no weight-training program (*A2*). Subsequently, these patients are randomly assigned to one of three programs designed to improve cardiovascular functioning (*B1, B2,* or *B3*). Complete the ANOVA, using the data below and $\alpha = .05$.

Weight-training program

A1			A2		
Cardiovascular program			*Cardiovascular program*		
B1	*B2*	*B3*	*B1*	*B2*	*B3*
19	43	53	30	49	64
10	42	51	24	43	61
21	41	57	25	49	68
15	44	57	30	53	56
20	42	68	28	44	60
24	49	60	34	46	55
16	46	48	31	46	54
22	39	47	32	56	68
18	48	60	27	54	59
18	39	60	32	53	57

a. State the hypotheses.

b. Set the criterion for rejecting each H_0.

c. Complete the ANOVA and compute the test statistics.

d. Compute the ω^2 for the main effects and the interaction.

e. Compute the Tukey procedure for the cardiovascular program (*B*) main effect.

f. Plot the interaction.

5. In preparing a report on faculty publications, a college dean looks at productivity over the past two years in relationship to (1) academic rank and (2) teaching load. Given the following numbers of publications by members of a randomly selected research sample, use analysis of variance procedures to test for differences among population means at the .05 level of significance.

		Academic rank		
		Assistant professor	*Associate professor*	*Full professor*
	Below average	6, 4, 3, 2	6, 4, 7, 8	8, 6, 10, 8
Teaching load	Average	3, 5, 4, 2	5, 4, 8, 4	7, 9, 5, 8
	Above average	3, 2, 4, 3	2, 4, 5, 1	3, 4, 6, 2

a. State the hypotheses.

b. Set the criterion for rejecting each H_0.

c. Complete the ANOVA and compute the test statistics.

d. Compute the ω^2 for the main effects and the interaction.

e. Compute the Tukey procedure for both main effects.

f. Plot the interaction.

Chapter 16 Exercises: Answers

1.

		Age Difference			
		Younger client	Same-age client	Older client	
Counseling approach	Directive	$T_{11} = 156$ $\bar{X}_{11} = 26.00$ $\Sigma X_i^2 = 4{,}098$	$T_{12} = 153$ $\bar{X}_{12} = 25.50$ $\Sigma X_i^2 = 3{,}959$	$T_{13} = 192$ $\bar{X}_{13} = 32.00$ $\Sigma X_i^2 = 6{,}178$	$T_{1.} = 501$ $\bar{X}_{1.} = 27.83$ $\Sigma X_i^2 = 14{,}235$
	Nondirective	$T_{21} = 197$ $\bar{X}_{21} = 32.83$ $\Sigma X_i^2 = 6{,}503$	$T_{22} = 171$ $\bar{X}_{22} = 28.50$ $\Sigma X_i^2 = 4{,}911$	$T_{23} = 148$ $\bar{X}_{23} = 24.67$ $\Sigma X_i^2 = 3{,}684$	$T_{2.} = 516$ $\bar{X}_{2.} = 28.67$ $\Sigma X_i^2 = 15{,}098$
	Combined	$T_{31} = 188$ $\bar{X}_{31} = 31.33$ $\Sigma X_i^2 = 5{,}930$	$T_{32} = 211$ $\bar{X}_{32} = 35.17$ $\Sigma X_i^2 = 7{,}441$	$T_{33} = 193$ $\bar{X}_{33} = 32.17$ $\Sigma X_i^2 = 6{,}249$	$T_{3.} = 592$ $\bar{X}_{3.} = 32.89$ $\Sigma X_i^2 = 19{,}620$
		$T_{.1} = 541$ $\bar{X}_{.1} = 30.06$ $\Sigma X_i^2 = 16{,}531$	$T_{.2} = 535$ $\bar{X}_{.2} = 29.72$ $\Sigma X_i^2 = 16{,}311$	$T_{.3} = 533$ $\bar{X}_{.3} = 29.61$ $\Sigma X_i^2 = 16{,}111$	$T = 1{,}609$ $\bar{X} = 29.80$ $\Sigma\Sigma\Sigma X_{ijk}^2 = 48{,}953$

a. $H_{01}: \mu_{1.} = \mu_{2.} = \mu_{3.}$

$H_{a1}: \mu_i \neq \mu_k$ for some i, k

$H_{02}: \mu_{.1} = \mu_{.2} = \mu_{.3}$

$H_{a2}: \mu_i \neq \mu_k$ for some i, k

$H_{03}:$ all $(\mu_{jk} - \mu_{j.} - \mu_{.k} + \mu) = 0$

$H_{a3}:$ all $(\mu_{jk} - \mu_{j.} - \mu_{.k} + \mu) \neq 0$

b. $F_{J_{cv}} = 5.11$

$F_{K_{cv}} = 5.11$

$F_{JK_{cv}} = 3.77$

c. $\Sigma T_{j.}^2 = (501)^2 + (516)^2 + (592)^2 = 867{,}721$

$\Sigma T_{.k}^2 = (541)^2 + (535)^2 + (533)^2 = 862{,}995$

$\Sigma\Sigma T_{jk}^2 = (156)^2 + (153)^2 + (192)^2 + (197)^2 + (171)^2 + (148)^2$

$\qquad + (188)^2 + (211)^2 + (193)^2 = 291{,}677$

$$SS_J = \frac{1}{(6)(3)}(867,721) - \frac{(1,609)^2}{54}$$

$$= 48,206.72 - 47,942.24 = 264.48$$

$$SS_K = \frac{1}{(6)(3)}(862,995) - \frac{(1,609)^2}{54}$$

$$= 47,944.17 - 47,942.24 = 1.93$$

$$SS_{JK} = \frac{1}{6}(291,677) - \frac{1}{(6)(3)}(867,721) - \frac{1}{(6)(3)}(862,995) + \frac{(1,609)^2}{54}$$

$$= 48,612.83 - 48,206.72 - 47,944.17 + 47,942.24$$

$$= 404.18$$

$$SS_W = 48,953 - \frac{1}{6}(291,677)$$

$$= 48,953 - 48,612.83 = 340.17$$

$$SS_T = 48,953 - \frac{(1,609)^2}{54}$$

$$= 48,953 - 47,942.24$$

$$= 1,010.76$$

Summary ANOVA

Source	SS	df	MS	F	F_{cv}
Rows	264.48	2	132.24	17.49	5.11
Columns	1.93	2	0.965	0.13	5.11
Interaction	404.18	4	101.045	13.37	3.77
Within	340.17	45	7.559		
Total	1,010.76	53			

d. For the row main effect

$$\omega^2 = \frac{264.48 - (2)(7.559)}{1,010.76 + 7.559} = .245$$

For the column main effect

$$\omega^2 = \frac{1.93 - (2)(7.559)}{1,010.76 + 7.559} = -.013$$

For the interaction

$$\omega^2 = \frac{404.18 - (2)(2)(7.559)}{1,010.76 + 7.559} = .367$$

e.

	$\bar{X}_i$		$(\bar{X}_i - \bar{X}_k)$		Q	
$\bar{X}_1$	27.83					
$\bar{X}_2$	28.67		0.84		1.30	
$\bar{X}_3$	32.89		5.06	4.22	7.81*	6.51*

$$*p < .01; \quad Q = \frac{\bar{X}_i - \bar{X}_k}{\sqrt{\dfrac{7.559}{18}}} \qquad Q_{cv(.01)} = 4.35 \text{ (for df } = 45)$$

f.

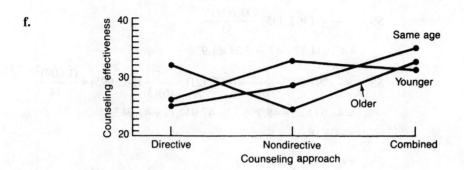

g.

$$SS_J \text{ at column } 1 = \frac{(156)^2}{6} + \frac{(197)^2}{6} + \frac{(188)^2}{6} - \frac{(541)^2}{18}$$

$$= 16,414.83 - 16,260.06 = 154.77$$

$$SS_J \text{ at column } 2 = \frac{(153)^2}{6} + \frac{(171)^2}{6} + \frac{(211)^2}{6} - \frac{(535)^2}{18}$$

$$= 16,195.17 - 15,901.39 = 293.78$$

$$SS_J \text{ at column } 3 = \frac{(192)^2}{6} + \frac{(148)^2}{6} + \frac{(193)^2}{6} - \frac{(533)^2}{18}$$

$$= 16,002.83 - 15,782.72 = 220.11$$

$$SS_K \text{ at row } 1 = \frac{(156)^2}{6} + \frac{(153)^2}{6} + \frac{(192)^2}{6} - \frac{(501)^2}{18}$$

$$= 14,101.50 - 13,944.50 = 157.00$$

$$SS_K \text{ at row } 2 = \frac{(197)^2}{6} + \frac{(171)^2}{6} + \frac{(148)^2}{6} - \frac{(516)^2}{18}$$

$$= 14,992.33 - 14,792.00 = 200.33$$

$$SS_K \text{ at row } 3 = \frac{(188)^2}{6} + \frac{(211)^2}{6} + \frac{(193)^2}{6} - \frac{(592)^2}{18}$$

$$= 19,519.00 - 19,470.22 = 48.78$$

Summary ANOVA

Source	SS	df	MS	F	F_{cv}
Rows (approach)	264.48	2	132.24	17.49	5.11
Rows at column 1	154.77	2	77.39	10.24	4.41
Rows at column 2	293.78	2	146.89	19.43	4.41
Rows at column 3	220.11	2	110.06	14.56	4.41
Columns (age diff.)	1.93	2	0.965	0.13	5.11
Columns at row 1	157.00	2	78.50	10.39	4.41
Columns at row 2	200.33	2	100.17	13.25	4.41
Columns at row 3	48.78	2	24.39	3.23	4.41
Interaction	404.18	4	101.045	13.37	3.77
Within	340.17	45	7.559		
Total	1,010.76	53			

2.

		Sunlight			
		Shade	Half sun	Full sun	Row totals
Soil nitrogen content	Low	$T_{11} = 46$ $\bar{X}_{11} = 11.5$ $\Sigma X_i^2 = 534$	$T_{12} = 57$ $\bar{X}_{12} = 14.25$ $\Sigma X_i^2 = 821$	$T_{13} = 66$ $\bar{X}_{13} = 16.5$ $\Sigma X_i^2 = 1,134$	$T_{1.} = 169$ $\bar{X}_{1.} = 14.08$ $\Sigma X_i^2 = 2,489$
	High	$T_{21} = 50$ $\bar{X}_{21} = 12.5$ $\Sigma X_i^2 = 630$	$T_{22} = 90$ $\bar{X}_{22} = 22.5$ $\Sigma X_i^2 = 2,060$	$T_{23} = 54$ $\bar{X}_{23} = 13.5$ $\Sigma X_i^2 = 742$	$T_{2.} = 194$ $\bar{X}_{2.} = 16.17$ $\Sigma X_i^2 = 3,432$
	Column totals	$T_{.1} = 96$ $\bar{X}_{.1} = 12$ $\Sigma X_i^2 = 1,164$	$T_{.2} = 147$ $\bar{X}_{.2} = 18.38$ $\Sigma X_i^2 = 2,881$	$T_{.3} = 120$ $\bar{X}_{.3} = 15$ $\Sigma X_i^2 = 1,876$	$T = 363$ $\bar{X} = 15.13$ $\Sigma\Sigma\Sigma X_{ijk}^2 = 5,921$

a. $H_{0_1}: \mu_{1.} = \mu_{2.}$

$H_{a_1}: \mu_{1.} \neq \mu_{2.}$

$H_{0_2}: \mu_{.1} = \mu_{.2} = \mu_{.3}$

$H_{a_2}: \mu_{.1} \neq \mu_{.k}$ for some i, k

$H_{0_3}:$ all $(\mu_{jk} - \mu_{j.} - \mu_{.k} + \mu) = 0$

$H_{a_3}:$ all $(\mu_{jk} - \mu_{j.} - \mu_{.k} + \mu) \neq 0$

b. $F_{J_{cv}} = 4.41$

$F_{K_{cv}} = 3.55$

$F_{JK_{cv}} = 3.55$

c.
$$\Sigma T_{j.}^2 = (169)^2 + (194)^2 = 66,197$$

$$\Sigma T_{.k}^2 = (96)^2 + (147)^2 + (120)^2 = 45,225$$

$$\Sigma \Sigma T_{jk}^2 = (46)^2 + (57)^2 + (66)^2 + (50)^2 + (90)^2 + (54)^2 = 23,237$$

$$T = \Sigma\Sigma\Sigma X_{ijk} = 363$$

$$\Sigma\Sigma\Sigma X_{ijk}^2 = 5921$$

$$SS_J = \frac{1}{(4)(3)}(66,197) - \frac{(363)^2}{24}$$
$$= 5516.42 - 5490.38 = 26.04$$

$$SS_K = \frac{1}{(4)(2)}(45,225) - \frac{(363)^2}{24}$$
$$= 5653.13 - 5490.38 = 162.75$$

$$SS_{JK} = \frac{23,237}{4} - \frac{66,197}{(4)(3)} - \frac{45,225}{(4)(2)} + \frac{(363)^2}{24}$$
$$= 5809.25 - 5516.42 - 5653.13 + 5490.38$$
$$= 130.08$$

$$SS_W = 5921 - \frac{23,237}{4} = 111.75$$

$$SS_T = 5921 - \frac{(363)^2}{24} = 430.62$$

Summary ANOVA

Source	SS	df	MS	F	F_{cv}
Fertilizer	26.04	1	26.04	4.19	4.41
Sun	162.75	2	81.38	13.10	3.55
Interaction	130.08	2	65.04	10.47	3.55
Within	111.75	18	6.21		
Total	430.62	23			

d. For the row main effect

$$\omega^2 = \frac{26.04 - (1)(6.21)}{430.62 + 6.21} = .045$$

For the column main effect

$$\omega^2 = \frac{162.75 - (2)(6.21)}{430.62 + 6.21} = .344$$

For the interaction

$$\omega^2 = \frac{130.08 - (1)(2)(6.21)}{430.62 + 6.21} = .269$$

e.

	$\bar{X}_i$	$(\bar{X}_i - \bar{X}_k)$		Q	
Shade	12.00				
Full sun	15.00	3.0		3.41	
Half sun	18.38	6.38	3.38	7.24*	3.84*

$*p < .05; \quad Q = \dfrac{\bar{X}_i - \bar{X}_k}{\sqrt{\dfrac{6.21}{8}}} \qquad Q_{cv(.05)} = 3.61$

f.

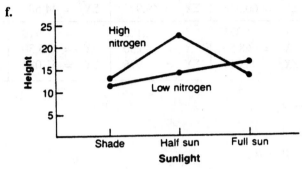

g.

SS_J at column $1 = \dfrac{(46)^2}{4} + \dfrac{(50)^2}{4} - \dfrac{(96)^2}{8}$
$= 1154.00 - 1152.00 = 2.00$

SS_J at column $2 = \dfrac{(57)^2}{4} + \dfrac{(90)^2}{4} - \dfrac{(147)^2}{8}$
$= 2837.25 - 2701.13 = 136.12$

SS_J at column $3 = \dfrac{(66)^2}{4} + \dfrac{(54)^2}{4} - \dfrac{(120)^2}{8}$
$= 1818.00 - 1800.00 = 18.00$

SS_K at row $1 = \dfrac{(46)^2}{4} + \dfrac{(57)^2}{4} + \dfrac{(66)^2}{4} - \dfrac{(169)^2}{12}$
$= 2430.25 - 2380.08 = 50.17$

SS_K at row $2 = \dfrac{(50)^2}{4} + \dfrac{(90)^2}{4} + \dfrac{(54)^2}{4} - \dfrac{(194)^2}{12}$
$= 3379.00 - 3136.33 = 242.67$

Summary ANOVA

Source	SS	df	MS	F	F_{cv}
Rows (fertilizer)	26.04	1	26.04	4.19	4.41
Rows at column 1	2.00	1	2.00	0.32	6.84
Rows at column 2	136.13	1	136.13	21.92	6.84
Rows at column 3	18.00	1	18.00	2.90	6.84
Columns (sun)	162.75	2	81.38	13.10	3.55
Columns at row 1	50.17	2	25.09	4.04	5.09
Columns at row 2	242.67	2	121.34	19.54	5.09
Interaction	130.08	2	65.04	10.47	3.55
Within	111.75	18	6.21		
Total	430.62	23			

3.

		Drug dosage			
		Level 1 Low	Level 2 Moderate	Level 3 High	
Drug	A	$T_{11} = 601$ $\bar{X}_{11} = 60.1$ $\Sigma X_i^2 = 37{,}703$	$T_{12} = 417$ $\bar{X}_{12} = 41.7$ $\Sigma X_i^2 = 17{,}979$	$T_{13} = 247$ $\bar{X}_{13} = 24.7$ $\Sigma X_i^2 = 6{,}503$	$T_{1.} = 1{,}265$ $\bar{X}_{1.} = 42.17$ $\Sigma X_i^2 = 62{,}185$
	B	$T_{21} = 770$ $\bar{X}_{21} = 77.0$ $\Sigma X_i^2 = 60{,}316$	$T_{22} = 703$ $\bar{X}_{22} = 70.3$ $\Sigma X_i^2 = 49{,}997$	$T_{23} = 663$ $\bar{X}_{23} = 66.3$ $\Sigma X_i^2 = 44{,}581$	$T_{2.} = 2{,}136$ $\bar{X}_{2.} = 71.20$ $\Sigma X_i^2 = 154{,}894$
		$T_{.1} = 1{,}371$ $\bar{X}_{.1} = 68.55$ $\Sigma X_i^2 = 98{,}019$	$T_{.2} = 1{,}120$ $\bar{X}_{.2} = 56.00$ $\Sigma X_i^2 = 67{,}976$	$T_{.3} = 910$ $\bar{X}_{.3} = 45.50$ $\Sigma X_i^2 = 51{,}084$	$T = 3{,}401$ $\bar{X} = 56.68$ $\Sigma\Sigma\Sigma X_{ijk}^2 = 217{,}079$

a. $H_{0_1}: \mu_{1.} = \mu_{2.}$

$H_{a_1}: \mu_{1.} \neq \mu_{2.}$

$H_{0_2}: \mu_{.1} = \mu_{.2} = \mu_{.3}$

$H_{a_2}: \mu_{.i} \neq \mu_{.k}$ for some i, k

$H_{0_3}:$ all $(\mu_{jk} - \mu_{j.} - \mu_{.k} + \mu) = 0$

$H_{a_3}:$ all $(\mu_{jk} - \mu_{j.} - \mu_{.k} + \mu) = 0$

b. $F_{J\text{cv}} = 4.03$

$F_{K\text{cv}} = 3.18$

$F_{JK\text{cv}} = 3.18$

c. $\Sigma T_{j.}^2 = (1265)^2 + (2136)^2 = 6{,}162{,}721$

$\Sigma T_{.k}^2 = (1371)^2 + (1120)^2 + (910)^2 = 3{,}962{,}141$

$\Sigma\Sigma T_{jk}^2 = (601)^2 + (417)^2 + (247)^2 + (770)^2 + (703)^2 + (663)^2 = 2{,}122{,}777$

$$SS_J = \frac{1}{(10)(3)}(6{,}162{,}721) - \frac{(3401)^2}{60}$$
$$= 205{,}424.033 - 192{,}780.017$$
$$= 12{,}644.016$$

$$SS_K = \frac{1}{(10)(2)}(3{,}962{,}141) - \frac{(3401)^2}{60}$$
$$= 198{,}107.050 - 192{,}780.017$$
$$= 5327.033$$

$$SS_{JK} = \frac{1}{10}(2{,}122{,}777) - \frac{1}{10(3)}(6{,}162{,}721) - \frac{1}{10(2)}(3{,}962{,}141) + \frac{(3401)^2}{60}$$
$$= 212{,}277.700 - 205{,}424.033 - 198{,}107.050 + 192{,}780.017$$
$$= 1526.634$$

$$SS_W = 217{,}079 - \frac{1}{10}(2{,}122{,}777) = 4801.300$$

$$SS_T = 217{,}079 - \frac{(3401)^2}{60} = 24{,}298.983$$

Summary ANOVA

Source	SS	df	MS	F	F_{cv}
Rows	12,644.016	1	12,644.016	142.207	4.03
Columns	5,327.033	2	2,663.517	29.956	3.18
Interaction	1,526.634	2	763.317	8.585	3.18
Within	4,801.300	54	88.913		
Total	24,298.983	59			

d. For the row main effect

$$\omega^2 = \frac{12,644.016 - (1)(88.913)}{24,298.983 + 88.913} = .515$$

For the column main effect

$$\omega^2 = \frac{5,327.033 - (2)(88.913)}{24,298.983 + 88.913} = .211$$

For the interaction

$$\omega^2 = \frac{1,526.634 - (1)(2)(88.913)}{24,298.983 + 88.913} = .055$$

e.

	$\bar{X}_i$	$(\bar{X}_i - \bar{X}_k)$		Q	
High	45.50				
Moderate	56.00	10.50		4.98*	
Low	68.55	23.05	12.55	10.93*	5.95*

$$*p < .05; \quad Q = \frac{\bar{X}_i - \bar{X}_k}{\sqrt{\frac{88.913}{20}}} \quad Q_{cv(.05)} = 3.41$$

f.

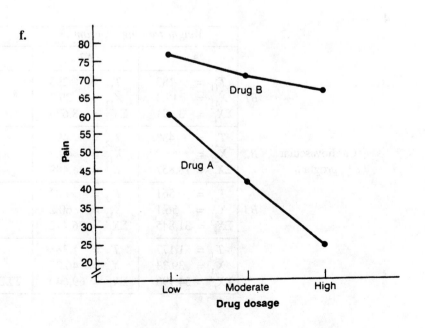

g.

$$SS_J \text{ at column } 1 = \frac{(601)^2}{10} + \frac{(770)^2}{10} - \frac{(1,371)^2}{20}$$
$$= 95,410.100 - 93,982.050 = 1,428.050$$

$$SS_J \text{ at column } 2 = \frac{(417)^2}{10} + \frac{(703)^2}{10} - \frac{(1,120)^2}{20}$$
$$= 66,809.800 - 62,720.000 = 4,089.800$$

$$SS_J \text{ at column } 3 = \frac{(247)^2}{10} + \frac{(663)^2}{10} - \frac{(910)^2}{20}$$
$$= 50,057.800 - 41,405.000 = 8,652.800$$

$$SS_K \text{ at row } 1 = \frac{(601)^2}{10} + \frac{(417)^2}{10} + \frac{(247)^2}{10} - \frac{(1,265)^2}{30}$$
$$= 59,609.900 - 53,340.833 = 6,269.067$$

$$SS_K \text{ at row } 2 = \frac{(770)^2}{10} + \frac{(703)^2}{10} + \frac{(663)^2}{10} - \frac{(2136)^2}{30}$$
$$= 152,667.800 - 152,083.200 = 584.600$$

Summary ANOVA

Source	SS	df	MS	F	F_{cv}
Rows (drug)	12,644.016	1	12,644.016	142.207	4.03
Rows at column 1	1,428.050	1	1,428.050	16.06	6.01
Rows at column 2	4,089.800	1	4,089.800	46.00	6.01
Rows at column 3	8,652.800	1	8,652.800	97.32	6.01
Columns (dosage)	5,327.033	2	2,633.517	29.956	3.18
Columns at row 1	6,269.067	2	3,134.534	35.25	4.33
Columns at row 2	584.600	2	292.300	3.29	4.33
Interaction	1,526.634	2	763.317	8.585	3.18
Within	4,801.300	54	88.913		
Total	24,298.983	59			

4.

		Weight-training program		
		A1	A2	
	B1	$T_{11} = 183$ $\bar{X}_{11} = 18.3$ $\Sigma X_i^2 = 3,491$	$T_{12} = 293$ $\bar{X}_{12} = 29.3$ $\Sigma X_i^2 = 8,679$	$T_{1.} = 476$ $\bar{X}_{1.} = 23.80$ $\Sigma X_i^2 = 12,170$
Cardiovascular program	B2	$T_{21} = 433$ $\bar{X}_{21} = 43.3$ $\Sigma X_i^2 = 18,857$	$T_{22} = 493$ $\bar{X}_{22} = 49.3$ $\Sigma X_i^2 = 24,489$	$T_{2.} = 926$ $\bar{X}_{2.} = 46.30$ $\Sigma X_i^2 = 43,346$
	B3	$T_{31} = 561$ $\bar{X}_{31} = 56.1$ $\Sigma X_i^2 = 31,845$	$T_{32} = 602$ $\bar{X}_{32} = 60.2$ $\Sigma X_i^2 = 36,472$	$T_{3.} = 1,163$ $\bar{X}_{3.} = 58.15$ $\Sigma X_i^2 = 68,317$
		$T_{.1} = 1,177$ $\bar{X}_{.1} = 39.23$ $\Sigma X_i^2 = 54,193$	$T_{.2} = 1,388$ $\bar{X}_{.2} = 46.27$ $\Sigma X_i^2 = 69,640$	$T = 2,565$ $\bar{X} = 42.75$ $\Sigma\Sigma\Sigma X_{ijk}^2 = 123,833$

$$\Sigma T_{j.}^2 = (476)^2 + (926)^2 + (1163)^2 = 2,436,621$$

$$\Sigma T_{.k}^2 = (1177)^2 + (1388)^2 = 3,311,873$$

$$\Sigma\Sigma T_{jk}^2 = (183)^2 + (293)^2 + (433)^2 + (493)^2 + (561)^2 + (602)^2$$
$$= 1,227,001$$

a. $H_{0_1}: \mu_{1.} = \mu_{2.} = \mu_{3.}$

$H_{a_1}: \mu_{1.} \neq \mu_{k.}$ for some i, k

$H_{0_2}: \mu_{.1} = \mu_{.2}$

$H_{a_2}: \mu_{.1} \neq \mu_{.2}$

$H_{0_3}:$ all $(\mu_{jk} - \mu_{j.} - \mu_{.k} + \mu) = 0$

$H_{a_3}:$ all $(\mu_{jk} - \mu_{j.} - \mu_{.k} + \mu) \neq 0$

b. $F_{J_{cv}} = 3.18$

$F_{K_{cv}} = 4.03$

$F_{JK_{cv}} = 3.18$

c. $SS_J = \dfrac{1}{(10)(2)}(2,436,621) - \dfrac{(2,565)^2}{60}$

$\qquad = 121,831.05 - 109,653.75$

$\qquad = 12,177.30$

$SS_K = \dfrac{1}{(10)(3)}(3,311,873) - \dfrac{(2,565)^2}{60}$

$\qquad = 110,395.77 - 109,653.75$

$\qquad = 742.02$

$SS_{JK} = \dfrac{1}{(10)}(1,227,001) - \dfrac{1}{(10)(2)}(2,436,621) - \dfrac{1}{(10)(3)}(3,311,873)$

$\qquad + \dfrac{(2,565)^2}{60}$

$\qquad = 122,700.1 - 121,831.05 - 110,395.77 + 109,653.75$

$\qquad = 127.03$

$SS_W = 123,833 - 122,700.1$

$\qquad = 1132.90$

$SS_T = 123,833 - 109,653.75$

$\qquad = 14,179.25$

Summary ANOVA

Source	SS	df	MS	F	F_{cv}
Rows	12,177.30	2	6,088.65	290.21	3.18
Columns	742.02	1	742.02	35.37	4.03
Interaction	127.03	2	63.52	3.03	3.18
Within	<u>1,132.90</u>	<u>54</u>	20.98		
Total	14,179.25	59			

d. For the row main effect

$$\omega^2 = \frac{12,177.30 - (2)(20.98)}{14,179.25 + 20.98} = .855$$

For the column main effect

$$\omega^2 = \frac{742.02 - (1)(20.98)}{14,179.25 + 20.98} = .051$$

For the interaction

$$\omega^2 = \frac{127.03 - (2)(1)(20.98)}{14,179.25 + 20.98} = .006$$

e.

	$\bar{X}_i$	$(\bar{X}_i - \bar{X}_k)$		Q	
$\bar{X}_1$	23.80				
$\bar{X}_2$	46.30	22.50		21.97*	
$\bar{X}_3$	58.15	34.35	11.85	33.54*	11.57*

$$*p < .05; Q = \frac{\bar{X}_i - \bar{X}_k}{\sqrt{\dfrac{20.98}{20}}} \qquad Q_{cv(.05)} = 3.41$$

f.

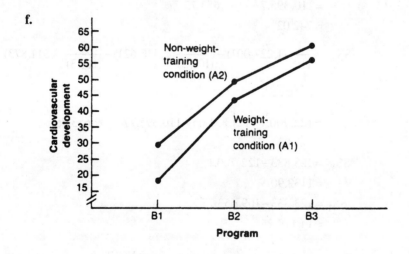

5.

		Academic rank			
		Assistant professor	Associate professor	Full professor	
	Below average	$T_{11} = 15$ $\bar{X}_{11} = 3.75$ $\Sigma X_i^2 = 65$	$T_{12} = 25$ $\bar{X}_{12} = 6.25$ $\Sigma X_i^2 = 165$	$T_{13} = 32$ $\bar{X}_{13} = 8.0$ $\Sigma X_i^2 = 264$	$T_{1.} = 72$ $\bar{X}_{1.} = 6.0$ $\Sigma X_i^2 = 494$
Teaching load	Average	$T_{21} = 14$ $\bar{X}_{21} = 3.50$ $\Sigma X_i^2 = 54$	$T_{22} = 21$ $\bar{X}_{22} = 5.25$ $\Sigma X_i^2 = 121$	$T_{23} = 29$ $\bar{X}_{23} = 7.25$ $\Sigma X_i^2 = 219$	$T_{2.} = 64$ $\bar{X}_{2.} = 5.33$ $\Sigma X_i^2 = 394$
	Above average	$T_{31} = 12$ $\bar{X}_{31} = 3.0$ $\Sigma X_i^2 = 38$	$T_{32} = 12$ $\bar{X}_{32} = 3.0$ $\Sigma X_i^2 = 46$	$T_{33} = 15$ $\bar{X}_{33} = 3.75$ $\Sigma X_i^2 = 65$	$T_{3.} = 39$ $\bar{X}_{3.} = 3.25$ $\Sigma X_i^2 = 149$
		$T_{.1} = 41$ $\bar{X}_{.1} = 3.42$ $\Sigma X_i^2 = 157$	$T_{.2} = 58$ $\bar{X}_{.2} = 4.83$ $\Sigma X_i^2 = 332$	$T_{.3} = 76$ $\bar{X}_{.3} = 6.33$ $\Sigma X_i^2 = 548$	$T = 175$ $\bar{X} = 4.86$ $\Sigma\Sigma\Sigma X_{ijk}^2 = 1037$

a. $H_{0_1}: \mu_{1.} = \mu_{2.} = \mu_{3.}$

$H_{a_1}: \mu_i \neq \mu_k$ for some i, k

$H_{0_2}: \mu_{.1} = \mu_{.2} = \mu_{.3}$

$H_{a_2}: \mu_i \neq \mu_k$ for some i, k

$H_{0_3}:$ all $(\mu_{jk} - \mu_{j.} - \mu_{.k} + \mu) = 0$

$H_{a_3}:$ all $(\mu_{jk} - \mu_{j.} - \mu_{.k} + \mu) = 0$

b. $F_{J_{cv}} = 3.35$

$F_{K_{cv}} = 3.35$

$F_{JK_{cv}} = 2.72$

c. $\Sigma T_{j.}^2 = (72)^2 + (64)^2 + (39)^2 = 10{,}801$

$\Sigma T_{.k}^2 = (41)^2 + (58)^2 + (76)^2 = 10{,}821$

$\Sigma\Sigma T_{jk}^2 = (15)^2 + (25)^2 + (32)^2 + (14)^2 + (21)^2 + (29)^2$

$\qquad + (12)^2 + (12)^2 + (15)^2 = 3{,}865$

$\text{SS}_J = \frac{1}{nK}\Sigma T_{j.}^2 - \frac{T^2}{N} = \frac{1}{(4)(3)}(10{,}801) - \frac{(175)^2}{36}$

$\qquad = 900.08 - 850.69$

$\qquad = 49.39$

$\text{SS}_K = \frac{1}{nJ}\Sigma T_{.k}^2 - \frac{T^2}{N} = \frac{1}{(4)(3)}(10{,}821) - \frac{(175)^2}{36}$

$\qquad = 901.75 - 850.69$

$\qquad = 51.06$

$$SS_{JK} = \frac{1}{n}\Sigma\Sigma T_{jk}^{\ 2} - \frac{1}{nK}\Sigma T_{j\cdot}^{\ 2} - \frac{1}{nJ}\Sigma T_{\cdot k}^{\ 2} + \frac{T^2}{N}$$

$$= \frac{1}{4}(3865) - \frac{1}{(4)(3)}(10{,}801) - \frac{1}{(4)(3)}(10{,}821) + \frac{(175)^2}{36}$$

$$= 966.25 - 900.08 - 901.75 + 850.69$$

$$= 15.11$$

$$SS_W = \Sigma\Sigma\Sigma X_{ijk}^{\ 2} - \frac{1}{n}\Sigma\Sigma T_{jk}^{\ 2}$$

$$= 1037 - \frac{1}{4}(3865)$$

$$= 1037 - 966.25$$

$$= 70.75$$

$$SS_T = \Sigma\Sigma\Sigma X_{ijk}^{\ 2} - \frac{T^2}{N} = 1037 - \frac{(175)^2}{36} = 186.31$$

Summary ANOVA

Source	SS	df	MS	F	F_{cv}
Rows	49.39	2	24.695	9.43	3.35
Columns	51.06	2	25.530	9.74	3.35
Interaction	15.11	4	3.778	1.44	2.72
Within	70.75	27	2.620		
Total	186.31	35			

d. For the row main effect

$$\omega^2 = \frac{49.39 - (2)(2.62)}{186.31 + 2.62} = .234$$

For the column main effect

$$\omega^2 = \frac{51.06 - (2)(2.62)}{186.31 + 2.62} = .243$$

For the interaction

$$\omega^2 = \frac{15.11 - (2)(2)(2.62)}{186.31 + 2.62} = .025$$

e.		$\bar{X}_i$		$(\bar{X}_i - \bar{X}_k)$			Q	
Assistant		3.42						
Associate		4.83		1.41			3.02	
Full Professor		6.33		2.91	1.50		6.23*	3.21

$$*p < .05;\ Q = \frac{\bar{X}_i - \bar{X}_k}{\sqrt{\dfrac{2.62}{12}}} \qquad Q_{cv(.05)} = 3.51$$

e.

	$\bar{X}_i$	$(\bar{X}_i - \bar{X}_k)$		Q	
Above	3.25				
Average	5.33	2.08		4.45*	
Below	6.00	2.75	0.67	5.89*	1.43

$$*p < .05; Q = \frac{\bar{X}_i - \bar{X}_k}{\sqrt{\dfrac{2.62}{12}}} \qquad Q_{\mathrm{cv}(.05)} = 3.51$$

f.

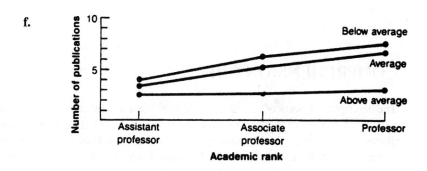

CHAPTER 17

Linear Regression: Estimation and Hypothesis Testing

COMPREHENSION CHECK

The descriptive aspects of __(1)__ regression were discussed in Chapter 6 and included the development and use of the linear regression equation in __(2)__ Y scores from X scores. In that discussion, __(3)__ distributions were defined as distributions of Y scores given a specific X score. For each of these distributions, the mean is equal to the __(4)__ score ($\hat{Y}$) for the given X and the standard deviation is called the standard error of __(5)__ . Under the assumption of __(6)__ , the standard errors are assumed to be equal for all the distributions. Further, under the assumptions of __(7)__ and homoscedasticity, we can make probability statements about the various predicted scores.

Confidence intervals can be developed for the predicted scores using the general formula for the confidence interval:

$$\text{CI} = \hat{Y} \pm (t_{cv})(s_{\hat{Y}})$$

where

$$t_{cv} = \text{the } \underline{\quad(8)\quad} \text{ value of } t \text{ for df} = n - 2$$
$$s_{\hat{Y}} = \text{the standard } \underline{\quad(9)\quad} \text{ of the predicted score}$$

In Chapter 7, we discussed the relationship between correlation and __(10)__ regression. In that discussion, we indicated that if $r = +1$ or -1, all points in the __(11)__ would be on the regression line. However, if $r = 0$, the regression line is a __(12)__ line that intercepts the Y axis at __(13)__ . This implies that, when $r = 0$, the __(14)__ value of Y for all values of X equals $\hat{Y}$.

The statistical test of all the null hypothesis $H_0: \beta = 0$ follows the same __(15)__ and involves the same __(16)__ that have been used throughout the text. The first step is to state the hypotheses, both the null hypothesis and the __(17)__ hypotheses ($H_a: \beta \neq 0$). The test statistic for testing this null hypothesis is defined by the general formula:

$$\text{Test statistic} = \frac{(18) - (19)}{(20)}$$

The sampling distribution for testing this null hypothesis is the t distribution with __(21)__ degrees of freedom. If the null hypothesis is rejected, the conclusion is that __(22)__ of scores on the X variable will enhance the __(23)__ of scores on the Y variable.

Testing the hypothesis $H_0: \beta = 0$ is identical to testing the null hypothesis __(24)__ . By rejecting the latter hypothesis, we would conclude that there is a statistically significant __(25)__ between the X variable and the Y variable. That is, with a statistically __(26)__ relationship between the X and Y variables, knowledge of the X variable __(27)__ the prediction of the Y scores.

Comprehension Check: Answers

1. linear
2. predicting
3. conditional
4. predicted
5. estimation
6. homoscedasticity
7. normality
8. critical
9. error

10. linear
11. scattergram
12. horizontal
13. $\bar{Y}$
14. predicted
15. logic
16. steps
17. alternative
18. statistic

19. parameter
20. standard error of the statistic
21. $n-2$
22. knowledge
23. prediction
24. $H_0: \rho = 0$
25. relationship
26. significant
27. enhances

CHAPTER 17 EXERCISES

1. Given the following regression equation, compute the predicted scores corresponding to the X scores.

$$\hat{Y} = .45(X) + 3.05$$

X	$\hat{Y}$
3	4.40
6	
8	
12	

$$\hat{Y} = .45(3) + 3.05 \ = 4.40$$
$$\hat{Y} = .45(\quad) + =$$
$$\hat{Y} = (\quad) + 3.05 \quad =$$
$$\hat{Y} = (\quad) + =$$

2. An employer requires each secretarial applicant to complete an on-site typing examination. Each applicant is provided with comparable material during a preliminary practice session and is informed of the results. The following data are the results of both the preliminary examination and the actual examination; the scores are the words per minute typed by the fifteen most recent applicants.

Applicant	Practice exam (X)	Actual exam (Y)
1	61	56
2	72	68
3	51	54
4	64	63
5	57	48
6	60	62
7	49	45
8	38	36
9	55	55
10	52	57
11	61	64
12	75	70
13	68	66
14	53	59
15	46	49

$$n = 15 \qquad \Sigma XY = 50{,}139$$
$$\bar{X} = 57.467 \qquad \bar{Y} = 56.800$$
$$\Sigma X = 862 \qquad \Sigma Y = 852$$
$$\Sigma X^2 = 50{,}920 \qquad \Sigma Y^2 = 49{,}622$$
$$SS_X = 1383.733 \qquad SS_Y = 1228.400$$
$$s_X = 9.942 \qquad s_Y = 9.367$$

a. Determine the regression equation for predicting actual examination scores (Y) from practice scores (X).

$$b = \frac{n\Sigma XY - \Sigma X \Sigma Y}{n\Sigma X^2 - (\Sigma X)^2}$$

$$= \frac{(15)(\qquad) - (862)(\qquad)}{15(\qquad) - (\qquad)^2}$$

$$= \underline{\qquad}$$

$$=$$

$$a = \bar{Y} - b(\bar{X})$$

$$= \qquad - (\qquad)(57.467)$$

$$=$$

Therefore, the regression equation is

$$\hat{Y} = \qquad X + $$

b. Predict the actual score for an applicant with a practice score of 68.

$$\hat{Y} = .851X + 7.896$$

$$= \qquad (\qquad) + $$

$$=$$

c. Compute the correlation between the practice scores and the actual exam scores. For these data, test the null hypotheses $H_0: \rho = 0$ using formula 10.7

$$r = \frac{n\Sigma XY - \Sigma X \Sigma Y}{\sqrt{[n\Sigma X^2 - (\Sigma X)^2][n\Sigma Y^2 - (\Sigma Y)^2]}}$$

$$= \frac{(15)(\qquad) - (\qquad)(852)}{\sqrt{[(15)(\qquad) - (862)^2][(15)(49{,}622) - (\qquad)^2]}}$$

$$= \frac{}{\sqrt{(\qquad)(\qquad)}}$$

$$=$$

$$t = r\sqrt{\frac{n-2}{1-r^2}}$$

$$= \sqrt{\frac{15-2}{1-\qquad^2}}$$

$$=$$

d. Compute the standard error of prediction using formula 6.11.

$$s_{Y \cdot X} = s_Y \sqrt{(1 - r^2)} \sqrt{(n-1)/(n-2)}$$

$$= 9.367 \sqrt{(1 - \quad^2)} \sqrt{(15-1)/(15-2)}$$

$$= \quad \sqrt{\quad / \quad}$$

$$=$$

e. If a group of applicants has a practice score of 56, what is the probability that they will have an actual score greater than 62?

$$\hat{Y} = \quad (\quad) +$$

$$=$$

$$z = \frac{62 - }{\quad}$$

$$=$$

Area beyond $z = 1.54$ is $.5000 - \quad =$

Therefore, the probability the group of applicants will have an actual score greater than 62 given a practice score of 56 is \quad .

f. Develop the CI_{95} for the predicted actual exam score $(\hat{Y})$ given a practice score (X) of 56.

$$s_{\hat{Y}} = s_{Y \cdot X} \sqrt{1 + \frac{1}{n} + \frac{(X - \bar{X})^2}{SS_X}}$$

$$= \sqrt{1 + \frac{1}{\quad} + \frac{\quad}{\quad}}$$

$$= \sqrt{1 + \quad + \quad}$$

$$= \sqrt{\quad}$$

$$=$$

$$\text{CI}_{95} = \hat{Y} \pm (1.96)(S_{\hat{Y}})$$

$$= 55.552 \pm (1.96)(4.316)$$

$$= 55.552 \pm$$

$$= (\quad , \quad)$$

g. Test the null hypothesis $H_0: \beta = 0$ using formula 17.5. Compare the results with part c of this exercise.

$$s_b = \frac{s_{Y \cdot X}}{\sqrt{SS_X}}$$

$$= \frac{\quad}{\sqrt{1383.733}}$$

$$=$$

$$t = \frac{b - \beta}{s_b}$$

$$= \frac{-0}{\rule{2cm}{0.4pt}}$$

$$=$$

3. For the data in question 2, suppose a group of applicants has a practice score of 60, compute the predicted score.

$$\hat{Y} = .851X + 7.896$$
$$= \quad (\quad) +$$
$$=$$

a. What is the probability that these applicants will have an actual score greater than 64?

$$z = \frac{-}{\rule{2cm}{0.4pt}}$$

$$=$$

Area beyond $z = 1.21$ is   .

Therefore, the probability these applicants will have an actual score greater than 64 given a practice of 60 is   .

b. What is the probability that these applicants will have an actual score less than 55?

$$z = \frac{-}{\rule{2cm}{0.4pt}}$$

$$=$$

Area beyond $z =$ is $-$ $=$

Therefore, the probability these applicants will have an actual score less than 55 given a practice of 60 is   .

4. For the data in question 2, compute the CI_{90}, $CI_{95,}$ and CI_{99} for the predicted actual exam score given a practice score of 54.

$$\hat{Y} = .851X + 7.896$$
$$= \quad (\quad) +$$
$$=$$

$$CI_{90} = \hat{Y} \pm (1.645)(s_{\hat{y}})$$
$$= 53.850 \pm (\qquad)(4.316)$$
$$= \qquad \pm$$
$$= (\qquad , \qquad)$$

$$CI_{95} = \hat{Y} \pm (1.96)(s_{\hat{y}})$$
$$= 53.850 \pm (\qquad)(\qquad)$$
$$= \qquad \pm$$
$$= (\qquad , \qquad)$$

$$\text{CI}_{99} = \hat{Y} \pm (2.576)(s_{\hat{Y}\cdot X})$$

$$= \qquad \pm (\qquad)(\qquad)$$

$$= \qquad \pm$$

$$= (\qquad , \qquad)$$

5. Consider the data in Question 1 of Chapter 6 in which the researcher investigated the relationship between written scores (*X*) and clinical scores (*Y*) on a professional licensing examination for 15 examinees. The summary data for this example are:

$n = 15$	$\Sigma XY = 96{,}514$
$\bar{X} = 78.267$	$\bar{Y} = 80.200$
$\Sigma X = 1{,}174$	$\Sigma Y = 1{,}203$
$\Sigma X^2 = 93{,}838$	$\Sigma Y^2 = 98{,}927$
$SS_X = 1952.933$	$SS_Y = 2446.400$
$s_X = 11.811$	$s_Y = 13.219$

a. Determine the regression equation for predicting clinical scores (*Y*) from written scores (*X*).

$$b = \frac{(\quad)(\qquad) - (\quad)(\quad)}{(\qquad) - (\quad)^2}$$

$$= \frac{}{\rule{2cm}{0.4pt}}$$

$$=$$

$$a = \qquad -(\quad)(\quad)$$

$$=$$

Therefore, the regression equation is

$$\hat{Y} = \qquad X +$$

b. For an examinee with a written score of 77, predict the clinical score.

$$\hat{Y} = \qquad (\quad) +$$

$$=$$

c. Compute the correlation between the written scores and the clinical scores. For these data, test the null hypothesis $H_0: \rho = 0$ using formula 10.7

$$r = \frac{(\quad)(\qquad) - (\quad)(\quad)}{\sqrt{[(\quad)(\quad) - (\quad)^2][(\quad)(\quad) - (\quad)^2]}}$$

$$= \frac{}{\sqrt{(\qquad)(\qquad)}}$$

$$=$$

$$t = \sqrt{\frac{15 - 2}{1 - \quad^2}}$$

$$=$$

d. Compute the standard error of prediction using formula 6.11

$$s_{Y \cdot X} = \sqrt{(1 - \qquad^2)} \sqrt{(\quad - 1)/(\quad - 2)}$$

$$= \sqrt{\quad /\quad}$$

$$=$$

e. If a group of examinees has a written score of 79, what is the probability that they will have a clinical score greater than 85?

$$\hat{Y} = \qquad (\quad) +$$

$$=$$

$$z = \frac{\quad - \quad}{\quad}$$

$$=$$

Area beyond $z = \qquad$ is $\qquad - \qquad =$

Therefore, the probability the group of examinees will have a clinical score greater than 85 given a written score of 79 is _____ .

f. Develop the CI_{95} for the predicted clinical score ($\hat{Y}$) given a written score (X) of 79.

$$s_{\hat{Y}} = s_{Y \cdot X} \sqrt{1 + \frac{1}{n} + \frac{(X - \bar{X})^2}{SS_X}}$$

$$= \sqrt{1 + \frac{1}{\quad} + \frac{\quad}{\quad}}$$

$$= \sqrt{1 + \quad + \quad}$$

$$= \sqrt{\quad}$$

$$=$$

$$CI_{95} = \qquad \pm (\quad)(\quad)$$

$$= \qquad \pm$$

$$= (\qquad , \qquad)$$

g. Test the null hypothesis $H_0: \beta = 0$ using formula 17.5. Compare the results with part c of this exercise.

$$s_b = \frac{\quad}{\sqrt{\quad}}$$

$$=$$

$$t = \frac{\quad - 0}{\quad}$$

$$=$$

6. For the data in question 5, suppose a group of examinees has a written score of 75, compute the predicted score.

$$\hat{Y} = 1.024X + 0.055$$

$$= \qquad (\quad) +$$

$$=$$

a. What is the probability that this group of examinees will have a clinical score greater than 85?

$$z = \dfrac{\quad - \quad}{\rule{3cm}{0.4pt}}$$

$$=$$

Area beyond $z = \qquad$ is $\qquad - \qquad =$

Therefore, the probability the group of examinees will have a clinical score greater than 85 given a written score of 75 is   .

b. What is the probability that this group of examinees will have a clinical score less than 70?

$$z = \dfrac{\quad - \quad}{\rule{3cm}{0.4pt}}$$

$$=$$

Area beyond $z = \qquad$ is $\qquad - \qquad =$

Therefore, the probability the group of examinees will have a clinical score greater than 85 given a written score of 75 is   .

7. For the data in question 5, compute the CI_{90}, $CI_{95,}$ and CI_{99} for the predicted clinical score given a written score of 82.

$$\hat{Y} = 1.024X + 0.055$$

$$= \qquad (\quad) +$$

$$=$$

$$CI_{90} = \qquad \pm (\qquad)(5.718)$$

$$= \qquad \pm$$

$$=$$

$$CI_{95} = \qquad \pm (\quad)(\quad)$$

$$= \qquad \pm$$

$$=$$

$$CI_{99} = \qquad \pm (\quad)(\quad)$$

$$= \qquad \pm$$

$$=$$

8. An experimental psychologist investigated the relationship between a stimulus (X) and performance (Y) for 12 subjects. The summary data for this exercise are:

$n =$	12	$\Sigma XY =$	2065
$\bar{X} =$	12.750	$\bar{Y} =$	12.917
$\Sigma X =$	153	$\Sigma Y =$	155
$\Sigma X^2 =$	2075	$\Sigma Y^2 =$	2095
$SS_X =$	124.250	$SS_Y =$	92.917
$s_X =$	3.361	$s_Y =$	2.906

a. Determine the regression equation for predicting performance scores (Y) from stimulus scores (X).

b. For a subject with a stimulus score of 14, predict the performance score.

c. Compute the correlation between the stimulus scores and the performance scores. For these data, test the null hypothesis H_0: $\rho = 0$ using formula 10.7.

d. Compute the standard error of prediction using formula 6.11.

e. If a group of subjects has a stimulus score of 10, what is the probability that the performance score will be greater than 13?

f. Develop the CI_{95} for the predicted performance score ($\hat{Y}$) given a stimulus score (X) of 10.

g. Test the null hypothesis H_0: $\beta = 0$ using formula 17.5. Compare the results with part c of this exercise.

Chapter 17 Exercises: Answers

1. $\hat{Y} = .45\,(X) + 3.05$

X	$\hat{Y}$
3	4.40
6	5.75
8	6.65
12	8.45

$\hat{Y} = .45\,(X) + 3.05$

$\hat{Y} = .45\,(3) + 3.05 = 4.40$
$\hat{Y} = .45\,(6) + 3.05 = 5.75$
$\hat{Y} = .45\,(8) + 3.05 = 6.65$
$\hat{Y} = .45\,(12) + 3.05 = 8.45$

2. a. $b = \dfrac{(15)(50{,}139) - (862)(852)}{15\,(50{,}920) - (862)^2}$

$= \dfrac{17{,}661}{20{,}756} = .851$

$a = 56.800 - (.851)(57.467)$

$= 7.896$

Therefore, the regression equation is

$\hat{Y} = .851X + 7.896$

b. $\hat{Y} = .851X + 7.896$

$= .851(68) + 7.896 = 65.764$

c. $r = \dfrac{(15)(50,139) - (862)(852)}{\sqrt{[(15)(50,920) - (862)^2][(15)(49,622) - (852)^2]}}$

$= \dfrac{17,661}{\sqrt{(20,756)(18,426)}} = .903$

$t = .903\sqrt{\dfrac{15-2}{1-.903^2}} = 7.578$

d. $s_{Y \cdot X} = 9.367\sqrt{(1-.903^2)}\sqrt{(15-1)/(15-2)}$

$= 4.024\sqrt{14/13} = 4.176$

e. $\hat{Y} = .851(56) + 7.896 = 55.552$

$z = \dfrac{62 - 55.552}{4.176} = 1.54$

Area beyond $z = 1.54$ is $.5000 - .4382 = .0618$

Therefore, the probability the group of applicants will have an actual score greater than 62 given a practice score of 56 is .0618.

f.

$s_{\hat{Y}} = s_{Y \cdot X}\sqrt{1 + \dfrac{1}{n} + \dfrac{(X - \bar{X})^2}{SS_X}}$

$= 4.176\sqrt{1 + \dfrac{1}{15} + \dfrac{(56 - 57.467)^2}{1383.733}}$

$= 4.176\sqrt{1 + 0.066667 + 0.001555}$

$= 4.176\sqrt{1.068222}$

$= 4.316$

$CI_{95} = 55.552 \pm (1.96)(4.316)$

$= 55.552 \pm 8.459$

$= (47.093, \ 64.011)$

g. $s_b = \dfrac{4.176}{\sqrt{1383.733}} = .1123$

$t = \dfrac{.851 - 0}{.1123} = 7.5805$

3. a. $\hat{Y} = .851(60) + 7.896 = 58.956$

$z = \dfrac{64 - 58.956}{4.176} = 1.21$

Area beyond $z = 1.21$ is $.5000 - .3869 = .1131$

Therefore, the probability the group of applicants will have an actual score greater than 64 given a practice score of 60 is .1131.

b. $z = \dfrac{55 - 58.956}{4.176} = -.95$

Area beyond $z = -.95$ is $.5000 - .3289 = .1711$

Therefore, the probability the group of applicants will have an actual score less than 55 given a practice score of 60 is .1711.

4. $\hat{Y} = .851(54) + 7.896$

$\quad\quad = 53.850$

$\text{CI}_{90} = 53.850 \pm (1.645)(4.316)$

$\quad\quad\quad = 53.850 \pm 7.100$

$\quad\quad\quad = (46.750, 60.950)$

$\text{CI}_{95} = 53.850 \pm (1.96)(4.316)$

$\quad\quad\quad = 53.850 \pm 8.459$

$\quad\quad\quad = (45.391, 62.309)$

$\text{CI}_{99} = 53.850 \pm (2.576)(4.316)$

$\quad\quad\quad = 53.850 \pm 11.118$

$\quad\quad\quad = (42.732, 64.968)$

5. a. $b = \dfrac{(15)(96,154) - (1174)(1203)}{15(93,838) - (1174)^2}$

$\quad\quad = \dfrac{29,988}{29,294} = 1.024$

$a = 80.200 - (1.024)(78.267)$

$\quad = 0.055$

Therefore, the regression equation is

$\hat{Y} = 1.024X + 0.055$

b. $\hat{Y} = 1.024(77) + 0.055$

$\quad\quad = 78.903$

c. $r = \dfrac{(15)(96,154) - (1174)(1203)}{\sqrt{[(15)(93,838) - (1174)^2][(15)(98,927) - (1203)^2]}}$

$\quad = \dfrac{29,988}{\sqrt{(29,294)(36,696)}} = .915$

$\quad\quad t = .915\sqrt{\dfrac{15-2}{1-.915^2}} = 8.177$

d. $s_{Y \cdot X} = 13.219\sqrt{(1-.915^2)}\sqrt{(15-1)/(15-2)}$

$\quad\quad\quad = 5.333\sqrt{14/13} = 5.535$

e. $\hat{Y} = 1.024(79) + 0.055$

$\quad\quad = 80.951$

$\quad\quad z = \dfrac{85 - 80.951}{5.535}$

$\quad\quad = .73$

Area beyond $z = .73$ is $.5000 - .2676 = .2327$

Therefore, the probability the group of examinees will have a clinical score greater than 85 given a written score of 79 is .2327.

f.
$$s_{\hat{Y}} = s_{Y \cdot X}\sqrt{1 + \frac{1}{n} + \frac{(X - \bar{X})^2}{SS_X}}$$

$$= 5.535\sqrt{1 + \frac{1}{15} + \frac{(79 - 78.267)^2}{1952.933}}$$

$$= 5.535\sqrt{1 + 0.066667 + 0.000275}$$

$$= 5.535\sqrt{1.066942}$$

$$= 5.718$$

$$CI_{95} = 80.951 \pm (1.96)(5.718)$$

$$= 80.951 \pm 11.207$$

$$= (69.744, \ 92.158)$$

g.
$$s_b = \frac{5.535}{\sqrt{1952.933}} = .1252$$

$$t = \frac{1.024 - 0}{.1252} = 8.1759$$

6. a. $\hat{Y} = 1.024(75) + 0.055$

$$= 76.855$$

$$z = \frac{85 - 76.855}{5.535} = 1.47$$

Area beyond $z = 1.47$ is $.5000 - .4292 = .0708$

Therefore, the probability the group of examinees will have a clinical score greater than 85 given a written score of 75 is .0708.

b.
$$z = \frac{70 - 76.855}{5.535} = -1.24$$

Area beyond $z = -1.24$ is $.5000 - .3925 = .1075$

Therefore, the probability the group of examinees will have a clinical score less than 70 given a written score of 75 is .1075.

7. $\hat{Y} = 1.024(82) + 0.055$

$$= 84.023$$

$$CI_{90} = 84.023 \pm (1.645)(5.718)$$

$$= 84.023 \pm 9.406$$

$$= (74.617, 93.429)$$

$$CI_{95} = 84.023 \pm (1.96)(5.718)$$

$$= 84.023 \pm 11.207$$

$$= (72.816, 95.230)$$

$$CI_{99} = 84.023 \pm (2.576)(5.718)$$

$$= 84.023 \pm 14.730$$

$$= (69.293, 98.753)$$

8. a. $b = \dfrac{(12)(2065) - (153)(155)}{12(2075) - (153)^2}$

$= \dfrac{1065}{1491} = .714$

$a = 12.971 - (.714)(12.750)$

$= 3.813$

Therefore, the regression equation is

$\hat{Y} = .714X + 3.813$

b. $\hat{Y} = .714(14) + 3.813$

$= 13.809$

c. $r = \dfrac{(12)(2065) - (153)(155)}{\sqrt{[(12)(2075) - (153)^2][(12)(2095) - (155)^2]}}$

$= \dfrac{1065}{\sqrt{(1491)(1115)}} = .826$

$t = .826\sqrt{\dfrac{12 - 2}{1 - .826^2}} = 4.634$

d. $s_{Y \cdot X} = 2.906\sqrt{(1 - .826^2)}\sqrt{(12 - 1)/(12 - 2)}$

$= 1.638\sqrt{11/10} = 1.718$

e. $\hat{Y} = .714(10) + 3.813$

$= 10.953$

$z = \dfrac{13 - 10.953}{1.718} = 1.19$

Area beyond $z = 1.19$ is $.5000 - .3830 = .1170$

Therefore, the probability the subject will have a performance score greater than 13 given a stimulus score of 10 is .1170.

f. $s_{\hat{Y}} = 1.718\sqrt{1 + \dfrac{1}{12} + \dfrac{(10 - 12.750)^2}{124.250}}$

$= 1.718\sqrt{1 + 0.083333 + 0.060865}$

$= 1.718\sqrt{1.1442}$

$= 1.838$

$CI_{95} = 10.953 \pm (1.96)(1.838)$

$= 10.953 \pm 3.602$

$= (7.351, \ 14.555)$

g. $s_b = \dfrac{1.718}{\sqrt{124.250}} = .1542$

$t = \dfrac{.714 - 0}{.1542} = 4.630$

CHAPTER 18
Multiple Linear Regression

COMPREHENSION CHECK

The concepts of bivariate linear regression (the case where there is a single __(1)__ variable and criterion variable) can be logically extended to multiple linear regression (the case with __(2)__ predictor variables). Geometrically, the bivariate regression equation is a __(3)__ line fit to a scattergram of points using the __(4)__ criterion, that is, $\Sigma(Y - \hat{Y})^2$ is a minimum. For multiple regression with k predictor variables, the multiple linear regression __(5)__ describes a __(6)__ solid that is to fit to a mass of points in $(k + 1)$ dimensional space. Again, the least squares criterion is used in this process. If only the relationship between Y and a set of X variables is of interest, multiple __(7)__ analysis is the appropriate procedure.

The __(8)__ score form of the multiple regression equation is

$$\hat{Y} = b_1 X_1 + b_2 X_2 + \ldots + b_k X_k + a$$

It is possible to develop the multiple regression equation in __(9)__ score form, that is,

$$z_{y'} = \beta_1 z_1 + \beta_2 z_2 + \ldots \beta_k z_k$$

In standard score form, the measurement scale of the hyperplane changes to a __(10)__ scale with the __(11)__ at the coordinate point $(0, 0, \ldots, 0)$. The regression coefficient in standard score form is called a __(12)__ (β) coefficient; in raw score form, the coefficients are b coefficients. The relationship between the __(13)__ score and raw score coefficients is as follows:

$$b_i = \beta_i (s_Y / s_i)$$

The regression __(14)__ in multiple linear regression is the point where the hyperplane __(15)__ the Y axis when $X_1 = X_2 = \ldots = X_K = 0$.

There are four steps for a complete multiple regression analysis. The first step is to __(16)__ the regression model, which involves computing the regression constant and regression coefficients. A second step is to calculate the __(17)__ correlation coefficient (R) and the __(18)__ of shared variance, that is, the coefficient of multiple determination (R^2). Third, the multiple __(19)__ is tested for statistical significance using the null hypothesis that, in the population, the multiple correlation coefficient equals __(20)__ . The fourth step is that of determining the relative importance of the individual __(21)__ variables.

One practical problem in multiple regression analysis is the __(22)__ of a set of predictor variables that are maximally effective in __(23)__ the criterion variable. One rule of thumb is to search for predictors that are __(24)__ with the criterion variable, but uncorrelated with __(25)__ . Oftentimes, researchers follow the practice of using a large number of predictor variables just to __(26)__ the multiple R. However, it is difficult to find a large number of predictor variables that are highly correlated with the __(27)__ variable and uncorrelated with each other.

Thus, in practice, using more than 5 or 6 __(28)__ variables rarely produces a larger multiple correlation coefficient. A predictor variable that *increases* the R^2 even though it has a low zero-order correlation with the criterion and high correlations with other predictors is a __(29)__ variable.

Variants of the Pearson correlation can be very useful for examining relationships among multiple predictors and a criterion variable. The correlation between two variables with the influence of a __(30)__ variable removed from both variables is called a __(31)__ correlation; the correlation between two variables with the influence of a third variable removed from only one variable is called a __(32)__ correlation.

Several different methods exist for selecting variables in a multiple regression equation. One method is the __(33)__ solution, in which all variables are initially included in the equation and certain variables are removed from the equation if they do not __(34)__ significantly. Two other approaches to variable selection are the forward solution and the __(35)__ solution. In the __(36)__ solution, variables are added one at a time, if they contribute significantly. In the stepwise solution, variables are also added one at a time, but a variable may be __(37)__ if it is not contributing at later stages in the analysis.

There is a mathematical relationship between multiple regression analysis and __(38)__ . In multiple regression analysis, the predictor variables are usually __(39)__ while the independent variables in ANOVA are __(40)__ . For both models the dependent/criterion variable is __(41)__ . To see the similarities, predictor variables can be created to represent the __(42)__ of the independent variable in ANOVA. In the multiple regression analysis using these predictor variables, $(R^2)(SS_T) =$ __(43)__ in ANOVA and $(1 - R^2)(SS_T) =$ __(44)__ in ANOVA. Thus, the calculated __(45)__ for testing the null hypothesis in multiple regression is exactly the same as the calculated F ratio for testing the __(46)__ in ANOVA.

Comprehension Check: Answers

1. predictor
2. multiple (> 1)
3. straight
4. least squares
5. equation
6. *k*-dimensional
7. correlation
8. raw
9. standard
10. standard
11. origin
12. beta
13. standard
14. intercept
15. intersects (crosses)
16. determine (estimate)

17. multiple
18. proportion
19. correlation
20. zero
21. predictor (*X*)
22. selection
23. predicting
24. correlated
25. other predictors
26. increase
27. criterion
28. predictor (*X*)
29. suppressor
30. third
31. partial
32. part

33. backward
34. contribute
35. stepwise
36. forward
37. removed
38. ANOVA
39. continuous
40. categorical
41. continuous
42. levels
43. SS_B
44. SS_W
45. *F* ratio
46. null hypothesis

CHAPTER 18 EXERCISES

1. A teacher wishes to check the relationship between performance on two prior tests and the final exam scores, as the criterion. Scores for her class follow.

ID	Final (Y)	Test 1 (X_1)	Test 2 (X_2)
1	75	77	66
2	78	82	78
3	88	97	92
4	83	68	79
5	65	86	88
6	72	81	77
7	92	75	84
8	89	72	84
9	88	92	90
10	81	73	77
11	79	58	72
12	100	88	98
13	75	79	75
14	92	87	84
15	86	78	82
16	91	81	83

$$\Sigma Y = 1{,}334.0 \qquad \Sigma X_1 = 1{,}274.0 \qquad \Sigma X_2 = 1{,}309.0$$
$$\bar{Y} = 83.375 \qquad \bar{X}_1 = 79.625 \qquad \bar{X}_2 = 81.8125$$
$$\Sigma Y^2 = 112{,}448 \qquad \Sigma X_1^2 = 102{,}808 \qquad \Sigma X_2^2 = 108{,}041$$
$$\Sigma X_1 Y = 106{,}480 \qquad \Sigma X_2 Y = 109{,}758 \qquad \Sigma X_1 X_2 = 104{,}980$$
$$SS_Y = 1{,}225.750 \qquad SS_1 = 1{,}365.7500 \qquad SS_2 = 948.4375$$
$$s_Y = 9.0397 \qquad s_1 = 9.5420 \qquad s_2 = 7.9517$$
$$r_{Y1} = 0.2011 \qquad r_{Y2} = 0.5751 \qquad r_{12} = 0.6597$$

a. Determine the regression model (standard score and raw score form). The standard score regression coefficients are

$$\beta_1 = \frac{r_{Y1} - (r_{Y2})(r_{12})}{1 - r_{12}^2}$$

$$= \frac{.2011 - (\quad)(\quad)}{1 - .6597^2}$$

$$\beta_2 = \frac{r_{Y2} - (r_{Y1})(r_{12})}{1 - r_{12}^2}$$

$$= \frac{-(\quad)(.6597)}{1 - (\quad)^2}$$

Thus the regression equation in standard score form is

$$z_{\hat{y}} = \quad z_1 + \quad z_2$$

The raw score regression coefficients and the regression constant are

$$b_1 = \beta_1 \left(\frac{s_Y}{s_1} \right)$$

$$= (\quad) \frac{9.0397}{\quad} =$$

$$b_2 = \beta_2 \left(\frac{s_Y}{s_2} \right)$$

$$= (\quad) \frac{}{7.9517} =$$

$$a = \bar{Y} - \sum_{i=1}^{k} b_i(\bar{X}_i)$$

$$a = 83.375 - [(\quad)(\quad) + (.8905)(\quad)]$$

$$=$$

Thus, the regression equation in raw score form is

$$\hat{Y} = \quad X_1 + \quad X_2 +$$

b. Determine R and R^2.

$$R_{Y \cdot 12} = \sqrt{\beta_1 r_{Y1} + \beta_2 r_{Y2}}$$

$$= \sqrt{(-.3157)(\quad) + (\quad)(\quad)}$$

$$=$$

$$R^2 =$$

c. Determine whether the multiple R is statistacally significant.

(Test $H_0: R_{pop} = 0$. Use $\alpha = .05$.)

$$F = \frac{R^2/k}{(1 - R^2)/(n - k - 1)}$$

$$= \frac{(\quad)^2/2}{(1 - .6221^2)/(\quad - 2 - 1)} =$$

F_{cv} (for 2, 13, df) =

Therefore, $\qquad H_0: R_{pop} = 0$

d. Determine the relative importance of the predictor variables (Test $H_0: \beta_i = 0$. Use $\alpha = .05$.)

$$s_{Y \cdot 12} = \sqrt{\frac{\Sigma(Y - \bar{Y})^2}{n - 2 - 1}} = \sqrt{\frac{SS_Y(1 - R^2)}{n - 2 - 1}}$$

$$= \sqrt{\frac{(1225.750)(1 - \quad^2)}{16 - 2 - 1}} \qquad =$$

$$s_{b_1} = \sqrt{\frac{s_{Y \cdot 12}^2}{SS_{X_1}(1 - r_{12}^2)}} \qquad =$$

$$= \sqrt{\frac{^2}{(1365.7500)(1 - \quad^2)}} \qquad =$$

$$s_{b_2} = \sqrt{\frac{s_{Y \cdot 12}^2}{SS_{X_2}(1 - r_{12}^2)}}$$

$$= \sqrt{\frac{7.6026^2}{(\quad)(1 - \quad^2)}} \qquad =$$

$$t = \frac{b_i}{s_{b_i}}$$

For the first predictor variable

$$t = \frac{}{} =$$

For the second predictor variable

$$t = \frac{}{} =$$

t_{cv} (for 13 df) =

Therefore, $H_0: \beta_i = 0$ for the   predictor
but not for the   .

e. Determine partial and part correlation coefficients:

$$r_{Y1 \cdot 2} \quad r_{Y2 \cdot 1} \quad \text{and} \quad r_{Y(1 \cdot 2)} \quad r_{Y(2 \cdot 1)}$$

For the partial correlations:

$$r_{Y1 \cdot 2} = \frac{r_{Y1} - (r_{Y2})(r_{12})}{\sqrt{(1 - r_{Y2}^2)(1 - r_{12}^2)}}$$

$$= \frac{-(\quad)(.6597)}{\sqrt{(1 - .5751^2)(1 - \quad^2)}} =$$

$$r_{Y2 \cdot 1} = \frac{r_{Y2} - (r_{Y1})(r_{12})}{\sqrt{(1 - r_{Y1}^2)(1 - r_{12}^2)}}$$

$$= \frac{.5751 - (\quad)(\quad)}{\sqrt{(1 - \quad^2)(1 - \quad^2)}} =$$

For the part correlations:

$$r_{Y(1 \cdot 2)} = \frac{r_{Y1} - (r_{Y2})(r_{12})}{\sqrt{(1 - r_{12}^2)}}$$

$$= \frac{.2011 - (\quad)(\quad)}{\sqrt{1 - \quad^2}} =$$

$$r_{Y(2 \cdot 1)} = \frac{r_{Y2} - (r_{Y1})(r_{12})}{\sqrt{(1 - r_{12}^2)}}$$

$$= \frac{-(\quad)(.6597)}{\sqrt{1 - \quad^2}} =$$

2. An exercise physiologist is studying the relationships among age and weight, as predictors, and oxygen intake as the criterion variable. The researcher measures these variables for a randomly selected sample of 16 males. The data follow.

ID	Age	Weight	Oxygen intake
	(X_1)	(X_2)	(Y)
1	43	89.5	44.6
2	33	80.3	52.5
3	38	81.8	60.0
4	48	91.6	46.7
5	43	85.8	54.2
6	38	89.0	49.8
7	33	77.8	59.2
8	48	61.2	47.9
9	51	69.6	40.8
10	51	91.6	39.2
11	54	83.1	51.8

ID	Age (X_1)	Weight (X_2)	Oxygen intake (Y)
12	54	79.3	46.0
13	57	73.3	39.4
14	57	59.1	50.5
15	60	83.8	44.7
16	60	87.2	45.5

$\Sigma X_1 =$ 768.0	$\Sigma X_2 =$ 1,284.0	$\Sigma Y =$ 772.8
$\bar{X}_1 =$ 48.00	$\bar{X}_2 =$ 80.25	$\bar{Y} =$ 48.30
$\Sigma X_1^2 =$ 38,104	$\Sigma X_2^2 =$ 104,541.86	$\Sigma Y^2 =$ 37,914.50
$\Sigma X_1 X_2 =$ 61,377.60	$\Sigma X_1 Y =$ 36,545.20	$\Sigma X_2 Y =$ 61,981.78
$SS_1 =$ 1,240.00	$SS_2 =$ 1,500.86	$SS_Y =$ 588.26
$s_1 =$ 9.0921	$s_2 =$ 10.0029	$s_Y =$ 6.2624
$r_{12} =$ −.1865	$r_{Y1} =$ −.6430	$r_{Y2} =$ −.0377

a. Determine the regression model (standard score and raw score form). The standard score regression coefficients are

$$\beta_1 = \frac{(\quad) - (\quad)(\quad)}{1 - (\quad)^2}$$

$$=$$

$$\beta_2 = \frac{(\quad) - (\quad)(\quad)}{1 - (\quad)^2}$$

$$=$$

Thus the regression equation in standard score form is

$$z_{\hat{y}} = (\quad)z_1 + (\quad)z_2$$

The raw score regression coefficients and the regression constant are

$$b_1 = (\quad)\frac{}{}$$

$$=$$

$$b_2 = (\quad)\frac{}{}$$

$$=$$

$$a = \quad - [(\quad)(\quad) + (\quad)(\quad)]$$

$$=$$

Thus, the regression equation in raw score form is

$$\hat{Y} = (\quad)X_1 + (\quad)X_2 +$$

b. Determine R and R^2.

$$R_{Y \cdot 12} = \sqrt{(\quad)(\quad) + (\quad)(\quad)}$$

$$=$$

$$R^2 =$$

c. Determine whether the multiple R is statistically significant.

(Test $H_0: R_{pop} = 0$. Use $\alpha = .05$.)

$$F = \frac{(\quad)^2/2}{(1-\quad^2)/(\quad -2-1)} =$$

F_{cv} (for 2, 13 df) =

Therefore, $H_0; R_{pop} = 0$.

d. Determine the relative importance of the predictor variables. (Test $H_0: \beta_i = 0$. Use $\alpha = .05$.)

$$s_{Y \cdot 12} = \sqrt{\frac{(\quad)(1-\quad^2)}{\quad -2-1}}$$

$$=$$

$$s_{b_1} = \sqrt{\frac{2}{(\quad)(1-(\quad)^2)}}$$

$$=$$

$$s_{b_2} = \sqrt{\frac{2}{(\quad)(1-(\quad)^2)}}$$

For the first predictor variable

$$t = \frac{}{} =$$

For the second predictor variable

$$t = \frac{}{} =$$

t_{cv} (for 13 df) =

Therefore, $H_0: \beta_i = 0$ for the   predictor but not for the

e. Determine partial and part correlation coefficients:

$r_{Y1 \cdot 2}$ $r_{Y2 \cdot 1}$ and $r_{Y(1 \cdot 2)}$ $r_{Y(2 \cdot 1)}$

For the partial correlations:

$$r_{Y1 \cdot 2} = \frac{(\quad)-(\quad)(\quad)}{\sqrt{(1-(\quad)^2)(1-(\quad)^2)}} =$$

$$r_{Y2 \cdot 1} = \frac{(\quad)-(\quad)(\quad)}{\sqrt{(1-(\quad)^2)(1-(\quad)^2)}} =$$

For the part correlations:

$$r_{Y(1 \cdot 2)} = \frac{(\quad)-(\quad)(\quad)}{\sqrt{1-(\quad)^2}} =$$

$$r_{Y(2 \cdot 1)} = \frac{(\quad)-(\quad)(\quad)}{\sqrt{1-(\quad)^2}} =$$

3. A psychological anthropologist wishes to examine the relationships between two content-coded variables (X_1, X_2) believed to represent the achievement motivation of a country and its gross national product (GNP). Data in correlation form for 15 countries follow.

$$r_{12} = .35 \qquad r_{Y1} = .67 \qquad r_{Y2} = .58$$

a. Determine the regression model in standard score form.

b. Determine R and R^2.

c. Determine whether the multiple R is statistically significant.
(Test H_0: $R_{pop} = 0$. Use $\alpha = .05$.)

d. Determine partial and part correlation coefficients:

$$r_{Y1\cdot2} \qquad\qquad r_{Y2\cdot1}$$

$$r_{Y(1\cdot2)} \qquad\qquad r_{Y(2\cdot1)}$$

4. An educational psychologist is interested in studying the effects of goals (X_1) and preexisting ability (X_2) on performance of a school-related reading comprehension task (Y). She obtains measures of existing ability, self-set goals, and subsequent performance from 20 randomly selected students. The data follow.

ID	Goal (X_1)	Ability (X_2)	Performance (Y)
1	17	12	21
2	16	15	14
3	12	11	13
4	14	12	14
5	15	13	13
6	19	15	12
7	17	16	20
8	10	8	11
9	13	10	12
10	12	15	20
11	9	8	10
12	11	10	12
13	10	8	8
14	14	12	14
15	10	11	9
16	20	10	20
17	7	7	5
18	14	13	10
19	18	10	15
20	10	15	15

$\Sigma X_1 = 268.0$	$\Sigma X_2 = 231.0$	$\Sigma Y = 268.0$
$\bar{X}_1 = 13.40$	$\bar{X}_2 = 11.55$	$\bar{Y} = 13.40$
$\Sigma X_1^2 = 3,840.0$	$\Sigma X_2^2 = 2,809.0$	$\Sigma Y^2 = 3,940.0$
$\Sigma X_1 X_2 = 3,187.0$	$\Sigma X_1 Y = 3,785.0$	$\Sigma X_2 Y = 3,221.0$
$SS_1 = 248.80$	$SS_2 = 140.95$	$SS_Y = 348.80$
$s_1 = 3.6187$	$s_2 = 2.7237$	$s_Y = 4.2846$
$r_{12} = .4891$	$r_{Y1} = .6579$	$r_{Y2} = .5665$

a. Determine the regression (raw score and standard score form).

b. Determine R and R^2.

c. Determine whether the multiple R is statistically significant.
(Test $H_0: R_{pop} = 0$. Use $\alpha = .05$.)

d. Determine the relative importance of the predictor variables.
(Test $H_0: \beta_i = 0$. Use $\alpha = .05$.)

e. Determine partial and part correlation coefficients:

$$r_{Y1\cdot2} \qquad r_{Y2\cdot1}$$
$$r_{Y(1\cdot2)} \qquad r_{Y(2\cdot1)}$$

5. A clinical psychologist is studying the relationship between self-reports of pain in response to a noxious stimulus (Y), as a criterion, and hypnosis level (X_1) and susceptibility to suggestion (X_2). A randomly selected sample of college students participated in the study; their data follow.

ID	Pain (Y)	Hypnosis (X_1)	Susceptibility (X_2)
1	29	8	4
2	22	5	3
3	37	9	5
4	33	4	2
5	41	8	4
6	32	6	3
7	42	9	5
8	28	6	2
9	18	3	1
10	38	7	3
11	22	4	4
12	30	7	5
13	38	9	4
14	34	5	3
15	27	4	2
16	28	7	4

$$\begin{aligned}
\Sigma Y &= 499.0 & \Sigma X_1 &= 101.0 & \Sigma X_2 &= 54.0 \\
\bar{Y} &= 31.1875 & \bar{X}_1 &= 6.3125 & \bar{X}_2 &= 3.3750 \\
\Sigma Y^2 &= 16{,}301.0 & \Sigma X_1^2 &= 697.0 & \Sigma X_2^2 &= 204.0 \\
\Sigma X_1 Y &= 3{,}307.0 & \Sigma X_2 Y &= 1{,}749.0 & \Sigma X_1 X_2 &= 369.0 \\
SS_Y &= 738.4375 & SS_1 &= 59.4375 & SS_2 &= 21.7500 \\
s_Y &= 7.0163 & s_1 &= 1.9906 & s_2 &= 1.2042 \\
r_{Y1} &= .7497 & r_{Y2} &= .5119 & r_{12} &= .7822
\end{aligned}$$

a. Determine the regression model (raw score and standard score form).

b. Determine R and R^2.

c. Determine whether the multiple R is statistically significant.
(Test $H_0: R_{pop} = 0$. Use $\alpha = .05$.)

d. Determine the relative importance of the predictor variables.
Test ($H_0: \beta_i = 0$. Use $\alpha = .05$.)

e. Determinal partial and part correlation coefficients:

$$r_{Y1\cdot2} \qquad r_{Y2\cdot1}$$
$$r_{Y(1\cdot2)} \qquad r_{Y(2\cdot1)}$$

Chapter 18 Exercises: Answers

1. a. The standard score regression coefficients are

$$\beta_1 = \frac{.2011 - (.5751)(.6597)}{1 - .6597^2} = -.3157$$

$$\beta_2 = \frac{.5751 - (.2011)(.6597)}{1 - .6597^2} = .7833$$

Thus the regression equation in standard score form is

$$z_{\hat{y}} = -.3157z_1 + .7833z_2$$

The raw score regression coefficients and the regression constant are

$$b_1 = (-.3157)\frac{9.0397}{9.5420} = -.2991$$

$$b_2 = (.7833)\frac{9.0397}{7.9517} = .8905$$

$$a = 83.375 - [(-.2991)(79.625) + (.8905)(81.8125)]$$
$$= 34.3368$$

Thus, the regression equation in raw score form is

$$\hat{Y} = -.2991X_1 + .8905X_2 + 34.3368$$

b. $R_{Y \cdot 12} = \sqrt{(-.3157)(.2011) + (.7833)(.5751)}$

$$= 0.6221$$

$$R^2 = .3870$$

c. $F = \dfrac{(.6221)^2/2}{(1 - .6221^2)/(16 - 2 - 1)} = 4.1037$

F_{cv} (for 2, 13 df) = 3.81

Therefore, reject H_0 $R_{pop} = 0$

d. $s_{Y \cdot 12} = \sqrt{\dfrac{(1225.750)(1 - .6221^2)}{16 - 2 - 1}} = 7.6026$

$$s_{b_1} = \sqrt{\frac{7.6026^2}{(1365.7500)(1 - .6597^2)}} = .2737$$

$$s_{b_2} = \sqrt{\frac{7.6026^2}{(948.4375)(1 - .6597^2)}} = .3285$$

For the first predictor variable

$$t = \frac{-.2991}{.2737} = -1.0928$$

For the second predictor variable

$$t = \frac{.8905}{.3285} = 2.7108$$

t_{cv} (for 13 df) = 2.160

Therefore, reject H_0: $\beta_i = 0$ for the second predictor but not for the first. The conclusion is that the first predictor variable (X_1) does not contribute to the regression when used in combination with the second predictor variable (X_2).

e. Partial correlations:

$$r_{Y1\cdot2} = \frac{.2011 - (.5751)(.6597)}{\sqrt{(1-.5751^2)(1-.6597^2)}} = -.2900$$

$$r_{Y2\cdot1} = \frac{.5751 - (.2011)(.6597)}{\sqrt{(1-.2011^2)(1-.6597^2)}} = .6009$$

Part correlations:

$$r_{Y(1\cdot2)} = \frac{.2011 - (.5751)(.6597)}{\sqrt{1-.6597^2}} = -.2372$$

$$r_{Y(2\cdot1)} = \frac{.5751 - (.2011)(.6597)}{\sqrt{1-.6597^2}} = .5887$$

2. a. The standard score regression coefficients are

$$\beta_1 = \frac{(-.6430) - (-.0377)(-.1865)}{1 - (-.1865)^2} = -.6734$$

$$\beta_2 = \frac{(-.0377) - (-.6430)(-.1865)}{1 - (-.1865)^2} = -.1633$$

Thus the regression equation in standard score form is

$$z_{\hat{y}} = (-.6734)z_1 + (-.1633)z_2$$

The raw score regression coefficients and the regression constant are

$$b_1 = (-.6734)\frac{6.2624}{9.0921} = -.4638$$

$$b_2 = (-.1633)\frac{6.2624}{10.0029} = -.1022$$

$$a = 48.30 - [(-.4638)(48.00) + (-.1022)(80.25)]$$
$$= 78.764$$

Thus, the regression equation in raw score form is

$$\hat{Y} = (-.4638)X_1 + (-.1022)X_2 + 78.764$$

b. $R_{Y \cdot 12} = \sqrt{(-.6734)(-.6430) + (-.1633)(-.0377)}$

$\qquad\qquad = 0.6627$

$\qquad R^2 = .4392$

c. $F = \dfrac{(.6627)^2 / 2}{(1 - .6627^2) / (16 - 2 - 1)} = 5.090$

F_{cv} (for 2, 13 df) = 3.81

Therefore, reject H_0: $R_{pop} = 0$.

d. $s_{Y \cdot 12} = \sqrt{\dfrac{(588.26)(1 - .6227^2)}{16 - 2 - 1}} \qquad = 5.0377$

$\qquad s_{b_1} = \sqrt{\dfrac{5.0377^2}{(1240.00)(1 - (-.1865)^2)}} \qquad = .1456$

$\qquad s_{b_2} = \sqrt{\dfrac{5.0377^2}{(1500.86)(1 - (-.1865)^2)}} \qquad = .1324$

For the first predictor variable

$\qquad t = \dfrac{-.4638}{.1456} = -3.1854$

For the second predictor variable

$\qquad t = \dfrac{-.1022}{.1324} = -.7719$

t_{cv} (for 13 df) = 2.160

Therefore, reject H_0: $\beta_i = 0$ for the first predictor but not for the second. The conclusion is that the second predictor variable (X_2) does not contribute to the regression when used in combination with the first predictor variable (X_1).

e. Partial correlations:

$\qquad r_{Y1 \cdot 2} = \dfrac{(-.6430) - (-.0377)(-.1865)}{\sqrt{(1 - (-.0377)^2)(1 - (-.1865)^2)}} = -.6621$

$\qquad r_{Y2 \cdot 1} = \dfrac{(-.0377) - (-.6430)(-.1865)}{\sqrt{(1 - (-.6430)^2)(1 - (-.1865)^2)}} = -.2095$

Part correlations:

$\qquad r_{Y(1 \cdot 2)} = \dfrac{(-.6430) - (-.0377)(-.1865)}{\sqrt{1 - (-.1865)^2}} = -.6616$

$\qquad r_{Y(2 \cdot 1)} = \dfrac{(-.0377) - (-.6430)(-.1865)}{\sqrt{1 - (-.1865)^2}} = -.1604$

3. a. The standard score regression coefficients are

$$\beta_1 = \frac{.67 - (.58)(.35)}{1 - .35^2} = -.5322$$

$$\beta_2 = \frac{.58 - (.67)(.35)}{1 - .35^2} = .3937$$

Thus the regression equation in standard score form is

$$z_{\hat{y}} = .5322z_1 + .3937z_2$$

b. $R_{Y\cdot12} = \sqrt{(.5322)(.67) + (.3937)(.58)}$

$$= .7648$$

$$R^2 = .5849$$

c. $F = \frac{(.7648)^2/2}{(1 - .7648^2)/(15 - 2 - 1)} = 8.455$

F_{cv} (for 2, 12 df) = 3.89

Therefore, reject H_0: $R_{pop} = 0$

d. Partial correlations:

$$r_{Y1\cdot2} = \frac{.67 - (.58)(.35)}{\sqrt{(1 - .58^2)(1 - .35^2)}} = .6120$$

$$r_{Y2\cdot1} = \frac{.58 - (.67)(.35)}{\sqrt{(1 - .67^2)(1 - .35^2)}} = .4968$$

Part correlations:

$$r_{Y(1\cdot2)} = \frac{.67 - (.58)(.35)}{\sqrt{1 - .35^2}} = .4985$$

$$r_{Y(2\cdot1)} = \frac{.58 - (.67)(.35)}{\sqrt{1 - .35^2}} = .3688$$

4. a. The standard score regression coefficients are

$$\beta_1 = \frac{.6579 - (.5665)(.4891)}{1 - .4891^2} = .5005$$

$$\beta_2 = \frac{.5665 - (.6579)(.4891)}{1 - .4891^2} = .3217$$

Thus the regression equation in standard score form is

$$z_{\hat{y}} = .5005z_1 + .3217z_2$$

The raw score regression coefficients and the regression constant are

$$b_1 = (.5005)\frac{4.2846}{3.6187} = .5926$$

$$b_2 = (.3217)\frac{4.2846}{2.7237} = .5061$$

$$a = 13.40 - [(.5926)(13.40) + (.5061)(11.55)]$$

$$= -0.3863$$

Thus, the regression equation in raw score form is

$$\hat{Y} = .5926X_1 + .5061X_2 - 0.3863$$

b. $R_{Y\cdot12} = \sqrt{(.5005)(.6579) + (.3217)(.5665)}$

$$= .7152$$

$$R^2 = .5115$$

c. $F = \dfrac{(.7152)^2/2}{(1-.7152^2)/(20-2-1)} = 8.9002$

F_{cv} (for 2, 17 df) = 3.59

Therefore, reject H_0: $R_{pop} = 0$

d. $s_{Y\cdot12} = \sqrt{\dfrac{(348.80)(1-.7152^2)}{20-2-1}} = 3.1659$

$$s_{b_1} = \sqrt{\dfrac{3.1659^2}{(248.80)(1-.4891^2)}} = .2301$$

$$s_{b_2} = \sqrt{\dfrac{3.1659^2}{(140.95)(1-.4891^2)}} = .3057$$

For the first predictor variable

$$t = \dfrac{.5926}{.2301} = 2.5754$$

For the second predictor variable

$$t = \dfrac{.5061}{.3057} = 1.6555$$

t_{cv} (for 17 df) = 2.110

Therefore, reject H_0: $\beta_i = 0$ for the first predictor but not for the second. The conclusion is that the second predictor variable (X_2) does not contribute to the regression when used in combination with the first predictor variable (X_1).

e. Partial correlations:

$$r_{Y1\cdot2} = \dfrac{.6579 - (.5665)(.4891)}{\sqrt{(1-.5665^2)(1-.4891^2)}} = .5298$$

$$r_{Y2\cdot1} = \dfrac{.5665 - (.6579)(.4891)}{\sqrt{(1-.6579^2)(1-.4891^2)}} = .3725$$

Part correlations:

$$r_{Y(1\cdot2)} = \dfrac{.6579 - (.5665)(.4891)}{\sqrt{(1-.4891^2)}} = .4366$$

$$r_{Y(2\cdot1)} = \dfrac{.5665 - (.6579)(.4891)}{\sqrt{(1-.4891^2)}} = .2805$$

5. a. The standard score regression coefficients are

$$\beta_1 = \frac{.7497 - (.5119)(.7822)}{1 - .7822^2} = .8999$$

$$\beta_2 = \frac{.5119 - (.7497)(.7822)}{1 - .7822^2} = -.1920$$

Thus the regression equation in standard score form is

$$z_{\hat{y}} = (.8999)z_1 + (-.1920)z_2$$

The raw score regression coefficients and the regression constant are

$$b_1 = (.8999)\frac{7.0163}{1.9906} = 3.1719$$

$$b_2 = (-.1920)\frac{7.0163}{1.2042} = -1.1187$$

$$a = 31.1875 - [(3.1719)(6.3125) + (-1.1187)(3.3750)]$$
$$= 14.9405$$

Thus, the regression equation in raw score form is

$$\hat{Y} = 3.1719X_1 + (-1.1187)X_2 + 14.9405$$

b. $\quad R_{Y \cdot 12} = \sqrt{(.8999)(.7497) + (-.1920)(.5119)}$

$$= .7592$$

$$R^2 = .5764$$

c. $\quad F = \dfrac{(.7592)^2/2}{(1 - .7592^2)/(16 - 2 - 1)} = 8.8447$

F_{cv} (for 2, 13 df) = 3.81

Therefore, *reject* $H_0; R_{pop} = 0$

d. $s_{Y \cdot 12} = \sqrt{\dfrac{(738.4375)(1 - .7592^2)}{16 - 2 - 1}} = 4.9052$

$$s_{b_1} = \sqrt{\frac{4.9052^2}{(59.4375)(1 - .7822^2)}} = 1.0212$$

$$s_{b_2} = \sqrt{\frac{4.9052^2}{(21.75)(1 - .7822^2)}} = 1.6882$$

For the first predictor variable

$$t = \frac{3.1719}{1.0212} = 3.1061$$

For the second predictor variable

$$t = \frac{-1.1187}{1.6882} = -.6627$$

t_{cv} (for 13 df) = 2.160

Therefore, reject H_0: $\beta_i = 0$ for the first predictor but not for the second. The conclusion is that the second predictor variable (X_2) does not contribute to the regression when used in combination with the first predictor variable (X_1).

e. Partial correlations:

$$r_{Y1\cdot2} = \frac{.7497 - (.5119)(.7822)}{\sqrt{(1-.5119^2)(1-.7822^2)}} = .6526$$

$$r_{Y2\cdot1} = \frac{.5119 - (.7497)(.7822)}{\sqrt{(1-.7497^2)(1-.7822^2)}} = -.1807$$

Part correlations:

$$r_{Y(1\cdot2)} = \frac{.7497 - (.5119)(.7822)}{\sqrt{(1-.7822^2)}} = .5606$$

$$r_{Y(2\cdot1)} = \frac{.5119 - (.7497)(.7822)}{\sqrt{(1-.7822^2)}} = -.1196$$

CHAPTER 19
Analysis of Covariance

___

COMPREHENSION CHECK

The analysis of covariance (ANCOVA) is used primarily for the ___(1)___ control of an extraneous variable, as opposed to ___(2)___ control, which is achieved through research design. By partitioning out the effects of an extraneous variable, called a ___(3)___ , a researcher can increase the statistical precision of the statistical test of the null hypothesis by ___(4)___ the error variance. A second application of ANCOVA is in the analysis of data from ___(5)___ groups of subjects, when treatments can be assigned at ___(6)___ to the intact groups but it is impossible to assign subjects randomly to the groups. In this application, there are two potential benefits. The first is an adjustment for preexisting ___(7)___ that may exist among the intact groups prior to the research; the second is an increase in ___(8)___ through reducing the error variance. However, the results of this second use of ANCOVA must be interpreted cautiously. If differences between the groups on the covariate are small, ANCOVA serves primarily to ___(9)___ the error variance. If the differences are ___(10)___ , the possibility of an interaction between the treatment and the covariate should be investigated. Such a finding invalidates the analysis.

The linear model for one-way ANCOVA is similar to the model for one-way ANOVA, but contains one additional source of ___(11)___ ; this component reflects the contribution of the covariate in the analysis. The linear model for ANCOVA is

$$Y_{ik} = \underline{\quad(12)\quad} + \underline{\quad(13)\quad} + \text{cov} + e_{ik},$$

where

$$\text{cov} = \underline{\quad(14)\quad} (X_{ik} - \mu_x)$$

The term *cov* illustrates how regression analysis is incorporated into ANCOVA for adjusting the scores on the ___(15)___ variable.

The null and alternative hypotheses for ANCOVA are stated in terms of the differences between ___(16)___ population means rather than the population means used in ANOVA. This adjustment for the covariate is also reflected in the degrees of freedom associated with the ___(17)___ and total sums of squares. The degrees of freedom are ___(18)___ and ___(19)___ , respectively. The F ratio for testing the null hypothesis in ANCOVA is the ratio of the adjusted MS_B and the adjusted MS_W, that is, ___(20)___ .

Before multiple comparisons can be performed following a significant F ratio in ANCOVA, ___(21)___ adjustments must be made. First, the sample means are adjusted using the ___(22)___ regression coefficient, which is calculated using the pooled correlation coefficient and the respective within-groups mean squares (MS_W) from the ___(23)___ on both the dependent variable and the covariate. Second, the within-groups means square (MS_W) is adjusted to take into account the ___(24)___ among means on the covariate. After making these two adjustments, the post hoc procedures are the same as in ANOVA.

There are ___(25)___ major assumptions that underlie the proper use of ANCOVA. Both are concerned with the relationship between the covariate and the dependent variable. The first assumption is that the relationship is __(26)__ ; the second is that the regression lines within each of the groups are __(27)__ . This latter assumption is necessary in order to use the pooled within-groups regression coefficient (b_w) to adjust the sample means. A statistical test of this assumption should be carried out __(28)__ the other analyses. If the test reveals an __(29)__ , ANCOVA is inappropriate and alternative techniques should be employed.

Comprehension Check: Answers

1. statistical	11. variance	21. two
2. experimental	12. μ	22. pooled within-group
3. covariate	13. α_k	23. ANOVAs
4. reducing	14. β_w	24. differences (variation)
5. intact	15. dependent	25. two
6. random	16. adjusted	26. linear
7. differences	17. within	27. parallel
8. precision	18. $(N - K - 1)$	28. before
9. reduce	19. $(N - 1)$	29. interaction
10. large	20. MS'_B / MS'_W	

CHAPTER 19 EXERCISES

1. A school psychologist wishes to compare the effectiveness of three teaching methods in raising the standardized test scores of junior high students. In addition, the psychologist has general ability scores for each student and decides to use these scores as a covariate. In this study, 24 students are selected and randomly assigned to one of two experimental treatments (Groups I and II) or to the control group (Group III). The study started at the beginning of the second semester and continued until the end of the school year. At the end of the school year, a standardized achievement test was administered; the following data were collected (X = covariate and Y = dependent variable).

	Group I		Group II		Group III			
	X	Y	X	Y	X	Y		
	11	21	13	36	17	26		
	13	27	18	37	19	31		
	16	32	12	31	15	30		
	15	29	12	24	12	23		
	12	27	15	36	20	33		
	18	34	12	29	14	29		
	14	28	12	33	15	26		
	12	33	19	34	19	23		
n	8		8		8		24	
$\Sigma X, \Sigma Y$	111	231	113	260	131	221	355	712
$\bar{X}, \bar{Y}$	13.875	28.875	14.125	32.500	16.375	27.625	14.7917	29.6667
$\Sigma X^2, \Sigma Y^2$	1,579	6,793	1,655	8,584	2,201	6,201	5,435	21,578
ΣXY	3,253		3,724		3,650		10,627	
SS_X, SS_Y	38.875	122.875	58.875	134.000	55.875	95.875	183.9583	455.3333
r	.6927		.5798		.4253		.3294	

a. Complete an ANOVA on both the dependent variable (achievement) and the covariate (ability) (see Chapter 14). Use $\alpha = .05$.

Summary ANOVA
for dependent variable (Y = *achievement*)

Source	SS	df	MS	F	F_{cv}
Between		2			3.46
Within	352.7500				
Total		23			

	$\bar{Y}$	s
Group 1	28.875	4.190
Group 2		
Group 3		
Grand Mean	29.667	

Summary ANOVA
for covariate (X = *ability*)

Source	SS	df	MS	F	F_{cv}
Between		2	15.1667		3.46
Within	153.625				
Total					

	$\bar{X}$	s
Group 1	13.875	2.357
Group 2		
Group 3		
Grand Mean	14.7917	

b. Compute the adjusted sums of squares.

$$SS'_T = SS_T(1 - r_T^2)$$
$$= 455.3333(1 - \quad ^2)$$
$$= 455.3333(\quad)$$
$$=$$

$$SS'_W = SS_W(1 - r_W^2)$$

$$r_W \frac{\Sigma[n\Sigma XY - \Sigma X\Sigma Y]}{\sqrt{[\Sigma(n\Sigma X^2 - (\Sigma X)^2)][\Sigma(n\Sigma Y^2 - (\Sigma Y)^2)]}}$$

$$\Sigma[n\Sigma XY - \Sigma X\Sigma Y] = [8(3253) - (111)(\quad)] +$$
$$[8(\quad) - (\quad)(260)] +$$
$$[8(\quad) - (131)(\quad)] +$$
$$= 383 + \quad +$$
$$=$$

$$\Sigma(n\Sigma X^2 - (\Sigma X)^2) = [8(1579) - (\quad)^2] +$$
$$[8(\quad) - (113)^2] +$$
$$[8(\quad) - (\quad)^2] +$$
$$= 311 + \quad +$$
$$=$$

$$\Sigma(n\Sigma Y^2 - (\Sigma Y)^2) = [8(\quad) - (231)^2] +$$
$$[8(8584) - (\quad)^2] +$$
$$[8(\quad) - (\quad)^2] +$$
$$= 983 + \quad +$$
$$=$$

$$r_W = \frac{\overline{}}{\sqrt{(1229)(\quad)}}$$
$$=$$

$$SS_W' = SS_W(1 - r_W^2)$$
$$= 352.7500(1 - \quad^2)$$
$$= \quad (\quad)$$
$$=$$

$$SS_B' = SS_T' - SS_W'$$
$$= \quad - 241.8940$$
$$=$$

c. Conduct the test of the assumption of homogeneity of regression.

$$H_0 : \beta_1 = \beta_2 = \cdots = \beta_k$$

$$SS_{hreg} = \Sigma SS_i(1 - r_i^2)$$
$$= 122.875(1 - \quad^2) + \quad (1 - .5798^2) +$$
$$(1 - \quad^2)$$
$$= 63.9155 + \quad +$$
$$=$$

$$F = \frac{(SS_W' - SS_{hreg})/(K - 1)}{SS_{hreg}/K(n - 2)}$$
$$= \frac{(241.8940 - \quad)/(3 - 1)}{231.4021/3(8 - 2)}$$
$$= 5.2459/$$
$$=$$

$$F_{cv} \text{ (for 2 and 18 df)} =$$

d. Complete the ANCOVA.

Step 1: State the hypotheses.
$$H_0 : \mu_1' = \mu_2' = \mu_3'$$
$$H_a : \mu_i' \neq$$

Step 2: Set the criterion for rejecting H_0.

For $K - 1 = 3 - 1 = 2$ and $N - K - 1 = 24 - 3 - 1 = 20$ degrees of freedom, the critical value of the test statistic (F_{cv}) is

Step 3: Compute the test statistic.

Test of the covariate

$H_0: \rho = 0$

$H_a:$

$$SS_{cov} = SS_T - SS'_T$$
$$= 455.3333 -$$
$$=$$

$$MS_{cov} = SS_{cov} / 1$$

$$F = \frac{MS_{cov}}{MS'_W}$$

$$= \frac{}{12.0947}$$

$$=$$

F_{cv} (for 1 and 20 df) =

Test of the group effect

$H_0: \mu'_1 = \mu'_2 = \mu'_3$

$H_a: \mu'_i \neq \mu'_k$ for some i, k

$$F = \frac{MS'_B}{MS'_W}$$

$$= \frac{/}{}$$

$$=$$

		Summary ANCOVA			
Source	SS	df	MS	F	F_{cv}
Covariate		1	49.4056		4.35
Between	164.0337				3.49
Within		20	12.0947		
Total		23			

e. Compute the adjusted means.

$$b_W = r_w \sqrt{\frac{MS_{W(Y)}}{MS_{W(X)}}}$$

$$= (\quad) \sqrt{\frac{}{153.625}}$$

$$=$$

$$\bar{Y}_k' = \bar{Y}_k - b_W(\bar{X}_k - \bar{X})$$

$$\bar{Y}_k' = \bar{Y}_k - (.8493)(\bar{X}_k - 14.7917)$$

$$\bar{Y}_1' = 28.875 - (\qquad)(13.875 - \qquad) =$$

$$\bar{Y}_2' = \qquad - (.8493)(\qquad - 14.7917) =$$

$$\bar{Y}_3' = \qquad - (\qquad)(\qquad - \qquad) =$$

f. Conduct the Tukey post hoc test on these adjusted means.

$$MS_W'' = MS_W'\left(1 + \frac{SS_{B(X)}}{(k-1)SS_{W(X)}}\right)$$

$$= 12.0947\left(1 + \frac{}{(3-1)153.625}\right)$$

$$= (1 + .0987)$$

$$=$$

$$Q = \frac{\bar{Y}_i' - \bar{Y}_k'}{\sqrt{MS_W''/n}}$$

Tukey post hoc tests

	$\bar{Y}_i'$	$(\bar{Y}_i' - \bar{Y}_j')$	Q
$\bar{Y}_3'$	26.28		
$\bar{Y}_1'$	29.65	3.37	
$\bar{Y}_2'$	33.07		5.265 *

$$\sqrt{MS_W''/n} = \sqrt{\qquad/8} =$$

$$Q_{cv} =$$

* Significant at .05 level.

2. An educational researcher is interested in testing the efficacy of three performance strategies on output rates on a verbal fluency task (Y). This researcher wishes to control statistically for existing creativity levels as measured by scores on the Remote Associates Test (X). The following data are based on random selection and assignment of 24 individuals to the three treatment groups (X = covariate and Y = dependent variable).

	Group					
	I		II		III	
	X	Y	X	Y	X	Y
	7	7	10	12	14	8
	10	11	11	14	12	9
	9	8	14	16	13	14
	11	10	12	13	11	13
	13	13	11	10	15	12
	9	11	9	12	10	10
	8	8	8	11	11	9
	7	10	8	10	9	11

	I		II		III			
n	8		8		8		24	
$\Sigma X, \Sigma Y$	74	78	83	98	95	86	252	262
$\bar{X}, \bar{Y}$	9.250	9.750	10.375	12.250	11.875	10.750	10.5000	10.9167
$\Sigma X^2, \Sigma Y^2$	714	788	891	1,230	1,157	956	2,762	2,974
ΣXY	743		1,040		1,023		2,806	
SS_X, SS_Y	29.500	27.500	29.875	29.500	28.875	31.500	116.000	113.833
r	.7549		.7832		.0580		.4786	

a. Complete an ANOVA on both the dependent variable (fluency) and the covariate (creativity) (see Chapter 14). Use $\alpha = .05$.

Summary ANOVA
for dependent variable (Y = fluency)

Source	SS	df	MS	F	F_{cv}
Between					
Within					
Total					

	$\bar{Y}$	s
Group 1		
Group 2		
Group 3		
Grand Mean		

Summary ANOVA
for covariate (X = creativity)

Source	SS	df	MS	F	F_{cv}
Between					
Within					
Total					

	$\bar{X}$	s
Group 1		
Group 2		
Group 3		
Grand Mean		

b. Compute the adjusted sums of squares.

$$SS_T' = \quad (1- \qquad {}^2)$$
$$= 87.759$$

$$SS_W' = SS_W(1 - r_W^2)$$

$$r_W = \frac{\Sigma(n\Sigma XY - \Sigma X\Sigma Y)}{\sqrt{[\Sigma(n\Sigma X^2 - (\Sigma X)^2)][\Sigma(n\Sigma Y^2 - (\Sigma Y)^2)]}}$$

$$
\begin{aligned}
\Sigma(n\Sigma XY - \Sigma X\Sigma Y) &= [(\quad) - (\quad)(\quad)] \\
&+ [(\quad) - (\quad)(\quad)] \\
&+ [(\quad) - (\quad)(\quad)] \\
&= \quad + \quad + \\
&=
\end{aligned}
$$

$$
\begin{aligned}
\Sigma(n\Sigma X^2 - (\Sigma X)^2) &= [(\quad) - (\quad)^2] \\
&+ [(\quad) - (\quad)^2] \\
&+ [(\quad) - (\quad)^2] \\
&= \quad + \quad + \\
&=
\end{aligned}
$$

$$
\begin{aligned}
\Sigma(n\Sigma Y^2 - (\Sigma Y)^2) &= [(\quad) - (\quad)^2] \\
&+ [(\quad) - (\quad)^2] \\
&+ [(\quad) - (\quad)^2] \\
&= \quad + \quad + \\
&=
\end{aligned}
$$

$$r_w = \frac{}{\sqrt{(\quad)(\quad)}}$$
$$=$$

$$SS_W' = \quad (1- \qquad {}^2)$$
$$=$$

$$SS_B' = \quad - $$
$$=$$

c. Conduct the test of the assumption of homogeneity of regression.

$$H_0: \beta_1 = \beta_2 = \cdots = \beta_k$$

$$SS_{hreg} = \quad (1- \qquad {}^2) + \quad (1- \qquad {}^2)$$
$$+ \quad (1- \qquad {}^2)$$
$$= \quad + \quad + $$
$$=$$

$$F = \frac{(\qquad - \qquad)/(\qquad - \qquad)}{\quad / (\qquad - \qquad)}$$
$$=$$

$$F_{cv} \text{ (for 2 and 18 df)} =$$

d. Complete the ANCOVA.

Step 1: State the hypotheses.

H_0:
H_a:

Step 2: Set the criterion for rejecting H_0.

For $K - 1$ and $N - K - 1$ degrees of freedom, the critical value of the test statistic (F_{cv}) is

Step 3: Compute the test statistic.

Test of the covariate

H_0:
H_a:

$SS_{cov} =$

$=$

$MS_{cov} = SS_{cov}/1$

$F = \underline{\qquad}$

$=$

F_{cv} (for   and   df) =

Test of the group effect

H_0:
H_a:

$$F = \frac{\qquad / \qquad}{\qquad / \qquad}$$

$=$

Summary ANCOVA

Source	SS	df	MS	F	F_{cv}
Covariate					
Between					
Within					
Total					

e. Compute the adjusted means.

$$b_w = (\qquad)\sqrt{\frac{\qquad}{\qquad}}$$

$=$

$\bar{Y}_1' = \qquad - (\qquad)(\qquad - \qquad) =$

$\bar{Y}_2' = \qquad - (\qquad)(\qquad - \qquad) =$

$\bar{Y}_3' = \qquad - (\qquad)(\qquad - \qquad) =$

f. Conduct the Tukey post hoc test on these adjusted means.

$$MS_W'' = \left(1 + \frac{}{(3-1)}\right)$$

$$= (\quad + \quad)$$

$$=$$

Tukey post hoc tests

	$\bar{Y}_i'$	$(\bar{Y}_i' - \bar{Y}_j')$	Q
$\bar{Y}_3'$			
$\bar{Y}_1'$			
$\bar{Y}_2'$			

$$\sqrt{MS_W''/n} = \sqrt{\quad / \quad} =$$

$$Q_{cv} =$$

* Significant at .05 level.

3. A biomechanical engineer is studying the effects of three muscle loading techniques on lactose levels in the blood. In designing the investigation, the researcher randomly selects 27 subjects and randomly assigns them to three different treatment groups. The researcher controls for the general physical fitness of the subjects by using the results of an extensive physical examination given before the study began. In the following data, X = fitness level and Y = lactose level.

	Group							
	I		II		III			
	X	Y	X	Y	X	Y	X	Y
	13	7	12	30	13	15		
	12	6	16	35	16	24		
	11	9	14	32	18	25		
	15	15	13	38	19	19		
	13	11	15	40	12	31		
	16	10	16	28	16	29		
	13	12	12	31	15	28		
	11	12	15	29	16	22		
	16	12	13	27	14	21		
n	9		9		9		27	
$\Sigma X, \Sigma Y$	120	94	126	290	139	214	385	598
$\bar{X}, \bar{Y}$	13.333	10.444	14.000	32.222	15.444	23.778	14.2593	22.1481
$\Sigma X^2, \Sigma Y^2$	1,630	1,044	1,784	9,508	2,187	5,298	5,601	15,850
ΣXY	1,270		4,068		3,292		8,630	
SS_X, SS_Y	30.000	62.222	20.000	163.556	40.222	209.556	111.1852	2,605.4074
r	.3858		.1398		−.1428		.1913	

a. Complete an ANOVA on both the dependent variable (lactose) and the covariate (fitness) (see Chapter 14). Use $\alpha = .05$.

b. Compute the adjusted sums of squares.

c. Conduct the test of the assumption of homogeneity of regression.

d. Complete the ANCOVA.

e. Compute the adjusted means.

f. Conduct the Tukey post hoc test on these adjusted means.

Chapter 19 Exercises: Answers

1. a.

Summary ANOVA
for dependent variable (Y = achievement)

Source	SS	df	MS	F	F_{cv}
Between	102.5833	2	51.2917	3.05	3.46
Within	352.7500	21	16.7976		
Total	455.3333	23			

	$\bar{Y}$	s
Group 1	28.875	4.190
Group 2	32.500	4.375
Group 3	27.625	3.701
Grand Mean	29.667	

Summary ANOVA
for covariate (X = ability)

Source	SS	df	MS	F	F_{cv}
Between	30.3333	2	15.1667	2.072	3.46
Within	153.6250	21	7.3155		
Total	183.9583	23			

	$\bar{X}$	s
Group 1	13.875	2.357
Group 2	14.125	2.900
Group 3	16.375	2.825
Grand Mean	14.7917	

b. $SS_T' = 455.3333(1 - .3294^2)$

$= 455.3333(.8915)$

$= 405.9277$

$$r_W = \frac{\Sigma[n\Sigma XY - \Sigma X\Sigma Y]}{\sqrt{[\Sigma(n\Sigma X^2 - (\Sigma X)^2)][\Sigma(n\Sigma Y^2 - (\Sigma Y)^2)]}}$$

$\Sigma[n\Sigma XY - \Sigma X\Sigma Y] = [8(3253) - (111)(231)]$

$+ [8(3724) - (113)(260)]$

$+ [8(3650) - (131)(221)]$

$= 383 + 412 + 249$

$= 1044$

$$\Sigma(n\Sigma X^2 - (\Sigma X)^2) = [8(1579) - (111)^2]$$
$$+ [8(1655) - (113)^2]$$
$$+ [8(2201) - (131)^2]$$
$$= 311 + 471 + 447$$
$$= 1229$$

$$\Sigma(n\Sigma Y^2 - (\Sigma Y)^2) = [8(6793) - (231)^2]$$
$$+ [8(8584) - (260)^2]$$
$$+ [8(6201) - (221)^2]$$
$$= 983 + 1072 + 767$$
$$= 2822$$

$$r_w = \frac{1044}{\sqrt{(1229)(2822)}} = .5605$$

$$SS'_W = 352.7500(1 - .5605^2)$$
$$= 352.7500(.6857)$$
$$= 241.8940$$

$$SS'_B = 405.9277 - 241.8940$$
$$- 164.0337$$

c. $H_0: \beta_1 = \beta_2 = \cdots = \beta_k$

$$SS_{hreg} = 122.875(1 - .6927^2) +$$
$$134.000(1 - .5798^2) +$$
$$95.875(1 - .4253^2)$$
$$= 63.9155 + 88.9535 + 78.5331$$
$$= 231.4021$$

$$F = \frac{(241.8940 - 231.4021)/(3-1)}{231.4021/3(8-2)}$$
$$= 5.2459/12.8557$$
$$= 0.4081$$

$$F_{cv} \text{ (for 2 and 18 df)} = 3.55$$

d. Step 1: State the hypotheses.

$$H_0: \mu'_1 = \mu'_2 = \mu'_3$$

$$H_a: \mu'_i \neq \mu'_k \text{ for some } i, k$$

Step 2: Set the criterion for rejecting H_0.

For $K - 1 = 3 - 1 = 2$ and $N - K - 1 = 24 - 3 - 1 = 20$ degrees of freedom, the critical value of the test statistic (F_{cv}) is 3.49.

Step 3: Compute the test statistic.

Test of the covariate

$H_0: \rho = 0$

$H_a: \rho \neq 0$

$SS_{cov} = 455.3333 - 405.9277$
$= 49.4056$

$MS_{cov} = SS_{cov}/1$

$F = \dfrac{49.4056}{12.0947} = 4.0849$

F_{cv} (for 1 and 20 df) = 4.35

Test of the group effect

$H_0: \mu_1' = \mu_2' = \mu_3'$

$H_a: \mu_i' \neq \mu_k'$ for some i, k

$F = \dfrac{164.0337/2}{241.8940/(24-2-2)} = 6.7812$

Summary ANCOVA

Source	SS	df	MS	F	F_{cv}
Covariate	49.4056	1	49.4056	4.0849	4.35
Between	164.0337	2	82.0169	6.7812	3.49
Within	241.8940	20	12.0947		
Total	455.3333	23			

e. $b_W = (.5605)\sqrt{\dfrac{352.750}{153.625}} = .8493$

$\bar{Y}_1' = 28.875 - (.8493)(13.875 - 14.7917) = 29.6536$

$\bar{Y}_2' = 32.500 - (.8493)(14.125 - 14.7917) = 33.0662$

$\bar{Y}_3' = 27.625 - (.8493)(16.375 - 14.7917) = 26.2803$

f. $MS_W'' = 12.0947\left(1 + \dfrac{30.3333}{(3-1)153.625}\right)$

$= 12.0947(1 + .0987) = 13.2884$

Tukey post hoc tests

	$\bar{Y}_i'$	$(\bar{Y}_i' - \bar{Y}_j')$		Q	
$\bar{Y}_3'$	26.28				
$\bar{Y}_1'$	29.65	3.37		2.618	
$\bar{Y}_2'$	33.07	6.79	3.41	5.265 *	2.648

$\sqrt{MS_W'' / n} = \sqrt{13.2884 / 8} = 1.2888$

$Q_{cv} = 3.58$

* Significant at .05 level.

2. a.

Summary ANOVA
for dependent variable (Y = fluency)

Source	SS	df	MS	F	F_{cv}
Between	25.333	2	12.667	3.01	3.46
Within	88.500	21	4.214		
Total	113.833	23			

	$\bar{Y}$	s
Group 1	9.750	1.982
Group 2	12.250	2.053
Group 3	10.750	2.121
Grand Mean	10.917	

Summary ANOVA
for covariate (X = creativity)

Source	SS	df	MS	F	F_{cv}
Between	27.750	2	13.875	3.30	3.46
Within	88.250	21	4.202		
Total	116.000	23			

	$\bar{X}$	s
Group 1	9.250	2.053
Group 2	10.375	2.066
Group 3	11.875	2.031
Grand Mean	10.500	

b.

$SS_T' = 113.833(1 - .4786^2)$
$\quad\quad = 87.759$

$\Sigma(n\Sigma XY - \Sigma X\Sigma Y) = [8(743) - (74)(78)]$
$\quad\quad\quad\quad\quad\quad\quad + [8(1040) - (83)(98)]$
$\quad\quad\quad\quad\quad\quad\quad + [8(1023) - (95)(86)]$
$\quad\quad\quad\quad\quad\quad\quad = 172 + 186 + 14$
$\quad\quad\quad\quad\quad\quad\quad = 372$

$$\Sigma(n\Sigma X^2 - (\Sigma X)^2) = [8(714) - (74)^2]$$
$$+ [8(891) - (83)^2]$$
$$+ [8(1157) - (95)^2]$$
$$= 236 + 239 + 231$$
$$= 706$$

$$\Sigma(n\Sigma Y^2 - (\Sigma Y)^2) = [8(788) - (78)^2]$$
$$+ [8(1230) - (98)^2]$$
$$+ [8(956) - (86)^2]$$
$$= 220 + 236 + 252$$
$$= 708$$

$$r_w = \frac{372}{\sqrt{(706)(708)}} = .5262$$

$$SS_W' = 88.500(1 - .5262^2)$$
$$= 63.999$$

$$SS_B' = 87.759 - 63.999$$
$$= 23.760$$

c. $H_0: \beta_1 = \beta_2 = \cdots = \beta_k$

$$SS_{hreg} = 27.500(1 - .7549^2) +$$
$$29.500(1 - .7832^2) +$$
$$31.500(1 - .0580^2)$$
$$= 11.828 + 11.405 + 31.394$$
$$= 54.627$$

$$F = \frac{(63.999 - 54.627)/(3-1)}{54.627/3(8-2)} = 1.544$$

F_{cv} (for 2 and 18 df) = 3.55

d. Step 1: State the hypotheses.

$H_0: \mu_1' = \mu_2' = \mu_3'$
$H_a: \mu_i' \neq \mu_k'$ for some i, k

Step 2: Set the criterion for rejecting H_0.

For $K - 1 = 3 - 1 = 2$ and $N - K - 1 = 24 - 3 - 1 = 20$ degrees of freedom, the critical value of the test statistic (F_{cv}) is 3.49.

Step 3: Compute the test statistic.

Test of the covariate

$H_0: \rho = 0$
$H_a: \rho \neq 0$

$$SS_{cov} = 113.833 - 87.759$$
$$= 26.074$$

$$MS_{cov} = SS_{cov}/1$$

$$F = \frac{26.074}{3.200}$$
$$= 8.148$$

F_{cv} (for 1 and 20 df) = 4.35

Test of the group effect

$H_0: \mu_1' = \mu_2' = \mu_3'$
$H_a: \mu_i' \neq \mu_k'$ for some i, k

$$F = \frac{23.760 / 2}{63.999 /(24 - 2 - 2)} = 3.712$$

Summary ANCOVA

Source	SS	df	MS	F	F_{cv}
Covariate	26.074	1	26.074	8.148	4.35
Between	23.760	2	11.880	3.712	3.49
Within	63.999	20	3.200		
Total	113.833	23			

e. $b_W = (.5262) \sqrt{\dfrac{4.214}{4.202}} = .5269$

$\bar{Y}_1' = 9.750 - (.5269)(9.250 - 10.500) = 10.409$
$\bar{Y}_2' = 12.250 - (.5269)(10.375 - 10.500) = 12.316$
$\bar{Y}_3' = 10.750 - (.5269)(11.875 - 10.500) = 10.026$

f. $MS_W'' = 3.200 \left(1 + \dfrac{27.750}{(3-1)88.250} \right)$

$\qquad = 3.200(1 + .157) = 3.703$

Tukey post hoc tests

	$\bar{Y}_i'$	$(\bar{Y}_i' - \bar{Y}_j')$		Q	
$\bar{Y}_3'$	10.03				
$\bar{Y}_1'$	10.41	0.38		0.559	
$\bar{Y}_2'$	12.32	2.29	1.91	3.366	2.808

$\sqrt{MS_W'' / n} = \sqrt{3.703 / 8} = 0.6803$

$Q_{cv} = 3.58$

3. a.

Summary ANOVA
for dependent variable (Y = lactose)

Source	SS	df	MS	F	F_{cv}
Between	2170.0741	2	1085.0370	59.82	3.40
Within	435.3333	24	18.1389		
Total	2605.4074	26			

	$\bar{Y}$	s
Group 1	10.444	2.789
Group 2	32.222	4.522
Group 3	23.778	5.118
Grand Mean	22.148	

Summary ANOVA
for covariate (X = fitness)

Source	SS	df	MS	F	F_{cv}
Between	20.9630	2	10.4815	2.79	3.40
Within	90.2222	24	3.7593		
Total	111.1852	26			

	$\bar{X}$	s
Group 1	13.333	1.936
Group 2	14.000	1.581
Group 3	15.444	2.242
Grand Mean	14.259	

b. $SS_T' = 2605.4074(1 - .1913^2)$
$\qquad = 2510.0607$

$$\Sigma(n\Sigma XY - \Sigma X\Sigma Y) = [9(1270) - (120)(94)]$$
$$+ [9(4068) - (126)(290)]$$
$$+ [9(3292) - (139)(214)]$$
$$= 150 + 72 + (-118)$$
$$= 104$$

$$\Sigma(n\Sigma X^2 - (\Sigma X)^2) = [9(1630) - (120)^2]$$
$$+ [9(1784) - (126)^2]$$
$$+ [9(2187) - (139)^2]$$
$$= 270 + 180 + 362$$
$$= 812$$

$$\Sigma(n\Sigma Y^2 - (\Sigma Y)^2) = [9(1044) - (94)^2]$$
$$+ [9(9508) - (290)^2]$$
$$+ [9(5298) - (214)^2]$$
$$= 560 + 1472 + 1886$$
$$= 3918$$

$$r_w = \frac{104}{\sqrt{(812)(3918)}} = .0583$$

$$SS'_W = 435.3333(1 - .0583^2)$$
$$= 433.8537$$

$$SS'_B = 2510.0607 - 433.8537$$
$$= 2076.2070$$

c. $H_0: \beta_1 = \beta_2 = \cdots = \beta_k$

$$SS_{hreg} = 62.2222(1 - .3858^2) +$$
$$163.5556(1 - .1398^2) +$$
$$209.5556(1 - (-.1428)^2)$$
$$= 52.9609 + 160.3591 + 205.2824$$
$$= 418.6024$$

$$F = \frac{(433.8537 - 418.6024)/(3-1)}{418.6024/3(9-2)} = 0.3826$$

F_{cv} (for 2 and 21 df) = 3.07

d. Step 1: State the hypotheses.

$H_0: \mu'_1 = \mu'_2 = \mu'_3$
$H_a: \mu'_i \neq \mu'_k$ for some i, k

Step 2: Set the criterion for rejecting H_0.

For $K - 1 = 3 - 1 = 2$ and $N - K - 1 = 27 - 3 - 1 = 23$ degrees of freedom, the critical value of the test statistic (F_{cv}) is 3.42.

Step 3: Compute the test statistic.

Test of the covariate

$H_0: \rho = 0$
$H_a: \rho \neq 0$

$$SS_{cov} = 2605.4074 - 2510.0607$$
$$= 95.3467$$

$$MS_{cov} = SS_{cov}/1$$

$$F = \frac{95.3467}{18.8632} = 5.055$$

F_{cv} (for 1 and 23 df) = 4.28

Test of the group effect

$H_0: \mu'_1 = \mu'_2 = \mu'_3$
$H_a: \mu'_i \neq \mu'_k$ for some i, k

$$F = \frac{2076.2070/2}{433.8537/(27-2-2)} = 55.033$$

Summary ANCOVA

Source	SS	df	MS	F	F_{cv}
Covariate	95.3467	1	95.3467	5.055	4.28
Between	2076.2070	2	1038.1035	55.033	3.42
Within	433.8537	23	18.8632		
Total	2605.4074	26			

e. $b_W = (.0583)\sqrt{\dfrac{18.1389}{3.7593}} = .1281$

$\bar{Y}_1' = 10.444 - (.1281)(13.333 - 14.2593) = 10.563$

$\bar{Y}_2' = 32.222 - (.1281)(14.000 - 14.2593) = 32.255$

$\bar{Y}_3' = 23.778 - (.1281)(15.444 - 14.2593) = 23.626$

f. $MS_W'' = 18.8632 \left(1 + \dfrac{20.9630}{(3-1)90.2222}\right)$

$= 18.8632(1 + .1162) = 21.055$

Tukey post hoc tests

	$\bar{Y}_i'$	$(\bar{Y}_i' - \bar{Y}_j')$		Q	
$\bar{Y}_1'$	10.563				
$\bar{Y}_3'$	23.626	13.063		8.541*	
$\bar{Y}_2'$	32.255	21.692	8.629	14.177*	5.642*

$\sqrt{MS_W''/n} = \sqrt{21.055/9} = 1.530$

$Q_{cv} = 3.54$

*Significant at .05 level.

CHAPTER 20
Other Correlation Coefficients

COMPREHENSION CHECK

An important consideration in selecting an appropriate correlation coefficient is the __(1)__ of measurement of the variables being correlated. Three types of measurement scales were considered in this chapter. For a __(2)__ scale, we distinguish between a variable with two levels and one with more than two levels. Nominal variables with two levels are called a __(3)__ , with measurement indicating __(4)__ or __(5)__ of a particular characteristic. Ordinal scales consist of __(6)__ values. A special case of the ordinal scale discussed in this chapter is a dichotomous variable that is assumed to have underlying __(7)__ and to be __(8)__ distributed. The __(9)__ and __(10)__ scales are combined in this discussion because they both exhibit __(11)__ degrees of __(12)__ in measurement. For both scales, the __(13)__ between levels of the __(14)__ on any part of the scale reflect __(15)__ in the characteristic being measured. Thus, both scales have what are called __(16)__ . The __(17)__ scale, however, has one additional property, that of a __(18)__ (2 words) point.

The type of correlation coefficient used to determine the relationship between two __(19)__ is dependent on the __(20)__ of __(21)__ variable. The appropriate correlation coefficient to use when both variables are measured at the interval or ratio level is the __(22)__ coefficient. The point-biserial correlation should be used when one variable is measured on an __(23)__ or __(24)__ scale and the other variable is a __(25)__ . The __(26)__ coefficient is appropriate when both variables are nominal dichotimies. Although presented earlier in Chapter 5, recall that __(27)__ (2 words) is appropriate when both variables are measured on ordinal scales, and is calculated by using the __(28)__ scores of the variables. The point-biserial, phi, and Spearman rho are all special cases of the __(29)__ correlation coefficient.

There are also indices of relationship other than the __(30)__ coefficients. These include __(31)__ that can be used instead of the ones discussed above as well as coefficients that are also __(32)__ given the __(33)__ of the two variables being correlated. When both variables are measured on a __(34)__ but are not dichotomous, a __(35)__ table greater than 2 × 2 is needed to display the data. For these data, one appropriate correlation coefficient is the __(36)__ . Another appropriate correlation for this case is Cramer's __(37)__ coefficient. A third coefficient that is appropriate in the case of a contingency table that is larger than 2 × 2 is the __(38)__ coefficient. This correlation can be calculated in two ways: one is called the __(39)__ version and the other the __(40)__ version. The difference between these two versions of lambda depends on whether the researcher is willing to __(41)__ the independent and dependent variables.

The __(42)__ coefficient is the appropriate correlation coefficient when both variables are dichotomous, but have __(43)__ continuity and are normally __(44)__ . When one variable is dichotomous but ordinal and the other variable is measured on at least an interval scale, the appropriate correlation coefficient is the __(45)__ . The rank-biserial correlation coefficient is used when one variable is measured on an __(46)__ scale and the other variable is a __(47)__ .

The use of the above correlations assumes that the relationship between the two variables is __(48)__ . This __(49)__ does not always hold for behavioral science data. When this assumption __(50)__ be met, the use of the above coefficients is not __(51)__ . Should a Pearson product-moment coefficient be applied when there is a __(52)__ trend in the data, the coefficient will __(53)__ the relationship between the two variables.

An index of the __(54)__ between two variables that can have a curvilinear relationship is the __(55)__ coefficient. Eta can only have positive values between __(56)__ and __(57)__ . Like the Pearson product-moment coefficient, the __(58)__ of the eta coefficient is that of the proportion of __(59)__ in the one variable that can be __(60)__ to the variance in the second variable.

Comprehension Check: Answers

1. scale (level)
2. nominal
3. dichotomy
4. presence
5. absence
6. ranked
7. continuity
8. normally
9. interval (ratio)
10. ratio (interval)
11. equivalent (similar)
12. precision
13. differences
14. categories
15. differences
16. equal units
17. ratio
18. known zero
19. variables
20. scale

21. each
22. Pearson
23. interval
24. ratio
25. dichotomy
26. phi
27. Spearman's ρ
28. ranked
29. Pearson
30. Pearson
31. coefficients
32. appropriate
33. measurement scale
34. nominal scale
35. contingency
36. contingency coefficient
37. *V*
38. lambda
39. asymmetric (symmetric)
40. symmetric (asymmetric)

41. specify
42. tetrachoric
43. underlying
44. distributed
45. biserial
46. ordinal
47. dichotomy
48. linear
49. assumption
50. cannot
51. appropriate
52. curvilinear
53. underestimate
54. relationship
55. eta
56. zero
57. one
58. square
59. variance
60. attributed

CHAPTER 20 EXERCISES

1. a. A child psychologist examined the impact of sibling status on the age at which infants begin to walk. The following data were obtained for 16 toddlers, with 1 or 0 indicating the presence or absence of an older child within the home. Compute the point-biserial correlation coefficient and explain the meaning of your answer.

Infant	Older sibling(s)	Walking age (months)
A	1	11.2
B	1	12.4
C	0	15.6
D	0	12.3
E	1	10.8
F	0	16.1
G	1	13.2
H	1	11.8
I	0	14.1
J	0	12.5
K	0	15.3
L	0	13.8

(*continued*)

Infant	Older sibling(s)	Walking age (months)
M	1	14.1
N	0	16.0
O	1	11.4
P	1	12.0

$$\bar{Y}_1 = \frac{11.2 + \cdots + 12.0}{8}$$

$$=$$

$$\bar{Y}_0 = \underline{\hspace{3cm}}$$

$$=$$

$$p = \underline{\hspace{1cm}} \quad ; q =$$

$$\sigma_Y = \sqrt{\frac{\Sigma Y^2 - \frac{(\Sigma Y)^2}{n}}{n}}$$

$$= \sqrt{\frac{2871.5 - \frac{(\quad)^2}{}}{}}$$

$$= \sqrt{\frac{2871.5 - }{}}$$

$$= \sqrt{\frac{}{16}}$$

$$=$$

$$r_{Pb} = \frac{\bar{Y}_1 - \bar{Y}_0}{\sigma_Y}\sqrt{pq}$$

$$= \frac{12.11 - }{}\sqrt{(0.5)(\quad)}$$

$$= (-1.37)(\quad)$$

$$=$$

b. A teacher has developed a new test of achievement, and believes that one question is strongly related to the amount of knowledge students have about the subject. The teacher wants to see if there is a relationship between the total test score and a correct answer to that question (1) rather than the incorrect answer (0). Compute the point-biserial correlation coefficient.

Student	Test score	Question
1	95	1
2	87	1
3	70	0
4	74	1
5	82	1
6	68	0
7	92	0
8	60	1
9	75	1
10	83	1

2. a. A political pollster wishes to provide some insight into an upcoming election. One hundred area residents are asked to indicate whether they voted for the incumbent candidate in the past election, and whether they favor the individual for re-election. Use the following information to compute the phi coefficient and explain the meaning of your answer.

Last election *voted for/will vote for* this election	46
Last election *voted for/will not vote for* this election	14
Last election *did not vote for/will vote for* this election	12
Last election *did not vote for/will not vote for* this election	28

This election

		Will not vote for	Will vote for	
	Voted for	14	46	60
Last election				
	Did not vote for	28	12	40
		42	58	100

$$\phi = \frac{BC - AD}{\sqrt{(A+B)(C+D)(A+C)(B+D)}}$$

$$= \frac{(46)(\quad) - (\quad)(\quad)}{\sqrt{(\quad)(\quad)(\quad)(\quad)}}$$

$$= \frac{-168}{\sqrt{}}$$

$$= \underline{}$$

$$=$$

b. A researcher in consumer products wants to see if there is a relationship between smoking and sex. A sample of 100 adults provided the following data. Compute the phi coefficient and explain the meaning of your answer.

Men, smokers	29
Men, nonsmokers	21
Women, smokers	18
Women, nonsmokers	32

3. a. The fifteen graduates of a dental hygiene program are ranked according to their scores on the clinical and written portions of their state board examination. Compute the Spearman rho correlation coefficient.

Graduate	Clinical rank	Written rank	d	d²
A	4	5	−1	1
B	12	11	1	1
C	8	8		
D	6	3		
E	5	10		
F	1	4		
G	15	13		
H	14	14		
I	11	15		
J	3	1		
K	2	2		
L	7	6		
M	9	7		
N	10	9		
O	13	12		

$$\Sigma d = \qquad \Sigma d^2 =$$

$$\rho = 1 - \frac{6\Sigma d^2}{n(n^2 - 1)}$$

$$= 1 - \frac{6(\quad)}{15[(\quad)^2 - \quad]}$$

$$= 1 - \frac{}{15(224)}$$

$$= 1 -$$

$$=$$

b. In a pet show, the judging of a particular breed of dog is determined by color and body shape. Use the results of the judging to compute rho.

Dog	Color	Body shape
1	4	3
2	8	7
3	1	4
4	5	8
5	2	1
6	6	5
7	3	2
8	7	6

4. a. A high school teacher examined the relationship between reading skill and typing speed. The following speeds were attained by 12 first-year students, with 1 indicating their ability and 0 their lack of ability to read at a given level of proficiency at the beginning of the course. Compute the biserial correlation coefficient.

Student	Reading proficiency	Typing speed (wpm)
A	1	45
B	0	32
C	0	35
D	0	26
E	1	38
F	1	41

(continued)

Student	Reading proficiency	Typing speed (wpm)
G	0	37
H	1	44
I	0	25
J	1	31
K	1	41
L	0	34

$\bar{Y}_1 =$

$\bar{Y}_0 =$

$p =$ ____ $; q =$ ____ $; u =$

$$\sigma_Y = \sqrt{\frac{(\quad)^2}{12}}$$

$$= \sqrt{\frac{}{12}}$$

$$= \sqrt{}$$

$$=$$

$$r_b = \left(\frac{\bar{Y}_1 - \bar{Y}_0}{\sigma_Y}\right)\left(\frac{pq}{u}\right)$$

$$= \left(\frac{}{}\right)\left(\frac{(\quad)(\quad)}{}\right)$$

$$= \left(\frac{8.5}{}\right)\left(\frac{}{}\right)$$

$$= (\quad)(\quad)$$

$$=$$

b. A teacher is interested in the relationship between hours of television watched in the week prior to an examination and whether students passed or failed the examination. Compute the biserial correlation coefficient.

Student	Television hours	Examination
A	6	1
B	14	0
C	9	1
D	20	0
E	22	0
F	17	1
G	13	1
H	4	1
I	11	1
J	19	0
K	8	0
L	16	1

5. a. The MDAC Survey Corporation has been asked to conduct a survey of registered voters to determine their attitude toward the Star Wars program. The following data were collected from 100 registered voters. Compute λ and λ_Y to determine the relationship between party affiliation and voter preference.

	Republican	Independent	Democrat	Total
Yes	26	13	12	51
No	12	14	23	49
	38	27	35	100

$$\lambda = \frac{\sum\limits_{j=1}^{J} N_{Mj} + \sum\limits_{i=1}^{I} N_{iM} - N_{M+} - N_{+M}}{2N - N_{M+} - N_{+M}}$$

$$= \frac{(26 + 14 + \quad) + (\quad + 23) - 51 - \quad}{2(\quad) - \quad - 38}$$

$$= \frac{63 + \quad - 51 -}{200 - \quad - 38}$$

$$=$$

$$\lambda_Y = \frac{\sum\limits_{j=1}^{J} N_{Mj} - N_{M+}}{N - N_{M+}}$$

$$= \frac{(26 + \quad + \quad) -}{\quad - 51}$$

$$=$$

b. The Academic Vice President of a small state university believes that the faculty will support a change from a quarter calendar to a semester calendar. A survey is conducted and the responses from 57 faculty follow. Compute λ and λ_Y to determine the relationship between faculty rank and their response.

	Full	Associate	Assistant	Total
Support	5	6	14	25
No opinion	6	4	3	13
Not support	3	12	4	19
	14	22	21	57

$\lambda =$

$\lambda_Y =$

6. a. A college mathematics instructor examined the impact of high school calculus exposure upon the level of achievement in the first-semester freshman course. Fifteen students are ranked according to their final scores, and categorized as to whether they have had (1) or have not had (0) previous exposure. Compute the rank-biserial correlation coefficient.

Student	Previous exposure	Class rank
A	1	1
B	1	2
C	0	3
D	1	4
E	0	5
F	0	6
G	0	7
H	1	8
I	0	9
J	1	10
K	1	11
L	0	12
M	0	13
N	0	14
O	1	15

$$\bar{Y}_1 =$$

$$\bar{Y}_0 =$$

$$r_{rb} = \frac{2}{n}(\bar{Y}_1 - \bar{Y}_0)$$

$$= \frac{2}{}(\quad - \quad)$$

$$= 0.133(\quad)$$

$$=$$

b. A graduate level course in a university has listed a recommended but not required lower level course. The instructor wants to determine if having taken the lower level course affects graduate class standing. Compute the appropriate correlation coefficient. Explain your answer.

Class standing	Course level
1	1
2	0
3	1
4	1
5	1
6	0
7	1
8	0
9	0

$$r_{rb} =$$

7. An industrial psychologist wants to investigate the relationship between the age of workers and their performance at a particular type of job. The workers' ages are categorized into intervals of equal width. The mean performance scores for each category are determined, as is the mean performance score for the total group. The sum of deviation scores squared for the categories is 48.32. The sum of deviation scores squared for the total group is 79.53. Compute the eta coefficient.

$$\eta = \sqrt{1 - \frac{\Sigma(Y - \mu_k)^2}{\Sigma(Y - \mu_t)^2}}$$

$$= \sqrt{1 - \underline{}}$$

$$=$$

8. On a ten-point spelling test, one word was spelled correctly (1) or incorrectly (0). What is the value of the appropriate correlation coefficient for the relationship between spelling the one word and a student's test score?

Student	One word	Test score
A	1	3
B	1	5
C	1	8
D	1	6
E	0	2
F	0	4
G	0	3
H	0	6
I	0	5
J	0	7
K	0	3
L	0	4

9. A special education teacher believes that there is a relationship between the popularity of students as rated by their peers and the comparative ranking of serious disruptions caused by the students. The following data were obtained, with 1 representing the most popular student, 2 the next most popular, and so on. Calculate the appropriate correlation coefficient.

Student	Peer-rated popularity	Number of disruptions
A	1	2
B	2	4
C	3	7
D	4	5
E	5	12
F	6	6
G	7	10
H	8	9

10. A psychologist is interested in the relationship between scholastic achievement and social achievement for ninth-grade students. A study of 100 students provided the following student characteristics. Compute the appropriate correlation coefficient.

High scholastic and high social achievement	35 students
High scholastic and low social achievement	20 students
Low scholastic and high social achievement	20 students
Low scholastic and low social achievement	25 students

11. If $p = 0.35$ and $r_{Pb} = 0.62$, find r_b.

Chapter 20 Exercises: Answers

1. a. $\bar{Y}_1 = \dfrac{11.2 + 12.4 + 10.8 + 13.2 + 11.8 + 14.1 + 11.4 + 12.0}{8}$

$= 12.11$

$\bar{Y}_0 = \dfrac{15.6 + 12.3 + 16.1 + 14.1 + 12.5 + 15.3 + 13.8 + 16.0}{8}$

$= 14.46$

$p = 0.50$

$q = 0.50$

$\sigma_Y = \sqrt{\dfrac{2871.5 - \dfrac{(212.6)^2}{16}}{16}}$

$= \sqrt{\dfrac{2871.5 - 2824.9}{16}}$

$= \sqrt{\dfrac{46.6}{16}}$

$= 1.71$

$r_{Pb} = \dfrac{12.11 - 14.46}{1.71} \sqrt{(0.5)(0.5)}$

$= (-1.37)(0.5)$

$= -0.685$

There is a moderate negative relationship between presence of an older child and walking age. Children with no older sibling(s) tend to walk at an older age, and children with older sibling(s) in the home tend to walk at a younger age.

b. $r_{Pb} = \dfrac{79.43 - 76.67}{10.57} \sqrt{(0.7)(0.3)}$

$= 0.12$

2. a.

		This election		
		Will not vote for	Will vote for	
Last election	Voted for	14	46	60
	Did not vote for	28	12	40
		42	58	100

$$\phi = \frac{(46)(28) - (14)(12)}{\sqrt{(60)(40)(42)(58)}}$$

$$= \frac{1288 - 168}{\sqrt{5846400}}$$

$$= \frac{1120}{2417.9}$$

$$= 0.46$$

There is a low positive correlation between people who voted for the incumbent last election and people who plan to vote the same way this election.

b.

	Men	Women	
Smokers	29	18	47
Nonsmokers	21	32	53
	50	50	100

$$\phi = \frac{(18)(21) - (29)(32)}{\sqrt{(47)(53)(50)(50)}}$$

$$= \frac{-550}{2495.5}$$

$$= -0.22$$

There is little correlation between sex and smoking.

3. a. $\Sigma d = 0 \qquad \Sigma d^2 = 76$

$$\rho = 1 - \frac{6(76)}{15[(15)^2 - 1]}$$

$$= 1 - \frac{456}{15(224)}$$

$$= 1 - .136$$

$$= 0.86$$

b. $\rho = 1 - \frac{6(24)}{8(64 - 1)}$

$$= 0.71$$

4. a. $\bar{Y}_1 = 40$

$\bar{Y}_0 = 31.5$

$$\sigma_Y = \sqrt{\frac{15,803 - \frac{(429)^2}{12}}{12}}$$

$$= \sqrt{\frac{15,803 - 15,336.75}{12}}$$

$$= \sqrt{38.85}$$

$$= 6.23$$

$p = 0.5$

$q = 0.5$

$u = 0.3989$

$$r_b = \left(\frac{40 - 31.5}{6.23}\right)\left[\frac{(0.5)(0.5)}{0.3989}\right]$$

$$= \left(\frac{8.5}{6.23}\right)\left(\frac{0.25}{0.3989}\right)$$

$$= (1.36)(0.627)$$

$$= 0.85$$

b. $r_b = \left(\frac{10.86 - 16.60}{5.52}\right)\left[\frac{(0.583)(0.417)}{0.3902}\right]$

$$= -0.65$$

5. a. $\lambda = \dfrac{(26 + 14 + 23) + (26 + 23) - 51 - 38}{2(100) - 51 - 38}$

$$= \frac{63 + 49 - 51 - 38}{200 - 89}$$

$$= .2072$$

$\lambda_Y = \dfrac{(26 + 14 + 23) - 51}{100 - 51}$

$$= \frac{63 - 51}{49}$$

$$= .2449$$

b. $\lambda = \dfrac{(6 + 12 + 14) + (14 + 6 + 12) - 25 - 22}{2(57) - 25 - 22}$

$$= \frac{32 + 32 - 25 - 22}{114 - 25 - 22}$$

$$= .254$$

$\lambda_Y = \dfrac{(6 + 12 + 14) - 25}{57 - 25}$

$$= \frac{32 - 25}{32}$$

$$= .2187$$

6. a. $r_{Pb} = \dfrac{2}{15}(7.29 - 8.63)$

$\qquad\qquad = 0.133(-1.34)$

$\qquad\qquad = -0.18$

b. $r_{rb} = -0.50$.

Having taken the lower level course has a moderate correlation with graduate class rank. Thus for this group, the students that took the lower level course tended to rank higher.

7. $\eta = \sqrt{1 - \dfrac{48.32}{79.53}}$

$\qquad = 0.63$

8. $r_{Pb} = 0.34$

9. $\rho = 0.74$

Note: The Spearman rho is used when both variables are measured on ordinal scales. The number of disruptions for students needs to be ranked with the least number of disruptions given a value of 1.

10.

		Social achievement	
		Low	*High*
Scholastic achievement	*High*	20	35
	Low	25	20

$r_{tet} = 0.30$

11. $r_b = 0.80$

CHAPTER 21
Chi-Square (χ^2) Tests for Frequencies

COMPREHENSION CHECK

The use of parametric statistical tests requires several __(1)__ , including normality and homogeneity of __(2)__ . If these assumptions are not satisfied, __(3)__ tests are available which require less restrictive __(4)__ . These nonparametric tests can be applied to __(5)__ , or categorical, data and __(6)__ , or ranked, data.

A commonly used test statistic in many nonparametric statistical procedures is __(7)__ (χ^2). The theoretrical __(8)__ distribution of χ^2 (chi-square), like the t distribution, is a family of distributions. Each distribution is determined by the degrees of freedom. The χ^2 distribution is __(9)__ skewed, with the skewness decreasing as the degrees of freedom __(10)__ . The degrees of freedom are calculated by subtracting __(11)__ from the number of __(12)__ of the nominal variable. As was the case for the parametric tests, if the observed value of χ^2 __(13)__ the __(14)__ value (χ^2_{cv}), the null hypothesis of no differences between the observed and expected frequencies, considered collectively, is __(15)__ .

The one-sample case for __(16)__ data is called the __(17)__ test; this test uses __(18)__ (χ^2) as the test statistic. To calculate the χ^2 value, the observed frequencies are compared to the theoretical or __(19)__ frequencies. A statistically significant χ^2 value does not indicate where the statistical significance lies. However, standardized __(20)__ can be computed. If a standardized residual is greater than __(21)__ , then the researcher can conclude that there is a statistically significant difference between the observed and expected frequencies for that particular __(22)__ .

In the two-sample case, the χ^2 (chi-square) statistic can be used to compare groups on a nominal variable with two or more __(23)__ . If there are only two groups and only two categories, the data can be depicted in a 2×2 contingency table and analyzed using the test for independent proportions (see Chapter 10) or the χ^2 test for homogeneity. If there are more than __(24)__ groups and/or more than two categories of the nominal variable, only the test of __(25)__ can be used. In this test, the observed __(26)__ frequencies are compared to the __(27)__ cell frequencies. The expected frequencies for the cells of the contingency table are calculated by multiplying the __(28)__ row and column frequencies that correspond to the specific cell and dividing by the __(29)__ frequency. The degrees of freedom for the two-sample case are the product of the number of rows minus __(30)__ and the number of columns minus __(31)__ . Thus, if comparing two groups on a nominal variable with five categories, we would have a 2×5 contingency table and there would be __(32)__ degrees of freedom, $(2-1)(5-1)$. For the k-sample case with nominal data, the contingency table has dimensions __(33)__ , where R is the number of rows and is equal to the number of __(34)__ , and C is the number of columns and is equal to the number of categories of the nominal measures. The degrees of freedom for the $R \times C$ case are __(35)__ . As before, the standardized residuals can be used to identify the __(36)__ that are contributing to the significant observed χ^2 (chi-square).

The procedures listed above are for __(37)__ samples, but one test that can be used with dependent samples is the __(38)__ test, which can be used with the pretest-posttest design. For this test, the data must be set up exactly as portrayed in the formula, with cells __(39)__ (2 cells) representing change between pretest and posttest and cells __(40)__ (2 cells) representing no change. Thus, only __(41)__ of the __(42)__ cells of the 2×2 table are used in this test. Another test, which is appropriate for __(43)__ contingency tables, is called the __(44)__ (2 words) test. The test statistic evaluates the __(45)__ between row and column totals.

Comprehension Check: Answers

1. assumptions
2. variance
3. nonparametric
4. assumptions
5. nominal
6. ordinal
7. chi-square
8. sampling
9. positively
10. increase
11. one
12. levels
13. exceeds
14. critical
15. rejected

16. nominal
17. goodness of fit
18. chi-square
19. expected
20. residuals
21. 2.00
22. category
23. categories (levels)
24. two
25. homogeneity
26. cell
27. expected
28. marginal
29. total
30. one (1)

31. one (1)
32. four (4)
33. $R \times C$
34. groups
35. $(R - 1)(C - 1)$
36. cells
37. independent
38. McNemar
39. A and D
40. B and C
41. two
42. four
43. 3×3
44. Stuart-Maxwell
45. difference

CHAPTER 21 EXERCISES

1. A sociologist is interested in the number of children in certain family units and hypothesizes the following proportions: no children — 15 percent, one child — 24 percent, two children — 30 percent, three children — 18 percent, four children — 8 percent, and more than four children — 5 percent. For a random sample of 400 couples, the following results were obtained; no children — 42, one child — 101, two children — 124, three children — 72, four children — 39, more than four children — 22. Test the validity of the sociologist's hypothesis at the .05 level of significance.

Number of children	O	E	O − E	(O − E)²	$\frac{(O - E)^2}{E}$
0	42	60	−18	324	5.40
1	101				
2	124				
3	72				
4	39				
5 or more	22				
Total	400	400	0		$= \chi^2$

a. State the hypotheses.
   The hypothesized distribution is 15 percent
   24 percent
   30 percent
   ____ percent
   ____ percent
   ____ percent

b. Set the criterion for rejecting H_0. χ^2_{cv} for 5 df at $\alpha = .05$ is

c. Compute the test statistic.

$$\chi^2 = \Sigma \frac{(O-E)^2}{E}$$

$$= \frac{(42-60)^2}{60} + \frac{(101- \quad)^2}{\quad} + \frac{(\quad - \quad)^2}{\quad}$$

$$+ \cdots + \frac{(\quad - \quad)^2}{\quad} =$$

d. Interpret the results.

$$H_0.$$

e. Compute the standardized residuals.

$$R = \frac{O-E}{\sqrt{E}}$$

$$R_1 = \frac{(42-60)}{\sqrt{60}} =$$

$$R_2 = \frac{(101- \quad)}{\sqrt{\quad}} =$$

$$R_3 =$$

$$R_4 =$$

$$R_5 =$$

$$R_6 =$$

2. A college board of trustees requests input from faculty members, students, alumni, and off-campus educators regarding a proposed change of academic policy. The responses from 50-member random samples selected from each of the four groups are summarized in the following table. At the .10 level of significance, test the hypothesis that opinion regarding the change in academic policy is independent of group membership.

	Favor	Oppose	Neutral
Faculty members	34( )	10( )	6( )
Students	39( )	8( )	3( )
Alumni	21( )	22( )	7( )
Off-campus educators	28( )	18( )	4( )

a. State the hypothesis.

$$H_0:$$

b. Set the criterion for rejecting H_0:

$$\chi^2_{cv} \text{ for } (R-1)(C-1) =$$

c. Compute the test statistic.

$$\chi^2 =$$

d. Interpret the results.

$$H_0$$

e. Compute the standardized residuals.

$$R = \frac{(O-E)}{\sqrt{E}}$$

3. A random sample of 75 parents is asked to give their opinions regarding a proposed program of sex education before and after hearing teachers and administrators discuss the curriculum content. Given the following results, determine at the .10 level of significance whether a change of sentiment occurred.

Before discussion

		Favor	*Oppose*
	Oppose	26	15
After discussion			
	Favor	23	11

a. State the hypothesis.

$$H_0:$$

b. Set the criterion for rejecting H_0.

$$\chi^2_{cv} \text{ for } \qquad df$$

c. Compute the test statistic.

$$\chi^2 = \frac{(A-D)^2}{A+D}$$

$$=$$

$$=$$

d. Interpret the results.

$$H_0.$$

Chapter 21 Exercises: Answers

1.

Number of children	O	E	O − E	(O − E)²	$\frac{(O - E)^2}{E}$
0	42	60	−18	324	5.40
1	101	96	5	25	0.26
2	124	120	4	16	0.13
3	72	72	0	0	0.00
4	39	32	7	49	1.53
5 or more	22	20	2	4	0.20
Total	400	400	0		7.52 = χ^2

a. The hypothesized distribution is 15 percent
24 percent
30 percent
18 percent
8 percent
5 percent

b. χ^2_{cv} for df = 5 and α = .05 is 11.07.

c. $\chi^2 = 7.52$

d. Fail to reject H_0. The observed frequencies do not depart significantly from the hypothesized frequencies.

e. $R_1 = \dfrac{(42-60)}{\sqrt{60}} = -2.32$

$R_2 = \dfrac{(101-96)}{\sqrt{96}} = 0.51$

$R_3 = \dfrac{(124-120)}{\sqrt{120}} = 0.37$

$R_4 = \dfrac{(72-72)}{\sqrt{72}} = 0.00$

$R_5 = \dfrac{(39-32)}{\sqrt{32}} = 1.24$

$R_6 = \dfrac{(22-20)}{\sqrt{20}} = 0.45$

2. a. H_0: There is no difference in the responses of the four groups.

b. χ^2_{cv} for $(4-1)(3-1) = 6$ df at $\alpha = .10$ is 10.64.

	Favor	Oppose	Neutral	
Faculty members	34(30.5)	10(14.5)	6(5.0)	50
Students	39(30.5)	8(14.5)	3(5.0)	50
Alumni	21(30.5)	22(14.5)	7(5.0)	50
Off-campus educators	28(30.5)	18(14.5)	4(5.0)	50
	122	58	20	200

O	E	O – E	(O – E)²	$\dfrac{(O-E)^2}{E}$
34	30.5	3.5	12.25	0.40
39	30.5	8.5	72.25	2.37
21	30.5	–9.5	90.25	2.96
28	30.5	–2.5	6.25	0.20
10	14.5	–4.5	20.25	1.40
8	14.5	–6.5	42.25	2.91
22	14.5	7.5	56.25	3.88
18	14.5	3.5	12.25	0.84
6	5.0	1.0	1.00	0.20
3	5.0	–2.0	4.00	0.80
7	5.0	2.0	4.00	0.80
4	5.0	–1.0	1.00	0.20
200	200	0		$16.96 = \chi^2$

d. Reject H_0. There is a difference in the responses of the four groups.

e. Standardized residuals.

0.634	–1.182	0.447
1.539	–1.706	–0.894
–1.721	1.969	0.894
–0.453	0.919	–0.447

3. a. H_0: There is no difference in parent opinions before and after the discussion.

b. χ^2_{cv} for 1 df at $\alpha = .10$ is 2.71.

c.
$$\chi^2 = \frac{(26-11)^2}{26+11}$$
$$= \frac{225}{37}$$
$$= 6.08$$

d. Reject H_0. More parents changed from favor to oppose after the discussion than from oppose to favor.

CHAPTER 22
Other Nonparametric Tests

COMPREHENSION CHECK

There are several additional nonparametric tests. Two tests for ordinal data were presented in the textbook: (1) the ___(1)___ test and (2) the ___(2)___ (3 words) test. The null hypothesis for the median test is that the two samples were selected from populations with the same ___(3)___ . To compute the test statistic for this test, a 2×2 table is developed based on the median computed on pooled data from both samples. This table is based on whether observations are above or below the ___(4)___ median and on ___(5)___ membership. The test statistic is ___(6)___ and the underlying sampling distribution is the χ^2 distribution with ___(7)___ degree(s) of freedom.

While the median test is sensitive to only the ___(8)___ of the scores for the two groups, the ___(9)___ test is sensitive to the central tendency as well as ___(10)___ of the scores for the two groups. The ___(11)___ hypothesis for the Mann-Whitney U test is stated in more general terms: there is no difference in the ___(12)___ of scores for the population from which the ___(13)___ were randomly selected. In this test, the scores are first ___(14)___ and then the ranks are ___(15)___ within each group. The test statistic is ___(16)___ , and critical values are available in table form. When the sample size (n) for both groups is greater than ___(17)___ , the ___(18)___ distribution of U approaches the ___(19)___ distribution and the test statistic is z.

A test of significance for the k-sample case with ordinal measures is the ___(20)___ one-way analysis of variance. This test is the nonparametric analogue to ___(21)___ , 1-way classification. The test statistic, ___(22)___ , is calculated much like the Mann-Whitney U. The underlying distribution of the test statistic is the χ^2 distribution with ___(23)___ degrees of freedom. In the case of tied ranks, there are appropriate ___(24)___ formulas for both the Kruskal-Wallis and the Mann-Whitney U tests; however, if the data include ___(25)___ tied ranks the use of either test is questionable.

The statistic for the two-sample case for dependent samples with ordinal data is the Wilcoxon matched-pairs signed-rank test. In this test, which can be used in ___(26)___ designs, the differences in scores from pretest to posttest are computed and the ___(27)___ of these differences are ranked disregarding the ___(28)___ of the difference. The test statistic is T, or the ___(29)___ of the ranks for the ___(30)___ frequent sign. The ___(31)___ distributions of T are defined, and tables of critical ___(32)___ are available. When the sample size is greater than 25, the sampling ___(33)___ of T is approximately ___(34)___ and the test statistic is ___(35)___ .

Comprehension Check: Answers

1. median	**5.** group	**9.** Mann-Whitney U
2. Mann-Whitney U	**6.** χ^2	**10.** variation
3. median	**7.** 1 (one)	**11.** null
4. common	**8.** central tendency (location)	**12.** distribution

13. samples	**21.** ANOVA	**29.** sum
14. ranked	**22.** *H*	**30.** less
15. summed	**23.** $(k - 1)$	**31.** underlying
16. *U*	**24.** correction	**32.** values
17. 20	**25.** many	**33.** distribution
18. sampling	**26.** pretest-posttest	**34.** normal
19. normal	**27.** ranks	**35.** *z*
20. Kruskal-Wallis	**28.** sign	

CHAPTER 22 EXERCISES

1. A research psychologist examines the relationship between the classroom behavior of elementary students and their tendency to "keep within the lines" in completing a coloring exercise. The researcher believes that students with satisfactory performance on the exercise will exhibit higher levels of classroom discipline than those who do not. A teacher is asked to provide behavioral ratings for ten students of each type, with such indices assumed to be (at most) ordinal in nature. Given the following data, use first the median test and then the Mann-Whitney *U* test to determine whether a group difference exists at the .01 level of significance.

Satisfactory performance	Unsatisfactory performance
20	17
25	19
26	21
28	22
31	24
36	27
37	29
38	32
40	34
42	35

Median Test

$$\text{Median} = \frac{\quad + \quad}{\quad} = \quad$$

	Satisfactory	Unsatisfactory
Above median		
Below median		

a. State the hypotheses.

H_0: $\text{Mdn}_1 =$

H_a: $\text{Mdn}_1 >$

b. Set the criterion for rejecting H_0.

χ^2_{cv} for ____ df is ____ .

c. Compute the test statistic.

$$\chi^2 = \frac{n(AD - BC)^2}{(A+B)(C+D)(A+C)(B+D)}$$

$$=$$

$$=$$

$$=$$

d. Interpret the results.

$H_0.$

Mann-Whitney U test

a. State the hypotheses.

$H_0:$
$H_a:$

b. Set the criterion for rejecting H_0.

$U_{cv} =$

c. Compute the test statistic.

Satisfactory performance		Unsatisfactory performance	
Score	Rank	Score	Rank
20	3	17	1
25		19	
26		21	
28		22	
31		24	
36		27	
37		29	
38		32	
40		34	
42	___	35	___

$$U_1 = n_1 n_2 + \frac{n_1(n_1 + 1)}{2} - R_1$$

$$= (\;\;)(\;\;) + \frac{(\;\;)(\;\;)}{} -$$

$$=$$

$$=$$

$$U_2 = n_1 n_2 + \frac{n_2(n_2 + 1)}{2} - R_2$$

$$= (\;\;)(\;\;) + \frac{(\;\;)(\;\;)}{} -$$

$$=$$

$$=$$

d. Interpret the results.

$H_0.$

2. A counseling psychologist examines the levels of confidence placed by high school students upon their career decisions in view of the major sources of influence on those decisions. Given the following confidence ratings (assumed to be ordinal in nature), determine if any population differences exist at the .05 level of significance.

Major source of influence

Counselor/teacher		Parent		Friend		Career participant		Self-initiated	
Rating	Rank	Rating	Rank	Rating	Rank	Rating	Rank	Rating	Rank
56		59		55		62		68	
48		64		43		57		61	
65		52		47		54		63	
58		49				67		66	
51		50						53	
60									
	$= R_1$		$- R_2$		$= R_3$		$= R_4$		$= R_5$

a. State the hypotheses.

H_0:

H_a:

b. Set the criterion for rejecting H_0.

$H_{cv} =$

c. Compute the test statistic.

$$H = \frac{12}{N(N+1)} \Sigma \frac{R_j^2}{nj} - 3(N+1)$$

$$H = \frac{}{(\ )}\left[\frac{(\ )^2}{} + \frac{(\ )^2}{} + \frac{(\ )^2}{} + \frac{(\ )^2}{} + \frac{(\ )^2}{} \right] - (\ )$$

$$=$$

$$=$$

$$=$$

d. Interpret the results.

H_0.

3. A public school administrator wishes to assess the impact of a compensatory education program on the classroom participation levels of chronic nonachievers. Two groups of 15 members each are selected for participation. Careful screening makes possible a matched-pairs format. The experimental treatment, a ten-week instructional program outside the traditional classroom, is applied to one of the groups. Three weeks after its initiation, the teacher is asked to specify a participation index (assumed to be measured on an ordinal scale) for each of the students. Given the following data, use the Wilcoxon matched-pairs signed-rank test to determine whether a difference exists between the experimental and control groups at the .01 level of significance. Use a directional alternative hypothesis.

a. State the hypotheses.

H_0:

H_a:

b. Set the criterion for rejecting H_0.

$$T_{cv} =$$

c. Compute the test statistic.

Matched-pair	Experimental group	Control group	Difference	Rank of difference	Rank with less frequent sign
1	18	14	4	6.5	
2	15	6	9	12	
3	20	10	10		
4	12	12			
5	15	16			
6	16	8			
7	18	12			
8	22	19			
9	14	4			
10	17	10			
11	9	13			
12	12	15			
13	21	16			
14	19	5			
15	10	12			
					$T =$

d. Interpret the results.

$$H_0:$$

Chapter 22 Exercises: Answers

1. Median $= \dfrac{28 + 29}{2} = 28.5$

	Satisfactory	Unsatisfactory
Above median	6	4
Below median	4	6

a. H_0: $\text{Mdn}_1 = \text{Mdn}_2$

H_a: $\text{Mdn}_1 > \text{Mdn}_2$

b. χ_{cv}^2 for 1 df is 6.635.

c. $\chi^2 = \dfrac{20[(6)(6) - (4)(4)]^2}{(6+4)(4+6)(6+4)(4+6)}$

$= \dfrac{8,000}{10,000}$

$= .80$

d. Fail to reject H_0.

Mann-Whitney U test

a. H_0: Behavior$_1$ = Behavior$_2$
H_a: Behavior$_1$ > Behavior$_2$

b. $U_{cv} = 20$

c.

Satisfactory performance		Unsatisfactory performance	
Score	*Rank*	*Score*	*Rank*
20	3	17	1
25	7	19	2
26	8	21	4
28	10	22	5
31	12	24	6
36	16	27	9
37	17	29	11
38	18	32	13
40	19	34	14
42	20	35	15
	$130 = R_1$		$80 = R_2$

$$U_1 = (10)(10) + \frac{(10)(11)}{2} - 130$$
$$= 100 + 55 - 130$$
$$= 25$$
$$U_2 = (10)(10) + \frac{(10)(11)}{2} - 80$$
$$= 100 + 55 - 80$$
$$= 75$$

Therefore, $U = 25$.

d. Fail to reject H_0.

2. a. H_0: There is no difference in the scores for the k groups.

b. $H_{cv} = 9.49$

c.

				Major source of influence					
Counselor/teacher		Parent		Friend		Career participant		Self-initiated	
Rating	Rank	Rating	Rank	Rating	Rank	Rating	Rank	Rating	Rank
56	11	59	14	55	10	62	17	68	23
48	3	64	19	43	1	57	12	61	16
65	20	52	7	47	2	54	9	63	18
58	13	49	4			67	22	66	21
51	6	50	5					53	8
60	15								
	$68 = R_1$		$49 = R_2$		$13 = R_3$		$60 = R_4$		$86 = R_5$

$$H = \frac{12}{23(24)}\left[\frac{(68)^2}{6} + \frac{(49)^2}{5} + \frac{(13)^2}{3} + \frac{(60)^2}{4} + \frac{(86)^2}{5}\right] - 3(24)$$

$$= \frac{12}{552}(770.67 + 480.2 + 56.33 + 900.0 + 1,479.2) - 72$$

$$= 8.14$$

d. Fail to reject H_0.

3. a. H_0: There is no difference between the experimental and control groups.

H_a: Experimental group is greater than the control group.

b. $T_{cv} = 20$

c.

Matched-pair	Experimental group	Control group	Difference	Rank of difference	Rank with less frequent sign
1	18	14	4	6.5	
2	15	6	9	12	
3	20	10	10	13.5	
4	12	12	0	1	
5	15	16	−1	−2	2
6	16	8	8	11	
7	18	12	6	9	
8	22	19	3	4.5	
9	14	4	10	13.5	
10	17	10	7	10	
11	9	13	−4	−6.5	6.5
12	12	15	−3	−4.5	4.5
13	21	16	5	8	
14	19	5	14	15	
15	10	12	−2	−3	3
					$T = 16$

d. Fail to reject H_0.

Computer Exercises and SPSS Printouts

This section includes computer exercises for Chapters 1, 2, 3, 5, 6, 8, 11, 14, 15, 16, 17, 18, 19, and 21. The SPSS procedures for these exercises can be found in the textbook, Appendix A, Part II – SPSS Procedures for Chapter Examples.

CHAPTER 1
Introduction

EXERCISE: **Set Up Data Set**
DATA: NLS.sav
TO DO: 1. Save the data set as "NLS.sav"
                2. Set the name, label, and value of the variables – see "Variable View" table below.
                3. Enter data into Data Editor sheet – see "Data Set" table below.
                (Please see the instructions in the textbook Appendix B, Part II, *Basic Skills*)

Variable View

Variable Names	Variable Values	Variable Labels	Description
RACE	2 = Nonwhite 7 = White	Race	
GENDER	1 = Male 2 = Female	Gender	
SES	1 = Lower Percent 2 = Middle 50 Percent 3 = Upper 25 Percent	Socioeconomic Status	
HSTRACK	1 = General 2 = Academic 3 = Vocational	High School Track	
ABLE	1 = Disagree Strongly 2 = Disagree 3 = No Opinion 4 = Agree 5 = Agree Strongly	Able to Do Things Well	"I am able to do things as well as most other people."
STOPPED	1 = Disagree Strongly 2 = Disagree 3 = No Opinion 4 = Agree 5 = Agree Strongly	Stopped by Something or Somebody	"Every time I try to get ahead, something or somebody stops me."
MONEY	1 = Not Important 2 = Somewhat Important 3 = Very Important	Importance of Money	"How important to your life is having a lot of money?"
FAMILY	1 = Not Important 2 = Somewhat Important 3 = Very Important	Marry Right Person	"How important to your life is finding the right person to marry and having a happy family life?"
ABILITY		Academic Ability	An overall academic ability measure created from four NLS variables.
EDATTN	12.00 = H S Only 12.50 =< 2 yrs Voc 13.00 => 2yrs Voc 15.00 =<2 yrs College 16.00 = 4 yrs College	Years of Schooling	Number of years of schooling
FATHED	7.55 = Less Than H S 12.00 = H S Degree 13.79 = Some College	Years of Father's Education	Number of years of father's education
SIBS		Number of Siblings	Number of siblings in family

Data Set

RACE	GENDER	SES	HSTRACK	ABLE	STOPPED	MONEY	FAMILY	ABILITY	EDATTN	FATHED	SIBS
2	2	1	2	4	2	3	3	49.00	13.00	7.55	5
7	2	1	3	4	2	2	3	58.00	12.00	12.00	4
7	2	2	2	4	2	2	3	63.25	13.00	13.79	3
7	2	2	2	4	3	2	3	57.57	13.00	13.79	2
7	1	2	2	4	2	3	3	54.50	12.00	13.79	3
7	1	2	2	3	3	2	3	61.75	16.00	12.00	7
7	1	1	1	4	2	2	3	50.25	15.00	7.55	0
7	2	3	2	5	2	1	3	48.00	6.00	13.79	2
7	1	2	2	4	4	3	3	55.00	13.00	2.00	0
7	2	1	2	4	1	1	3	55.50	13.00	7.55	5
7	1	2	2	5	2	2	3	60.75	15.00	12.00	8
7	2	2	1	1	4	1	1	53.00	12.00	7.55	5
7	1	1	2	4	4	2	3	57.00	13.00	7.55	2
7	2	2	1	4	5	2	3	50.50	12.00	7.55	7
7	2	2	1	4	2	2	3	40.00	12.00	12.00	4
7	2	1	1	4	2	2	3	49.25	16.00	12.00	4
7	2	2	1	4	2	2	3	55.24	16.00	12.00	2
7	1	2	2	5	2	3	3	58.00	12.00	12.00	5
7	2	1	3	4	2	1	3	42.50	12.00	7.55	5
7	2	2	2	3	2	1	2	54.75	12.50	7.55	3
7	1	1	1	4	4	1	3	40.25	12.00	7.55	6
7	2	1	1	4	2	1	3	54.75	16.00	7.55	6
7	2	1	3	2	2	2	3	35.00	12.00	7.55	6
7	2	1	1	4	2	2	3	59.75	15.00	7.55	4
7	1	2	2	4	2	3	3	61.25	12.00	13.79	1
7	1	1	1	4	3	2	3	55.00	16.00	7.55	2
7	2	3	1	5	2	2	3	50.00	12.00	13.79	6
7	1	2	1	5	2	3	3	43.25	12.50	12.00	7
7	2	2	1	4	2	2	3	51.50	12.50	2.00	4
7	2	3	2	5	1	1	2	64.25	16.00	13.79	2
7	2	2	2	4	2	2	3	54.25	13.00	12.00	2
7	2	1	1	4	3	2	3	47.75	12.00	13.79	3
2	2	1	2	5	2	3	3	45.50	12.00	7.55	7
2	2	2	3	5	2	3	3	36.00	12.00	13.79	3
2	1	2	1	5	5	3	1	41.50	12.00	7.55	1
7	2	2	2	4	2	3	3	46.25	16.00	12.00	2
7	2	1	1	4	5	2	3	46.25	12.00	7.55	1
7	2	2	1	5	1	3	3	38.25	12.50	12.00	4
7	2	2	3	4	4	2	3	46.50	12.00	7.55	1
7	1	3	2	5	2	3	3	61.00	15.00	13.79	1
7	1	2	2	4	2	2	3	49.50	12.00	12.00	3
7	2	1	1	2	3	1	2	53.25	12.00	7.55	6
7	1	2	1	5	2	3	3	45.25	12.00	7.55	4
7	2	2	1	4	2	1	3	56.00	15.00	12.00	2
2	2	1	2	4	4	2	3	36.25	16.00	7.55	9
2	2	1	2	5	1	2	3	44.75	16.00	7.55	0
2	2	1	1	5	2	2	2	39.75	12.00	7.55	1
2	2	1	1	4	4	2	3	41.25	12.00	7.55	1
7	2	2	3	2	4	2	3	47.00	12.00	7.55	1
7	2	1	3	4	4	2	2	46.25	12.00	7.55	2

CHAPTER 2
Organizing and Graphing Data

EXERCISE: **Frequencies**
DATA: NLS.sav
TO DO: Run SPSS and display the frequency distributions for all the variables except ABILITY.
RESULTS:

Frequency Table

RACE Race

		Frequency	Percent	Valid Percent	Cumulative Percent
Valid	2 Black	8	16.0	16.0	16.0
	7 White	42	84.0	84.0	100.0
	Total	50	100.0	100.0	

GENDER Gender

		Frequency	Percent	Valid Percent	Cumulative Percent
Valid	1 Male	15	30.0	30.0	30.0
	2 Female	35	70.0	70.0	100.0
	Total	50	100.0	100.0	

SES Socioeconomic Status

		Frequency	Percent	Valid Percent	Cumulative Percent
Valid	1 Lower 25 Percent	21	42.0	42.0	42.0
	2 Middle 50 Percent	25	50.0	50.0	92.0
	3 Upper 25 Percent	4	8.0	8.0	100.0
	Total	50	100.0	100.0	

HSTRACK High School Track

		Frequency	Percent	Valid Percent	Cumulative Percent
Valid	1 General	22	44.0	44.0	44.0
	2 Academic	21	42.0	42.0	86.0
	3 Vocational	7	14.0	14.0	100.0
	Total	50	100.0	100.0	

ABLE Able to Do Things Well

		Frequency	Percent	Valid Percent	Cumulative Percent
Valid	1 Disagree Strongly	1	2.0	2.0	2.0
	2 Disagree	4	8.0	8.0	10.0
	3 No Opinion	2	4.0	4.0	14.0
	4 Agree	30	60.0	60.0	74.0
	5 Agree Strongly	13	26.0	26.0	100.0
	Total	50	100.0	100.0	

STOPPED Stopped by Somthing or Somebody

		Frequency	Percent	Valid Percent	Cumulative Percent
Valid	1 Disagree Strongly	4	8.0	8.0	8.0
	2 Disagree	29	58.0	58.0	66.0
	3 No Opinion	5	10.0	10.0	76.0
	4 Agree	9	18.0	18.0	94.0
	5 Agree Strongly	3	6.0	6.0	100.0
	Total	50	100.0	100.0	

MONEY Importance of Money

		Frequency	Percent	Valid Percent	Cumulative Percent
Valid	1 Not Important	10	20.0	20.0	20.0
	2 Somewhat Important	27	54.0	54.0	74.0
	3 Very Important	13	26.0	26.0	100.0
	Total	50	100.0	100.0	

FAMILY Marry Right Person

		Frequency	Percent	Valid Percent	Cumulative Percent
Valid	1 Not Important	2	4.0	4.0	4.0
	2 Somewhat Important	5	10.0	10.0	14.0
	3 Very Important	43	86.0	86.0	100.0
	Total	50	100.0	100.0	

EDATTN Years of Schooling

		Frequency	Percent	Valid Percent	Cumulative Percent
Valid	6.00	1	2.0	2.0	2.0
	12.00 H S Only	24	48.0	48.0	50.0
	12.50 =< 2yrs Voc	4	8.0	8.0	58.0
	13.00 => 2yrs Voc	7	14.0	14.0	72.0
	15.00 =< 2yrs College	5	10.0	10.0	82.0
	16.00 =4yrs College	9	18.0	18.0	100.0
	Total	50	100.0	100.0	

FATHED Years of Father's Education

		Frequency	Percent	Valid Percent	Cumulative Percent
Valid	2.00	2	4.0	4.0	4.0
	7.55 Less Than H S	25	50.0	50.0	54.0
	12.00 H S Degree	13	26.0	26.0	80.0
	13.79 Some College	10	20.0	20.0	100.0
	Total	50	100.0	100.0	

SIBS Number of Siblings

		Frequency	Percent	Valid Percent	Cumulative Percent
Valid	0	3	6.0	6.0	6.0
	1	8	16.0	16.0	22.0
	2	10	20.0	20.0	42.0
	3	6	12.0	12.0	54.0
	4	7	14.0	14.0	68.0
	5	5	10.0	10.0	78.0
	6	5	10.0	10.0	88.0
	7	4	8.0	8.0	96.0
	8	1	2.0	2.0	98.0
	9	1	2.0	2.0	100.0
	Total	50	100.0	100.0	

CHAPTER 3
Describing Distributions: Individual Scores, Central Tendency and Variation

EXERCISE 1:   **Descriptive Statistics**
DATA: NLS.sav
TO DO: Run SPSS and produce the measures of central tendency and variation for the
following variables: RACE, GENDER, HSTRACK, ABLE, STOPPED,
MONEY, FAMILY, ABILITY, EDATTN, FATHED, and SIBS.
RESULTS:

Descriptive Statistics

	N	Minimum	Maximum	Mean	Std. Deviation	Variance
RACE Race	50	2	7	6.20	1.852	3.429
GENDER Gender	50	1	2	1.70	.463	.214
SES Socioeconomic Status	50	1	3	1.66	.626	.392
HSTRACK High School Track	50	1	3	1.70	.707	.500
ABLE Able to Do Things Well	50	1	5	4.00	.904	.816
STOPPED Stopped by Something or Somebody	50	1	5	2.56	1.072	1.149
MONEY Importance of Money	50	1	3	2.06	.682	.466
FAMILY Marry Right Person	50	1	3	2.82	.482	.232
ABILITY Academic Ability	50	35.00	64.25	50.2262	7.69237	59.173
EDATTN Years of Schooling	50	6.00	16.00	13.0800	1.88809	3.565
FATHED Years of Father's Education	50	2.00	13.79	9.7330	3.09753	9.595
SIBS Number of Siblings	50	0	9	3.48	2.279	5.193
Valid N (listwise)	50					

EXERCISE 2: **Compute the Standard Scores**
DATA: NLS.sav
TO DO: Run SPSS and produce the standard scores for ABILITY, and SIBS.
RESULTS:

ABILIT	Z-ABILITY	ABILIT	Z-ABILITY	SIBS	Z-SIBS	SIBS	Z-SIBS
49.00	-.15940	5.00	.62059	5	.66698	2	-.64943
58.00	1.01059	50.00	-.02941	4	.22818	6	1.10579
63.25	1.69308	43.25	-.90690	3	-.21063	7	1.54459
57.57	.95469	51.50	.16559	2	-.64943	4	.22818
54.50	.55559	64.25	1.82308	3	-.21063	2	-.64943
61.75	1.49808	54.25	.52309	7	1.54459	2	-.64943
50.25	.00309	47.75	-.32190	0	-1.52704	3	-.21063
48.00	-.28940	45.50	-.61440	2	-.64943	7	1.54459
55.00	.62059	36.00	-1.84939	0	-1.52704	3	-.21063
55.50	.68559	41.50	-1.13440	5	.66698	1	-1.08824
60.75	1.36808	46.25	-.51690	8	1.98340	2	-.64943
53.00	.36059	6.25	-.51690	5	.66698	1	-1.08824
57.00	.88059	38.25	-1.55689	2	-.64943	4	.22818
50.50	.03559	46.50	-.48440	7	1.54459	1	-1.08824
40.00	-1.32940	61.00	1.40058	4	.22818	1	-1.08824
49.25	-.12690	49.50	-.09441	4	.22818	3	-.21063
55.24	.65179	53.25	.39309	2	-.64943	6	1.10579
58.00	1.01059	45.25	-.64690	5	.66698	4	.22818
42.50	-1.00440	56.00	.75059	5	.66698	2	-.64943
54.75	.58809	36.25	-1.81689	3	-.21063	9	2.42220
40.25	-1.29690	44.75	-.71190	6	1.10579	0	-1.52704
54.75	.58809	39.75	-1.36190	6	1.10579	1	-1.08824
35.00	-1.97939	41.25	-1.16690	6	1.10579	1	-1.08824
59.75	1.23808	47.00	-.41940	4	.22818	1	-1.08824
61.25	1.43308	46.25	-.51690	1	-1.08824	2	-.64943

EXERCISE: **Correlation**
DATA: NLS.sav
TO DO: Run SPSS and compute the Pearson correlation coefficients between the variables ABLE, STOPPED, MONEY, FAMILY, ABILITY, EDATTN, and FATHED.

RESULTS:

Correlations

		ABLE Able to Do Things Well	STOPPED Stopped by Something or Somebody	MONEY Importance of Money	FAMILY Marry Right Person	ABILITY Academic Ability	EDATTN Years of Schooling	FATHED Years of Father's Education
ABLE Able to Do Things Well	Pearson Correlation	1	-.274	.397**	.375**	.032	.054	.325*
	Sig. (2-tailed)		.054	.004	.007	.824	.710	.021
	N	50	50	50	50	50	50	50
STOPPED Stopped by Something or Somebody	Pearson Correlation	-.274	1	-.019	-.275	-.183	-.189	-.406**
	Sig. (2-tailed)	.054		.896	.053	.203	.189	.003
	N	50	50	50	50	50	50	50
MONEY Importance of Money	Pearson Correlation	.397**	-.019	1	.220	-.148	.004	.133
	Sig. (2-tailed)	.004	.896		.125	.304	.977	.359
	N	50	50	50	50	50	50	50
FAMILY Marry Right Person	Pearson Correlation	.375**	-.275	.220	1	.026	.117	.183
	Sig. (2-tailed)	.007	.053	.125		.856	.418	.203
	N	50	50	50	50	50	50	50
ABILITY Academic Ability	Pearson Correlation	.032	-.183	-.148	.026	1	.307*	.259
	Sig. (2-tailed)	.824	.203	.304	.856		.030	.069
	N	50	50	50	50	50	50	50
EDATTN Years of Schooling	Pearson Correlation	.054	-.189	.004	.117	.307*	1	-.002
	Sig. (2-tailed)	.710	.189	.977	.418	.030		.987
	N	50	50	50	50	50	50	50
FATHED Years of Father's Education	Pearson Correlation	.325*	-.406**	.133	.183	.259	-.002	1
	Sig. (2-tailed)	.021	.003	.359	.203	.069	.987	
	N	50	50	50	50	50	50	50

**. Correlation is significant at the 0.01 level (2-tailed).

*. Correlation is significant at the 0.05 level (2-tailed).

EXERCISE: Linear Regression
DATA: NLS.sav
TO DO: Run SPSS and develop the regression equation for predicting EDATTN from ABILITY. Then develop a different regression for predicting ABILITY from FATHED.
RESULTS:

Regression (I)

Variables Entered/Removed[b]

Model	Variables Entered	Variables Removed	Method
1	ABILITY Academic Ability[a]	.	Enter

a. All requested variables entered.

b. Dependent Variable: EDATTN Years of Schooling

Model Summary

Model	R	R Square	Adjusted R Square	Std. Error of the Estimate
1	.307[a]	.094	.075	1.81558

a. Predictors: (Constant), ABILITY Academic Ability

ANOVA[b]

Model		Sum of Squares	df	Mean Square	F	Sig.
1	Regression	16.457	1	16.457	4.993	.030[a]
	Residual	158.223	48	3.296		
	Total	174.680	49			

a. Predictors: (Constant), ABILITY Academic Ability

b. Dependent Variable: EDATTN Years of Schooling

Coefficients[a]

Model		Unstandardized Coefficients		Standardized Coefficients	t	Sig.
		B	Std. Error	Beta		
1	(Constant)	9.296	1.713		5.427	.000
	ABILITY Academic Ability	.075	.034	.307	2.234	.030

a. Dependent Variable: EDATTN Years of Schooling

Regression Equation:

$$Y = 0.075X + 9.296$$

Regression (II)

Variables Entered/Removed[b]

Model	Variables Entered	Variables Removed	Method
1	FATHED Years of Father's Education [a]	.	Enter

a. All requested variables entered.

b. Dependent Variable: ABILITY Academic Ability

Model Summary

Model	R	R Square	Adjusted R Square	Std. Error of the Estimate
1	.259[a]	.067	.048	7.50706

a. Predictors: (Constant), FATHED Years of Father's Education

ANOVA[b]

Model		Sum of Squares	df	Mean Square	F	Sig.
1	Regression	194.370	1	194.370	3.449	.069[a]
	Residual	2705.084	48	56.356		
	Total	2899.454	49			

a. Predictors: (Constant), FATHED Years of Father's Education

b. Dependent Variable: ABILITY Academic Ability

Coefficients[a]

Model		Unstandardized Coefficients		Standardized Coefficients		
		B	Std. Error	Beta	t	Sig.
1	(Constant)	43.968	3.533		12.445	.000
	FATHED Years of Father's Education	.643	.346	.259	1.857	.069

a. Dependent Variable: ABILITY Academic Ability

The model is not significant. Therefore, it is not appropriate to use FATHED to predict ABILITY.

CHAPTER 8
Hypothesis Testing: One-Sample Case for the Mean

EXERCISE: **One-Sample t-test**
DATA: NLS.sav
TO DO: Run SPSS and test the hypothesis that the population mean of the Academic Ability (ABILITY) is 55.6. Use alpha = .05. Consider this a two-tailed test, assuming that the hypothesis was formulated before the sample was measured.
RESULTS:

T-Test

One-Sample Statistics

	N	Mean	Std. Deviation	Std. Error Mean
ABILITY Academic Ability	50	50.2262	7.69237	1.08787

One-Sample Test

	Test Value = 55.6					
					95% Confidence Interval of the Difference	
	t	df	Sig. (2-tailed)	Mean Difference	Lower	Upper
ABILITY Academic Ability	-4.940	49	.000	-5.3738	-7.5599	-3.1877

CHAPTER 11
Hypothesis Testing: Two-Sample Cases for the Mean

EXERCISE: **t-test**
DATA: NLS.sav
TO DO: Run SPSS and conduct *t* tests to determine the differences (A) between males and females and (B) between whites and nonwhites on ABILITY.

RESULTS:

T-Test (A)

Group Statistics

	GENDER Gender	N	Mean	Std. Deviation	Std. Error Mean
ABILITY Academic Ability	1 Male	15	52.9500	7.51023	1.93913
	2 Female	35	49.0589	7.57477	1.28037

Independent Samples Test

| | | Levene's Test for Equality of Variances | | t-test for Equality of Means | | | | | |
| | | F | Sig. | t | df | Sig. (2-tailed) | Mean Difference | Std. Error Difference | 95% Confidence Interval of the Difference | |
									Lower	Upper
ABILITY Academic Ability	Equal variances assumed	.040	.842	1.669	48	.102	3.8911	2.33183	-.79732	8.57961
	Equal variances not assumed			1.675	26.773	.106	3.8911	2.32370	-.87859	8.66088

T-Test (B)

Group Statistics

	RACE Race	N	Mean	Std. Deviation	Std. Error Mean
ABILITY Academic Ability	2 Nonwhite	8	41.7500	4.52375	1.59939
	7 White	42	51.8407	7.10883	1.09692

Independent Samples Test

		Levene's Test for Equality of Variances		t-test for Equality of Means					95% Confidence Interval of the Difference	
		F	Sig.	t	df	Sig. (2-tailed)	Mean Difference	Std. Error Difference	Lower	Upper
ABILITY Academic Ability	Equal variances assumed	2.713	.106	-3.851	48	.000	-10.0907	2.62061	-15.35980	-4.82163
	Equal variances not assumed			-5.203	14.583	.000	-10.0907	1.93940	-14.23476	-5.94667

CHAPTER 14
Hypothesis Testing, *K*-Sample Case: Analysis of Variance, One-Way Classification

EXERCISE: **One-Way ANOVA**
DATA: NLS.sav
TO DO: Run SPSS and compute the ANOVA, using ABILITY as the dependent variable, and SES as the independent variable.
RESULTS:

Oneway

Descriptives

ABILITY Academic Ability

	N	Mean	Std. Deviation	Std. Error	95% Confidence Interval for Mean		Minimum	Maximum
					Lower Bound	Upper Bound		
1 Lower 25%	21	47.9643	7.20776	1.57286	44.6834	51.2452	35.00	59.75
2 Middle 50%	25	51.2324	7.66463	1.53293	48.0686	54.3962	36.00	63.25
3 Upper 25%	4	55.8125	8.01918	4.00959	43.0522	68.5728	48.00	64.25
Total	50	50.2262	7.69237	1.08787	48.0401	52.4123	35.00	64.25

Test of Homogeneity of Variances

ABILITY Academic Ability

Levene Statistic	df1	df2	Sig.
.129	2	47	.880

ANOVA

ABILITY Academic Ability

	Sum of Squares	df	Mean Square	F	Sig.
Between Groups	257.579	2	128.790	2.291	.112
Within Groups	2641.875	47	56.210		
Total	2899.454	49			

CHAPTER 15
Multiple-Comparison Procedures

EXERCISE: **One-Way ANOVA, Multiple Comparisons**
DATA: NLS.sav
TO DO: Run SPSS and compute the ANOVA and multiple comparisons, using ABILITY as the dependent variable, and SES as the independent variable.
RESULTS:

Oneway

ANOVA

ABILITY Academic Ability

	Sum of Squares	df	Mean Square	F	Sig.
Between Groups	257.579	2	128.790	2.291	.112
Within Groups	2641.875	47	56.210		
Total	2899.454	49			

Post Hoc Tests

Multiple Comparisons

Dependent Variable: ABILITY Academic Ability
Tukey HSD

(I) SES Socioeconomic Status	(J) SES Socioeconomic Status	Mean Difference (I-J)	Std. Error	Sig.
1 Lower 25%	2 Middle 50 Percent	-3.2681	2.21925	.313
	3 Upper 25 Percent	-7.8482	4.09013	.145
2 Middle 50%	1 Lower 25 Percent	3.2681	2.21925	.313
	3 Upper 25 Percent	-4.5801	4.03744	.498
3 Upper 25%	1 Lower 25 Percent	7.8482	4.09013	.145
	2 Middle 50 Percent	4.5801	4.03744	.498

Homogeneous Subsets

ABILITY Academic Ability

Tukey HSD [a,b]

SES Socioeconomic Status	N	Subset for alpha = .05
		1
1 Lower 25 Percent	21	47.9643
2 Middle 50 Percent	25	51.2324
3 Upper 25 Percent	4	55.8125
Sig.		.080

Means for groups in homogeneous subsets are displayed.

  a. Uses Harmonic Mean Sample Size = 8.886.

  b. The group sizes are unequal. The harmonic mean of the group sizes is used. Type I error levels are not guaranteed.

CHAPTER 16
Analysis of Variance, Two-Way Classification

EXERCISE: **Two-Way ANOVA**
DATA: NLS.sav
TO DO: Run SPSS and compute a 2 X 3 ANOVA, using ABILITY as the dependent variable, and GENDER and SES as the independent variable.
RESULTS:

Between-Subjects Factors

			Value Label	N
GENDER Gender	1		Male	15
	2		Female	35
SES Socioeconomic Status	1		Lower 25 Percent	21
	2		Middle 50 Percent	25
	3		Upper 25 Percent	4

Tests of Between-Subjects Effects

Dependent Variable: ABILITY Academic Ability

Source	Type III Sum of Squares	df	Mean Square	F	Sig.
Corrected Model	385.026ᵃ	5	77.005	1.348	.262
Intercept	55248.825	1	55248.825	966.800	.000
GENDER	97.417	1	97.417	1.705	.198
SES	187.097	2	93.549	1.637	.206
GENDER * SES	9.957	2	4.979	.087	.917
Error	2514.428	44	57.146		
Total	129033.013	50			
Corrected Total	2899.454	49			

a. R Squared = .133 (Adjusted R Squared = .034)

CHAPTER 17
Linear Regression: Estimation and Hypothesis Testing

EXERCISE: **Linear Regression**
DATA: NLS.sav
TO DO: Run SPSS and develop the regression equation for predicting ABILITY from EDATTN.
RESULTS:

Regression

Variables Entered/Removed[b]

Model	Variables Entered	Variables Removed	Method
1	EDATTN Years of Schooling[a]	.	Enter

a. All requested variables entered.

b. Dependent Variable: ABILITY Academic Ability

Model Summary

Model	R	R Square	Adjusted R Square	Std. Error of the Estimate
1	.307[a]	.094	.075	7.39692

a. Predictors: (Constant), EDATTN Years of Schooling

ANOVA[b]

Model		Sum of Squares	df	Mean Square	F	Sig.
1	Regression	273.163	1	273.163	4.993	.030[a]
	Residual	2626.291	48	54.714		
	Total	2899.454	49			

a. Predictors: (Constant), EDATTN Years of Schooling

b. Dependent Variable: ABILITY Academic Ability

Coefficients[a]

Model		Unstandardized Coefficients		Standardized Coefficients	t	Sig.
		B	Std. Error	Beta		
1	(Constant)	33.869	7.395		4.580	.000
	EDATTN Years of Schooling	1.251	.560	.307	2.234	.030

a. Dependent Variable: ABILITY Academic Ability

Regression Equation:

$$Y = 1.251X + 33.869$$

CHAPTER 18
Multiple Linear Regression

EXERCISE: **Multiple Linear Regression**
DATA: NLS.sav
TO DO: Run multiple regression to determine whether ABILITY could be predicted by the
               three variables FATHED, EDATTN, and SES, or any combination of them.
RESULTS:

Regression – First Run

Variables Entered/Removed[b]

Model	Variables Entered	Variables Removed	Method
1	SES Socioeconomic Status, EDATTN Years of Schooling, FATHED Years of Father's Education[a]	.	Enter

a. All requested variables entered.

b. Dependent Variable: ABILITY Academic Ability

Model Summary

Model	R	R Square	Adjusted R Square	Std. Error of the Estimate
1	.477[a]	.227	.177	6.97871

a. Predictors: (Constant), SES Socioeconomic
Status, EDATTN Years of Schooling, FATHED
Years of Father's Education

ANOVA[b]

Model		Sum of Squares	df	Mean Square	F	Sig.
1	Regression	659.142	3	219.714	4.511	.007[a]
	Residual	2240.313	46	48.702		
	Total	2899.454	49			

a. Predictors: (Constant), SES Socioeconomic Status, EDATTN Years of
Schooling, FATHED Years of Father's Education

b. Dependent Variable: ABILITY Academic Ability

Coefficients[a]

Model		Unstandardized Coefficients		Standardized Coefficients	t	Sig.
		B	Std. Error	Beta		
1	(Constant)	22.376	8.091		2.766	.008
	FATHED Years of Father's Education	.277	.372	.112	.745	.460
	EDATTN Years of Schooling	1.455	.538	.357	2.706	.010
	SES Socioeconomic Status	3.687	1.864	.300	1.978	.054

a. Dependent Variable: ABILITY Academic Ability

** In this run, the variable FATHED is not significant to the model ($p < 0.46$). We may delete this variable and test the other two (EDATTN, and SES) to see whether a better model will be produced – see the second run:

Regression – Second Run

Variables Entered/Removed[b]

Model	Variables Entered	Variables Removed	Method
1	SES Socioeconomic Status, EDATTN Years of Schooling [a]	.	Enter

a. All requested variables entered.

b. Dependent Variable: ABILITY Academic Ability

Model Summary

Model	R	R Square	Adjusted R Square	Std. Error of the Estimate
1	.467[a]	.218	.185	6.94563

a. Predictors: (Constant), SES Socioeconomic Status, EDATTN Years of Schooling

ANOVA[b]

Model		Sum of Squares	df	Mean Square	F	Sig.
1	Regression	632.092	2	316.046	6.551	.003[a]
	Residual	2267.362	47	48.242		
	Total	2899.454	49			

a. Predictors: (Constant), SES Socioeconomic Status, EDATTN Years of Schooling

b. Dependent Variable: ABILITY Academic Ability

Coefficients[a]

Model		Unstandardized Coefficients		Standardized Coefficients	t	Sig.
		B	Std. Error	Beta		
1	(Constant)	23.431	7.928		2.955	.005
	EDATTN Years of Schooling	1.492	.533	.366	2.800	.007
	SES Socioeconomic Status	4.383	1.607	.357	2.728	.009

a. Dependent Variable: ABILITY Academic Ability

** In the second run, the two variables are significant to the model, so we will include them into the model.

Regression Equation:

$$Y = 1.492X_1 + 4.383X_2 + 23.431$$

Where X_1 is EDATTN, and X_2 is SES

CHAPTER 19
Analysis of Covariance

EXERCISE: ANCOVA
DATA: NLS.sav
TO DO: Conduct an ANCOVA using SES as the independent variable, ABILITY as the dependent variable, and FATHED as the covariate.
RESULTS:

Between-Subjects Factors

		Value Label	N
SES Socioeconomic Status	1	Lower 25 Percent	21
	2	Middle 50 Percent	25
	3	Upper 25 Percent	4

Tests of Between-Subjects Effects

Dependent Variable: ABILITY Academic Ability

Source	Type III Sum of Squares	df	Mean Square	F	Sig.
Corrected Model	303.981[a]	3	101.327	1.796	.161
Intercept	6174.150	1	6174.150	109.425	.000
FATHED	46.401	1	46.401	.822	.369
SES	109.611	2	54.805	.971	.386
Error	2595.474	46	56.423		
Total	129033.013	50			
Corrected Total	2899.454	49			

a. R Squared = .105 (Adjusted R Squared = .046)

CHAPTER 21
Chi Square (χ^2) Tests for Frequencies

EXERCISE: **Chi Square (χ^2) Test**
DATA: NLS.sav
TO DO: Conduct a Chi-Square test to determine whether the two ratings – MONEY and FAMILY – are independent.
RESULTS:

Crosstabs

Case Processing Summary

	Cases					
	Valid		Missing		Total	
	N	Percent	N	Percent	N	Percent
MONEY Importance of Money * FAMILY Marry Right Person	50	100.0%	0	.0%	50	100.0%

MONEY Importance of Money * FAMILY Marry Right Person Crosstabulation

Count

		FAMILY Marry Right Person			
		1 Not Important	2 Somewhat Important	3 Very Important	Total
MONEY Importance of Money	1 Not Important	1	3	6	10
	2 Somewhat Important		2	25	27
	3 Very Important	1		12	13
Total		2	5	43	50

Chi-Square Tests

	Value	df	Asymp. Sig. (2-sided)
Pearson Chi-Square	8.887[a]	4	.064
Likelihood Ratio	9.603	4	.048
Linear-by-Linear Association	2.365	1	.124
N of Valid Cases	50		

a. 6 cells (66.7%) have expected count less than 5. The minimum expected count is .40.